THE FORESTER'S LOG

The Forester's Log

MUSINGS FROM THE WOODS

Mary Stuever

UNIVERSITY OF NEW MEXICO PRESS
ALBUQUERQUE

© 2009 by the University of New Mexico Press
All rights reserved. Published 2009
Printed in the United States of America
14 13 12 11 10 09   2 3 4 5 6 7 8

LIBRARY OF CONGRESS CATALOGING-IN-PUBLICATION DATA
Stuever, Mary.
The forester's log : musings from the woods / Mary Stuever.
p. cm.
Includes index.
ISBN 978-0-8263-4458-8 (PBK. : ALK. PAPER)
1. Forest fires—West (U.S.)—Prevention and control—Anecdotes.
2. Foresters—United States.
3. Forests and forestry—West (U.S.)—Anecdotes.
4. Stuever, Mary. I. Title.
SD421.32.W47S774   2009
634.9092—dc22
[B]

2008043599

Book and jacket design and type composition by Kathleen Sparkes.
This book was composed using Minion Pro OTF 11/14, 26P.
Display type is Trump Mediaeval OTF

FOR

THE LAND

AND

THE PEOPLE

CONTENTS

❧

INTRODUCTION   xi

CHAPTER ONE ❧ Fire   1

Freezing Fires   4

Fire Triangles   6

Respect Fire   9

When Firefighters Start Fires   11

Smokey's Wisdom   13

Nothing Gray about Fire Starting   15

A Visit with Harry Kallander   17

Bernalillo Watershed Prescribed Burn   19

Musings at Grand Canyon National Park   22

The Perfect Fire on Powell Plateau   24

Burning Piles   26

Burning Questions   29

SEATs Take No Back Seat in Air Tanker Business   30

Southwest Fire Fighters   33

Who Pays the Bill?   34

Addressing the Wildland Urban Interface   36

Fire in the Bosque   39

Oklahoma Fire Response   41

Farewell to My Fire Boots   42

Alaska Adventures   45

Remembering Sam Tobias   49

Thoughts on Fire and Mortality   51

CHAPTER TWO ∾ Forestry   57

Red Belt of 1984   61

Circle A Thinning   62

Betty Jane Curry: An American Tree Farmer   63

Wildlife Inspires Backyard Tree Farmers   68

An Argument for Keeping the Baca Ranch Private   70

This Year, Get a Patriotic Christmas Tree   73

Green Side Up, Okay?   76

Creating Cottonwoods   77

Survivor Tree Symmetry   79

Living in a Log Home   82

Forester's Confession   84

Cutting through the Tangle of Private Timber Sales   86

Divining Healthy Forests   88

A Common Vision for Jemez Mountain Elk   90

Dying Pinyons   92

Observations of a Dying Pinyon Tree   94

Pining for Pinyon   96

Habitat Typing   98

White Mountain Stewardship Program   101

In Defense of Informed, Intuitive Forestry   103

Logging in on Forestry   105

CHAPTER THREE ∾ Burn Area Recovery   109

Rehabbing the Rodeo-Chediski Fire   112

Mixing in Mexico   114

Gathering the BAER Clan   116

Laying a Log Erosion Barrier Legacy   118

She Ran Calling "Godiłtła'" 120

Stream Sense 123

Sowing the Seeds of a Future Forest 125

Fencing Feats 126

Land Lessons 128

Chasing the Chainsaws 130

Tribal Tree Planting Camp 132

Reflections on a Burned Landscape 134

Cibecue Native Manages Rodeo-Chediski Recovery Activities 136

BAER Fairs Showcase Burn Restoration 138

On the National Fire Plan Awards 140

Remembering Judith 142

Frightening Lightning 143

Flash Floods 145

Bear Scare 147

Cone Counting 149

Chediski Origin Myth 151

Moist Microsites 153

Cooking Reports—A Culinary Approach 155

Transitioning to Tribal Forestry 157

A Visit to Yale 159

Confidence and Competence 161

Sawing into the Tribal Forest Protection Act 163

Five Years after Rodeo-Chediski 166

Greening the Super Bowl 169

BAER Growls 171

Changing Woman 173

CHAPTER FOUR ∾ Environmental Education 177

Instilling That Love for the Land 180

New Mexico Forestry Camp 183

Rivers of Colorado Water Watch Network 185

Project del Rio 187

Pilgrimage to Boca Chica 190

Exploring the Hundred-Acre Wood 192

A Winter's Day in the Pueblo of Santa Ana's Bosque 193

The Bosque Education Guide 195

The BEMP Intern Program 197

Alameda Tai Chi 200

Philmont Forestry 202

Contemplating Closures 204

Lessons in Fall Foliage 206

Field Guide to the Sandia Mountains 208

Striving to Follow in the Footsteps of Carson and Bruchac 210

CHAPTER FIVE ∾ Recreation 213

Pico de Orizaba: 1985–1986 Seldom Seen Expedition 215

Tomorrow's Adventurers 226

Rocky Canyon Trail Building 227

Opportunity, Privilege, and Respect 230

Mount Taylor Winter Quadrathlon 238

Rescue Training in the World of Whitewater 240

Tree Spirits in Thailand 243

Leopold Retires from Forestry Career 245

Copper and Condors 247

ACKNOWLEDGMENTS 249

CHRONOLOGICAL LIST OF ARTICLES 253

INDEX 257

INTRODUCTION

Breathe in the musty decay of dead leaves and pine needles turning to soil. Notice the mottled shadows on the forest floor as the sun moves above tree canopy and cloud cover. Listen to wind whistling through branches overhead while warblers add their harmonies. Feel the soft bounce of the forest floor beneath your step. Then marvel at the opportunity to be in this moment.

THE POPULAR BLESSING "MAY YOU LIVE IN INTERESTING TIMES" could be a theme for foresters in the last quarter century. When I graduated from forestry school in the early 1980s, American forests were in serious decline and poised for crises that would include catastrophic wildfires, massive insect outbreaks, and an unprecedented invasion of suburban human dwellings. Not only did my profession face incredible challenges out on the land, but more than ever before in the history of our century-old profession, we needed to involve the public in solving the complex troubles facing our forests. It was an opportune time to be both forester and writer.

Throughout my career, I have written about my work and my profession, including penning a syndicated column called *The Forester's Log*. The *Log* appears in semi monthly and monthly newspapers in rural forested communities, and has shown up in national magazines, newsletters, anthologies, and websites. Gathered in this collection, these writings tell the poignant story of the conditions of our forests and our efforts to address what has become a national crisis of forest health.

The collection also weaves a story of a woman's career in the woods in an era when women were claiming their place in a profession where "diameter breast high" was more often "diameter chin level" to this new

Mary on the Mogollon Rim near Forest Lakes, with the Rodeo-Chediski fire in the background. July 2002. Photographer unknown.

class of foresters. I worked for federal and state agencies, spent twelve years as a consultant, worked almost five years for a tribal forestry program, and now am returning to state government.

In addition to handling the stereotypical forester assignments of monitoring timber sales and planting trees, my career has involved firefighting, fire rehabilitation, environmental education, collaborative projects, and forest planning. In 2003 I was hired to direct one of the largest Burn Area Emergency Rehabilitation (Rodeo-Chediski Fire, White Mountain Apache Tribe) programs in the nation. I also worked for the tribe as the acting tribal forest manager.

This compilation spans over two decades and captures changes within the field of forestry in the last quarter century. The columns are grouped into five chapters: Fire, Forestry, Burn Area Rehabilitation, Environmental Education, and Recreation. The first four chapters begin with a tale—a glimpse into a day of my life as a forester—and an introduction to the chapter. The last chapter is full of stories, thus its introduction is simply that. Within most chapters, the articles are grouped by subtopics, and then appear chronologically. My twins, Katie and Roland, permeate these pages, showing up at various ages and providing another marker of time. The original date of publication is included at the front of each piece, and an appendix in the back lists the articles in chronological order.

These stories are about places, people, and experiences. These are tales that honor the beautiful relationship between land and people. These pages tell about the bosque, the Rio Grande, aspen groves, ponderosa pine and mixed conifer stands, spruce-fir forests, alpine tundra on high mountaintops, meadows, deserts, and woodlands, mostly in New Mexico and Arizona but also reaching out to Alaska, Thailand, the Gulf of Mexico, and the Pacific Ocean. There are people in these pages, both named and not named: friends, family, colleagues, teachers, students, heroes and heroines. The experiences here are mine. These are stories of just one forester and offer only a glimpse of forestry in the Southwest at the turn of the new millennium.

Come on into the woods. Explore the mountains and valleys of the Southwest with this forester. Although these stories are meant to inform and educate, I hope you'll find some smiles and inspiration along the way.

CHAPTER ONE

Fire

1

Winter 1988

Louie's voice has a sharp edge as he issues directions over the radio on his location in the burning bosque. Having fought fires for the New Mexico State Forestry Division for several years, on this cold winter day I am engine boss of a 1971 International Model 70 fire engine. The truck had been transferred to our state agency from the neighboring Cibola National Forest. With a classy air horn mounted on the hood and a white State Penitentiary paint job, our Bernalillo District staff lovingly refers to the beast as the "Albino Rhino."

Louie Casaus, our district fire management officer, has been on the rural Valencia County fire south of Albuquerque for hours. My engine is just arriving at the riverside blaze burning in the cottonwood and salt cedar along the Rio Grande. Louie is concerned that the fire is an immediate threat to a mobile home parked within the thick wooded area.

As we arrive, Louie grabs the nozzle on the hose reel before I even set the brake and races off into the thick salt cedar. A wall of flames is heading our way. I scream at him to slow down, but realize that I must get water into the line as fast as possible. After engaging the power take-off so the truck engine can run the water pump, I quickly adjust valves so water will flow to the nozzle he is holding. Priming the pump, I pray the aged equipment works on the first attempt. My crew yells that flames are reaching Louie's position in the woods.

The hose jerks as water pours through the line. A fog of mist surrounds my co-worker as he adjusts the nozzle to protect himself.

The Albino Rhino, a Model 70 International fire engine, the third engine out on the Bernalillo District, New Mexico State Forestry. Courtesy of Fred Rossbach.

Once the flames immediately around him have fallen back, he narrows the stream and knocks down the flames.

He is grinning as he heads back to the pump panel.

"What were you thinking?" I am shaking with rage and adrenaline. "What if I hadn't been able to get you water right then?"

"Come on, Stuever, I have faith in you. Besides, we did a good job."

"Well, you have more faith in me than I have in myself. I haven't operated this beast in months!"

Still, Louie admits that his next stop is to check in with the ambulance crew on scene to be sure he is fine. Meanwhile, under the direction of the county fire marshal who has assumed the role of incident commander, our crew continues through the night to stomp out flames with the Albino Rhino. Thanks to the quick action by my colleague, the trailer home, beneath tree branches and immediately next to brush, has survived this fire.

IN THE LAST DECADE, WILDFIRES HAVE ESCALATED TO THE FRONT BURNER of western American issues. With a century of fire exclusion, several decades of extensive home building in the forest, and a decade of severe drought, today's wildfires are burning hundreds of homes, charring thousands of acres, and killing millions of trees. The following collection of stories provides one forester's perspective on fire over a period of twenty years.

I started fighting fires in college, but really didn't sink my teeth into the job until I worked as a forester with New Mexico State Forestry on the Bernalillo District. For six years I chased wildfires, mostly as the engine boss on the Albino Rhino. A small state agency with large responsibility, our district had four permanent employees to cover six million acres.

Through these years, firefighting evolved. In the "bad ol' days" we had a credo of succeeding at great personal risk. This "can do" attitude often shadowed our judgment and was based on the precept that bad things only happened to other people. We found ourselves taking quick, decisive actions when we had no experience or training that prepared us for the emergency situations we were facing.

My firefighting career coevolved with the Incident Command System (ICS). With ICS, positions and job tasks are clearly defined. Emergency responders form immediately organized, well-functioning teams based on well-defined expectations of each member's job assignment. Firefighters participate in a training system where experience is documented in formal task books. Task books are completed under the guidance of more experienced mentors before a firefighter can be assigned to various fire roles. I have joked with my staff that the task book system was created specifically because of people like me who often had no choice back then but to go out on a limb and rely on common sense and a degree of good luck to get our job accomplished.

As a small State Forestry agency, we always needed help and much of my job was coordinating various resources arriving to put out fires. We worked with volunteer fire departments, "pick-up" firefighters who were hired temporarily only for the incident, and other cooperating agencies. In 1986 I joined my hometown fire department to better understand the sixty-six rural fire departments in my district. After leaving State Forestry in 1991, I continued to fight fire for the Placitas Volunteer Fire Brigade, and served as their wildland fire captain. Occasionally

I was picked up by State Forestry as an engine boss and initial attack incident commander.

Although I love the actual firefighting role—what in ICS is called the "Operations Section"—my role was often as spokesperson whenever media or members of the public showed up. Eventually we had the first formal trainings designed for fire information officers. The fire information officer is now a standard position working directly for the incident commander.

As a fire information officer, my assignments have also included nonfire events such as flash floods, wind events, and fire prevention assignments. For years I was associated with the New Mexico Type 2 Incident Management Team, which handled fires that had exceeded the local unit's fire management resources.

Most of these fire stories come from the field as a fire information officer or, as I once described the job to the Mescalero Tribal Council, as a fire storyteller.

2 FREEZING FIRES
March 2002

Snake Tank Camp, Mescalero Reservation—March is a generally cold month in the southern New Mexico mountains and tonight is no exception. As my breath condenses in the cool air, I am amazed to find myself bunking down in a fire camp. I started this month fighting a chimney fire as a volunteer in Placitas. It was so cold that night icicles formed inside the house from the water we were spraying. Tonight I am on a wildland fire near Ruidoso, New Mexico, where already over ten thousand acres have burned in several area fires. It's an early start to what could be a serious fire season in the Southwest.

A few weeks ago, fire behavior experts published a seasonal outlook that suggests above normal levels of fires in April, May, and June. Fires are expected to start more readily; fuels are expected to burn more quickly. Records may be set for low moisture values in larger pieces of wood. These conditions are related to weather variations in the Pacific Ocean, a continuance of drought for several years, and low amounts of winter precipitation.

Already in Ruidoso this week, close to thirty homes have been destroyed. As a volunteer firefighter, I have watched friends and strangers grapple with the tragedy of losing their homes and belongings. After 2000, I hoped I'd never see another fire season displace so many families. Unfortunately, this year is shaping up to also be tragic.

When I started my career fighting forest fires over twenty years ago, forest firefighters were separate from structural firefighters. With today's forests full of houses, we now cross-train and work side by side. *New Challenges*

This human migration to living in the forests presents a serious challenge. When houses are threatened, we must allocate firefighting resources to protect structures rather than direct those resources to fire suppression. Conversely, we are obligated to suppress fires in areas that, without the presence of homes, we would allow to burn naturally.

There are no easy answers to the dilemma facing our "wildland-urban" areas. Homeowners can improve the chance that their house will survive a forest fire by managing vegetation on their property and choosing fire-resistant building materials. Developers can improve property protection and evacuation by limiting dead ends and providing multiple access routes. County officials can improve the situation through reasonable zoning and regulations. Forest managers can reduce risks to communities by developing fuel breaks between forests and subdivisions. None of these activities work alone; to be effective, they must be done in a coordinated fashion. The major solution to protecting homes in the forest revolves around teamwork. *& Prevention*

Teamwork requires training and communication. My volunteer fire department saved a house on that cold, March morning because we knew what we were doing and we worked toward a common goal. It was satisfying to see our years of training come through. The incident management team on this fire includes people I have known and fought fires with for many years. I have the same confidence in our ability to contain this fire before more resources are lost.

Our hope for saving homes in the forest is in creating communities committed to teamwork. All players need to communicate and train together. We must talk about evacuation procedures before we ever need to evacuate. We should hold seminars and workshops for homeowners. We need reasonable building regulations and subdivision planning. When we choose to live in the forests, we must recognize the additional risks.

Throughout the Southwest these community teams are forming. We *cannot* help our weather patterns that create conditions of low winter moisture and extended drought. We *can* manage the fuels and, through prevention programs, cut down on the sources of ignition. Some years conditions will come together to give us these freezing fires in March, but hopefully as the years go by, we will lose fewer—not more—homes in the wildland.

FIRE TRIANGLES
September 2002

When thinking about fire, triangles are a familiar shape for firefighters. All firefighters know the fire triangle and the fire behavior triangle, but here is another three-sided image: the fire disaster triangle.

The standard fire triangle consists of three necessary components to have a fire: heat, oxygen, and fuel. Remove any leg of the triangle, and the fire will go out. Although structural firefighters use water to cool and smother the flames, wildland firefighters generally attempt to remove fuel through the construction of fire lines and by burning fuels between control lines and the main fire.

Wildland firefighters refer to the fire behavior triangle (weather, topography, and fuels) to describe factors that affect how fires burn on the landscape. As with the fire triangle, the easiest leg to influence is the fuel. Forest managers are keenly aware that areas that have recently been thinned or burned are less likely to sustain long-term damage from wildfires.

This third fire disaster triangle helps us understand the crises of today's fires. The three legs include 1) excessive fuel accumulations, 2) prolonged drought conditions, and 3) increased construction of homes and businesses in fire-prone forests and woodlands. In the past century, fire spread was significantly reduced. In the absence of regular, light-intensity burning, both live and dead fuels have reached unprecedented levels. Meanwhile, in the last decade we have experienced one of the worst droughts within the past five hundred years.

Before this drought, however, we experienced one of the wettest periods of the last few millennia. Under this wet regime, and even continuing into this drought, the number of buildings in fire-prone forests

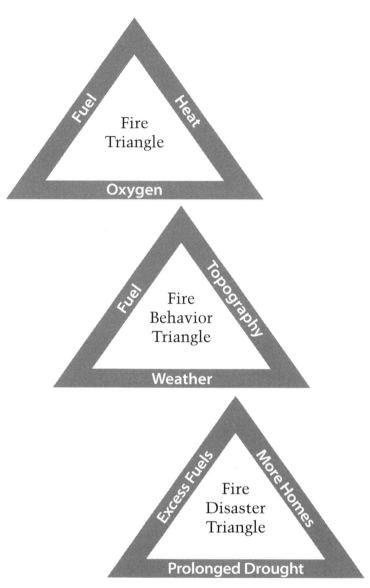

Fire Triangles: The Fire Triangle is used by both structural and wildland firefighters to illustrate basic fire principles. The Fire Behavior Triangle, used in wildland fire situations, emphasizes critical components that influence how wildfires burn. The Fire Disaster Triangle is suggested by the author as a way to understand critical issues with fire in forested suburban areas. Illustration by Kathleen Sparkes.

exploded, with miles of extensive communities and subdivisions spreading through what were once regularly burning wildlands.

As with the other two triangles, the vulnerable leg where we can mitigate the fire impact is the fuels. The people who are more likely to save homes from burning this summer are not firefighters but homeowners who take action to make their properties more fire resistant.

In preparing for the fire season, homeowners should view their property as fuel for fire and recognize what is more likely to burn. Obviously construction materials like metal roofs, stucco siding, and rock foundations are less likely to ignite. Conversely, wood shake shingles and siding are a clear invitation for disaster.

For most homeowners, tasks around the house include removing flammable vegetation near the home, closing in open decks and porches, and clearing areas around propane tanks. Projects might include relocating wood piles away from homes, propane tanks, and power lines, clearing weeds away from outbuildings, thinning thick forests and undergrowth, and cleaning gutters and roofs of leaves and woody debris. Homes are more likely to survive fire when these types of efforts are applied throughout the neighborhood.

At a recent fire training session in my hometown of Placitas, New Mexico, we talked about the future fire we dread. This is the wildfire that moves through our village. Homes here are tightly packed by rural standards and surrounded by dense vegetation, especially sumac bushes and weeds. This fire has not yet happened, but it is only a matter of time until it will.

As we developed a strategy for such a scenario, we realized that, like firefighters all over the West, we will have to pick and choose our battles. We will not be able to save every house, and we will have to put our energies where homeowners had already done their part to make their properties less fire prone. At least our village has multiple roads leading in and out. This will make evacuations safer and allow emergency equipment to come on scene faster.

When homeowners understand the fire triangles, and seriously address the "fuel" legs, our communities will have better chances for coexisting in fire-prone ecosystems.

❧

Postscript: Each community has unique features and concerns. Most fire issues for communities surrounded by forests, woodlands, and grasslands are similar. A national Firewise program (visit www.firewise.org) offers information and free materials for homeowners and community leaders. There are many examples to encourage homeowners to invest an afternoon or two now that might make a difference in whether their home burns or survives during this year's wildfires.

3 RESPECT FIRE
April 1997

I stop at a red light, and suddenly a man is standing at my window. He doesn't look like a typical panhandler, and as I glance in my rearview mirror, I notice the car behind me is driverless. The driver is knocking on my window and he seems irritated. I roll the window down.

"What is this?" he demands. "Why do you have a bumper sticker that says 'Help Smokey *promote* forest fires'?" He starts to tell me of his firefighting career in Oregon in years past.

"I am a firefighter, too," I reply, nodding back to the red packs (one for structures, one for wildfires) in back of my Subaru station wagon. My nine-year-old son gives a deep sigh. I know he is wondering how much of a fire ecology lecture I am going to slip in before the light turns green. I decide to make a stab at it.

"Fires can be beneficial for our forests, too," I add. "That's my job, I am a fire ecologist. I promote using fire in the forests."

The light turns green, and the disgruntled man wanders back to his car, grimly shaking his head, as if the world is making no sense.

"How did I do?" I ask my son.

"I don't think you made any friends," he replies. We wave as the man passes us, but he won't even look our way.

He is an ex-firefighter, brethren . . . but not enlightened on the good that fire can do. To him, and to many people, fire is an awful monster, the villain that desperately needs destroying, the evil enemy to be battled. Can't say I blame him much for holding such an attitude. I've seen thousands of moonscape acres resulting from catastrophic crown fires. I've seen the walls of silt and water coming down canyons below burned-over watersheds. I've walked around foundations of homes completely destroyed during last summer's busy fire season. Fire has earned its nasty reputation.

If my experiences stopped here, I, too, would be shaking my head and wondering about the sanity of my custom bumper sticker. Yet other images crowd my mind. Cross-section after cross-section of ponderosa pine, Douglas-fir, and southwestern white pine collected throughout Arizona and New Mexico have fire scars that tell remarkably the same story: that fires were once frequent throughout the Southwest, but this pattern stopped around a hundred years ago. Research demonstrates that there are many more trees closer together now than in our forests prior to European settlement. Where we have forest glades with large pine trees, lush grasses, and little shrub undergrowth, we find forests that have repeated fires, usually due to prescribed burning. Fire doesn't always have a nasty reputation.

Lately, I have been musing about the role of fire ecology in fire prevention programs. This month, I am on the Mescalero Reservation in south-central New Mexico working with the Bureau of Indian Affairs to develop and support existing fire prevention programs. The task is rather daunting. Here is an agency that easily burns ten thousand acres a year with prescribed fire, asking me to go tell the people not to start fires! This is not just any group of people, either. These are Apaches. If several prominent geographers have their story straight, the Apaches' ancestors have used fire for hundreds to thousands of years, and have been credited with molding ecosystems!

When I met with my client for an initial briefing, they understood my dilemma. It is theirs, too.

"That's why we asked you (a fire ecologist) here."

It's okay to include fire ecology in fire prevention programs. In fact, it is vital to include fire ecology in fire prevention programs. The public needs to understand that fire is a tool to be used. That some fires can do "good things" that will prevent "bad things" from happening. Trouble is, the message is complex, and it just doesn't lend itself well to a bumper sticker.

Before I started roaming around the reservation delivering my complex fire message, I removed the "Help Smokey *Promote* Forest Fires" slogan from my bumper. My job is tough enough without being misunderstood.

Yet the Apaches have given me the idea for the next bumper sticker I'll have. I was explaining to a tribal council member why I was calling my program "Fire Education" rather than "Fire Prevention," and he started nodding his head in agreement.

"In our culture," he explained to me, "we teach our children to respect fire."

Respect fire. That's got all the makings of a bumper sticker slogan. It's short and catchy. It doesn't deny a role for fire in our forests, but it does imply the serious attitude one needs when approaching the issue of wildland fires. There's one drawback, though, in adopting such a motto: not only will fire education programs need to teach about fire, they will need to address "respect" as well. And frankly, that's what fire education should be all about.

WHEN FIREFIGHTERS START FIRES
July 2002

I just returned last week from working on the Rodeo-Chediski Fire in central Arizona. Two separate fires, started two days apart on the Fort Apache Indian Reservation, burned together forming the largest fire in Arizona's history, covering 468,638 acres with a fire perimeter of 218 miles. This combined fire burned 423 homes and businesses in communities as far as 50 miles apart, not to mention leaving miles and miles of devastated natural resources. One of the disturbing features of the event was that people intentionally started both of these blazes.

During our suppression efforts, one of the firefighters working on the blaze was arrested for starting the Rodeo portion of the fire. Since arson investigations often take months or years before a case is cracked, it was unusual for an arrest to be made before the fire was contained. As a result, people—especially the media—started asking how firefighters feel about firefighters starting fires. There is no simple answer, and each of the almost five thousand responders involved in this particular incident probably has her or his unique opinion. For the record, here are a few of my own thoughts.

First, it is important to keep the issue in perspective. With a nod to Sebastian Junger's book *The Perfect Storm*, Arizona State University fire researcher Stephen Pyne dubbed this fire "The Perfect Fire." Conditions surrounding the weather, fuels, and topography combined for the most extreme fire behavior ever witnessed in the Southwest. Even so, I doubt the emergency firefighter who is said to have started this blaze had any idea of how "perfect" these conditions were. If he started the fire to get a job, he probably expected only a few days' worth of work and a few acres burned. What made this fire international news was not the source of ignition, but the ferocity and pace with which it marched across the Arizona landscape.

It is hard to point fingers at dry weather and steep canyons when fuel conditions throughout much of the Southwest are influenced by human actions. For decades, managers have been anxiously promoting aggressive fuel treatments in the form of thinning and prescribed fire. In many places, substantial roadblocks such as limited budgets or objections from environmentalists have stalled thinning projects. Some politicians are suggesting environmental organizations are responsible for this fire's destructive nature.

Early observations show that where previous timber sales, prescribed burns, or thinning were conducted before the area burned, the crown fire dropped back down to the ground. Even though the fire burned through these acres, it did little damage.

Still one of the initial ignitions of this blaze involved a firefighter. On the day the arrest was announced, I was on the phone, live on national television. The anchorwoman asked me point blank what I thought about a firefighter starting this fire. She tried to get me to say I was sickened of and disappointed in my fellow workers.

I did not feel this way. On the contrary, I was pretty darn proud of the firefighters. The men and women on the front lines had saved many homes and even whole neighborhoods. For days, we had been on pins and needles worried about what more the flames would claim. Hard work had paid off and we had rounded a significant corner in containing the fire. There was no way I was going say I was disappointed in firefighters. They are my heroes. The anchorwoman finally gave up.

In every population, there are a few people who make bad choices and do bad things. We had roughly five thousand firefighters involved in this incident, and that does not include the thousands of firefighters working on other fires in New Mexico, Colorado, Utah, and South

Dakota at the same time. Personally, I see no reason to lose my faith in the firefighting community because of one person. Whether the fire-starter was also a firefighter is not significant. The actions of one person do not reflect on his gender, his race, his family, his profession, or any other group with which he may be associated.

I am as sickened by this ignition as by any other ignition caused by ignorance and lack of respect for fire conditions. When someone starts a fire in the dry, vulnerable forest for personal reasons, whether it is to signal help, create a job, salvage a relationship, or whatever sad justification is given, that person has committed a crime against the land and the people. As a society, we need to clearly communicate intolerance for this type of behavior.

So what about firefighters starting fires? Honestly, we do start fires all the time, using fires in both suppression and management activities. For the vast majority of us, we just would not start a fire outside of these situations. I, for one, remain extremely proud of the men and women fighting fires today.

4 SMOKEY'S WISDOM
May 2005

As we head into fire season I worry that stupid people will start forest fires this year. I have this big, furry friend who wears a ridiculous, pointy-topped round hat. Although he does not talk (at least according to the official instructions that come with the costume), many preschoolers can tell you that Smokey's message is "don't play with fire." So if a four-year-old can get it straight, why are American adults responsible for starting so many wildfires each year?

The White Mountain Apache community, where I work, values the wisdom of *elders*, but as I get older, I sometimes wonder whether I am getting any wiser. It seems the more I learn, the less I actually know. The world out there is complicated and all those youthful impressions of black and white are, like my hair, fading to gray. Gray may be a theme color for *fire information*. Fire has a beneficial role in the forest, but people should not start fires. How do we explain that using fire requires extensive knowledge and experience?

Recently I was at the Point Reyes National Seashore north of San Francisco, California, exploring a ten-year-old burn, the Mount Vision Fire. While visiting with National Park Service employee Jennifer Chapman, who specializes in "fire education" at the park, I was reminded of the bosque along the Rio Grande in Albuquerque, New Mexico. Besides the gross concept of trees growing next to water, these forests are very different.

The cottonwood forest of the bosque lies on a flat floodplain next to a meager trickle of fresh water we desert folks call a river. Point Reyes sports a dense evergreen carpet of bishop pine and Douglas-fir on steep hillsides overlooking the vast Pacific Ocean. What these diverse forests have in common shows up in the fire ignition statistics. Only 2 percent of fires in both ecosystems start naturally. That means the rest are started by people. Jennifer explained, rather delicately, that the Mount Vision Fire, the largest fire in the history of the park, was started by an illegal campfire.

I work on a large, catastrophic burn: actually two fires started by two people. Daily I face the devastating impact of these fires. Still, I believe fire belongs in our forests in many situations. This ambiguous attitude I share with many of my colleagues must be confusing to the American public.

In 1998 I worked on a fire prevention assignment in Texas. The Texas Forest Service had gone to the effort of reprinting some Smokey Bear posters from the 1960s that called fire "bad." I questioned one of the program leaders about the wisdom of labeling all fire "bad" when decades later we knew there were important ecological benefits from fire. He shrugged off my concerns.

"This message is clear," he retorted. "In Texas, we don't need fire."

At the time, I knew of research being done at a Texas university on using fire to control mesquite, but I bit my tongue. Could a mute Smokey really navigate the gray area of fire use, or did his message have to be black and white?

When I first started listening to what the elders were saying about the Rodeo-Chediski burn and fire in general, I thought many of their remarks were simplistic. I wondered if I was missing their wisdom by not speaking their native tongue. However, I have come to appreciate the inherent wisdom in their commonsense answers that, although they seem simple initially, are deep-rooted in years of living.

Smokey's advice to be careful with fire has the similar quality of a simple message with a very deep and powerful meaning. Fire season is upon us. We need to respect fire. We need to be careful. We need to make sure that none of us earn the title of "stupid people who start forest fires."

5 NOTHING GRAY ABOUT FIRE STARTING
June 2007

I reread the last sentence of the guidebook section on "What to do if lost or injured" again. I cannot believe the statement is there in print. It reads, "A note of warning: in case of extreme fire conditions in the forest, making any kind of fire could be considered illegal."

Excuse me. I think that needs to be rewritten. The more accurate warning should read: "in case of extreme fire conditions in the forest, making any kind of fire could kill people, destroy property, and devastate the forest!"

I live in the White Mountains of Arizona. I am relatively new to this area, thus my interest in a guidebook to the hiking trails of the region. I came here to work as a burn area emergency coordinator, because five years ago, two people who felt they were in desperate situations started some fires. It is an action both individuals have publicly regretted.

The Rodeo Fire, started by Leonard Gregg, and the Chediski Fire, started by Valinda Jo Elliott, burned together to scorch nearly a half-million acres of forests and woodlands, destroy over four hundred buildings, and cost almost $200 million for suppression, rehabilitation, and property loss costs.

Elliott trespassed in a closed section of tribal lands without a permit. She got lost and started a signal fire on a steep hillside, only a ten-minute scramble from flat clearings and roads that would have provided safer locations for her fire. While the White Mountain Apache Tribe took her to court, she has yet to pay a fine or serve a day of community service.

I check the trail guide, *Walking the Edge,* by Laurie Dee Acree, for a publishing date: 2004, two years after the Chediski Fire wreaked havoc in Heber and Overgaard. Since Elliott was "rescued" and continues to contest her fines, perhaps Acree, a White Mountain resident before, during, and after the Rodeo-Chediski Fire, believes that fire starting while lost should merely "be considered illegal."

Gregg, a White Mountain Apache tribal member, was a part-time firefighter with limited fire experience. Jobless in a community that had 60 percent unemployment, Gregg had few ways to make money. He did not feel he had any other options but to get a part-time job fighting fire. He wanted a day or two of work, and lit a fire that he hoped might provide that. Gregg is serving a ten-year jail sentence and owes $28 million in restitution.

Earlier this month, another firefighter was sentenced for the similar crime of starting a fire. Van Bateman was not only a full-time wildland firefighter with extensive experience, he had been one of the key incident commanders during the Rodeo-Chediski Fire. The fires he started did not destroy homes or devastate vast expanses of forest. In fact, Bateman tried to explain to the public that he felt his intentions in starting the fires were good. In a story in the *Arizona Republic*, Bateman was quoted as saying, "I wasn't trying to start an arson fire. I was just trying to clean this piece of country up."

Still, as U.S. Forest Service Southwest Regional Forester Harv Forsgren wrote in a letter to the *Arizona Republic* editor, "[Bateman] set the fires during a time when prescribed burning was not done because forest conditions were too dangerous. He did not arrange for other firefighters to manage the fires. He did not report the fires. He did not stay at the fires to make certain they were under control."

Bateman was sentenced to two years in jail.

The act of starting a fire evokes the responsibility for that fire, to insure that it does no harm and to be responsible for any harm that it may cause. Like any other citizen, firefighters, who often double as fire starters for prescribed burning activities, need to cherish this societal value that we do not start fires during extreme conditions. That should go for people who are lost or injured as well.

Relying on our legal system to allow a lost individual the right to endanger others by starting a wildfire seems ludicrous. A better solution would be to encourage anyone going into the woods to carry a signal mirror. At least, that is what trail guides should suggest.

9 A VISIT WITH HARRY KALLANDER
August 1996

When Interior Secretary Bruce Babbitt addressed a convention of ecologists in Albuquerque a few days ago, he included "Fire Ecology" as one of the five important ecological issues facing the Clinton administration. The other four were the president's Forest Plan for the Pacific Northwest, the Everglades in Florida, the Endangered Species Act, and the upcoming Kyoto Conference on the Environment.

Today land managers are actively recognizing fire as a part of natural forest ecosystems. Yet, Secretary Babbitt astutely reminded the crowd that Aldo Leopold had already written about the importance of fire in 1924. As national politicians are endorsing the importance of fire in maintaining forest health, we should acknowledge those foresters, including Leopold, who, although in the minority, bravely supported the use of fire in the forests through this past century.

While many of these observant professionals wrote and spoke eloquently of fire's importance in shaping the ecosystem, few people actually practiced prescribed burning. In August, I visited with a forester who worked on the ground during the 1950s igniting and managing some of the Southwest's largest prescribed fires in this century.

Harry Kallander came to Fort Apache Reservation in east-central Arizona in 1950. He moved to the Southwest from the Klamath Reservation in Oregon following his friend and fellow forester, Harold Weaver. Kallander and Weaver attended forestry school together at Oregon State University. Kallander described Weaver as a "top-notch" scholar who graduated in 1929. Kallander, a self-described "poorer student," followed a year later. When Kallander failed to pass a Forest Service entrance exam, his friend Weaver helped him land a position with the Bureau of Indian Affairs (BIA) at Klamath.

Kallander experimented with prescribed burning, often at night so as to escape detection by critics who were less than enthusiastic about the merits of using fire. When Weaver, an active spokesperson for prescribed fire, moved to the BIA area office in Phoenix, he asked Kallander to come to the Southwest to implement burning programs.

In 1950, Kallander's first burn, ignited in late November, covered forty thousand acres and was still burning until December 20.

"Clarence Spaulding, the (Sitgreaves National Forest) forest supervisor, allowed us to burn from the Rim Road across Forest Service land and then onto the reservation," Kallander explained. "The Forest Service had the authority to use fire then, and Spaulding even agreed that fire belonged in the forest, but the Forest Service was afraid to light fires."

Kallander explained that for several years after this prescribed burn, firefighters were rarely dispatched when fires occurred in this burn area. They knew additional fires wouldn't cause any real damage but would aid in keeping fuels reduced.

Today, Kallander lives alone in his home in Pinetop, Arizona. The ninety-two-year-old retired forester is surrounded by books, mostly about the outdoors, and trees he transplanted from the reservation. Many friends drop in to check on him, share a meal, and listen to his stories. His stories are pretty amazing.

"We used kitchen matches," he told me, the gleam in his eyes dancing across the room. "We burned in strips. Sent the first man out on horseback. He'd follow the contour, just dropping lit matches as he rode. His matches would fall and ignite a strip of fire behind him that would burn up to the road. Another firefighter ran behind him dropping his string of fire. They'd both replenish their matches from an ample supply carried in the horse's saddle bags." Kallander then explained that more firefighters would follow staggered behind, each burning a strip below and behind the man ahead of him.

"We would burn thousands of acres each day this way."

Kallander paused to laugh at the current Forest Service prescribed burns that are only a few hundred acres in size. I comment that a New Mexico forest recently pushed the accepted norm and burned sixteen thousand acres.

"We'd do twice that the years we were burning."

I can tell another story is coming.

"We used to fill Phoenix with smoke," the story started. "Even had the governor calling the Tribal Chairman to complain. They had a nice discussion about sovereignty," he said, referring to the tribe's status as a sovereign nation.

Prescribed fire wasn't the only idea Kallander pushed in his years at Fort Apache. He also urged the tribe to build a sawmill to process the tribe's vast timber resources. Fort Apache Timber Company is now a thriving business employing hundreds of people and grossing several million dollars per year.

I am honored by my friendship with this elder of my forestry *tribe*. If we have the wisdom to act as decisively today as these foresters did forty years ago, we can address the excessive fuel concerns that Secretary Babbitt has brought before us. I dream of visiting my friend Harry to tell him of the hundreds of thousands of acres of prescribed burning we have been doing.

BERNALILLO WATERSHED PRESCRIBED BURN
February 1997

In January, firefighters were in the mountain suburb of Placitas just outside of Albuquerque, New Mexico, with drip torches and fuses blackening a portion of the grassland. Nationwide, firefighters regularly start fires as well as fight them. These fires, known as prescribed burns, are management activities to reduce fuels contributing to potential catastrophic fires or to improve ecological health. Last month's prescribed burn was one event in a long-range plan for improving the health of the grasslands and woodlands on national forest property.

The vegetation around Placitas, like many grasslands, woodlands, and forests throughout the West, has undergone significant change in the last two centuries. Many vegetation changes occur because of historical shifts in climate patterns, such as retreating glaciers or shifts in long-term weather patterns. These changes, however, are the direct impact of fire suppression and grazing, which have vastly affected the ecology of millions of acres throughout the West.

Scientific studies and early written records suggest there were fewer trees and shrubs and more grasses in Placitas before European settlement. Wildfires were more frequent, probably started by lightning and also by people. These fast-burning fires were carried by rich mats of grasses and swept across vast areas. Since grasses grow from their bases, they recover quickly because their regenerative tissue is at ground level and often not damaged by fast-moving fires. Nutrients are also released when leaves and dead plant parts burn.

Small trees, which grow from the top and tips of branches, were often killed in these blazes. When chance allowed, some trees would grow large enough between fires to be able to withstand future fires. Therefore, in the past, the area supported scattered trees.

As Albuquerque and vicinity were settled, large numbers of domestic livestock were introduced to the region. As grasses were reduced through grazing, fires were unable to spread across the landscape. Pinyon pine and juniper seedlings that would have been killed by fire became prolific shrubs, establishing the thick woodlands we have today. At lower elevations, short, woody plants such as snakeweed and cactus replaced grasses. As a result, deeper rooted trees and shrubs dominate available moisture in the soil, limiting grass reestablishment even decades after grazing pressure is reduced.

Grass prevents erosion by holding the soil in place with shallow roots and a compact growth form. As grasslands transition to shrub lands and woodlands, soil that developed over tens of thousands of years is eroded from the area. In addition to reducing the productivity of these lands, sediment is the largest source of water pollution in New Mexico. In order to reverse this decline in ecosystem health, these lands need to be covered by grass.

An obvious solution is to reintroduce fire into these ecosystems. This is not a simple operation. Fire is complex, varying in intensities that can be beneficial or destructive. Fires produce smoke, causing air pollution concerns. The effects of fire on vegetation, soil, and animal life vary with fire intensity. When managers apply fire on the land, they need to understand how to use fire in the ecosystem to achieve positive results.

This is why the Sandia Ranger District of the Cibola National Forest is working with researchers from the University of New Mexico and the Forest Service's Rocky Mountain Research Station. The Placitas prescribed burn provides researchers the opportunity to study the effects of burning in the grasslands.

The 420-acre study site was first burned in November of 1995. Prior to the prescribed burn, researchers set up eight plots for intensive study. They took various measurements of soil and vegetation. Four plots were burned, while fire was kept out of four control plots. Comparisons were made between the burned and non-burned areas. Since the first fire, researchers have been collecting information to see how rapidly the vegetation responds and how much soil erosion occurs.

"To say that the weather conditions before and after the prescribed fire (of 1995) were less than optimal would be an understatement," explained UNM researcher Dr. Carl White.

Dry conditions the summer before the first burn in 1995 yielded less than normal growth of grasses and plants, providing less than ideal fuel levels to carry the burn. Under the best conditions, the fire should have been followed by a light rain that would leach minerals released in the ash into the soil and make them available to the plants. Instead, the drought continued for seven more months. Much of the ash was moved about by wind. When the rains did come in late June of 1996, they were torrential thunderstorm-related downpours.

Although no significant differences in plant productivity were seen as a result of the 1995 burn, the study had some good news to report. Even under severe drought conditions, there was not a significant difference in soil erosion rates between the burned and non-burned areas. The researchers concluded that prescribed fire for reducing shrub and tree cover may pose minimal adverse risk even under drought conditions.

The plan is to study how repeated fires affect the landscape. The decision of when next to burn the area is based on plant recovery. Following the first burn, grass cover returned to preburn levels after the first growing season. Therefore, the Forest Service decided to burn the area a second time last month.

Forest Service crews were assisted by New Mexico State Forestry Division inmate crews and by members of the Placitas Volunteer Fire Brigade. Firefighters were somewhat frustrated by high relative humidity and fuel moisture. The fire did not burn as well as expected, and a portion of the site was left unburned due to time constraints.

Researchers will continue to monitor the effects of the burning, and when they determine it is time, firefighters will once again return to Placitas with drip torches to blacken the land. As more information is compiled on the effects of fire on the landscape, we can hopefully see fire used more often to restore the health of our environment.

MUSINGS AT GRAND CANYON NATIONAL PARK
September 2001

It is a beautiful evening on the South Rim of the Grand Canyon. I am alone, but surrounded by people. The sun is setting. I wander among the visitors, eavesdropping on conversations, looking for an opportunity to discuss fire ecology. The nearly full moon is creeping up the eastern sky. The sunset over the canyon is spectacular. The crowd at Mather Point acts like a feeding frenzy. Everyone is jockeying for position.

Along with the standard firefighter costume—yellow shirt, green pants, and big black boots—a radio is strapped to my chest. My gloves, hardhat, and fire shelter are in the car. There is no point in going overboard. The fires are a thousand feet higher and twelve to twenty miles away.

Here to mingle, my goal is to encourage people to think about the fires burning on the North Rim. Looking official, visitors ask me questions that have nothing to do with fires. A gracious host, I dispense details on bathrooms, lodging opportunities, bus schedules, and trail distances.

Before us stretches a canyon whose very magic is tied to the enormity of its scale, and yet people are asking about the "best view." They give an incredulous expression when I reply that any spot is magnificent.

What constitutes a "best spot"? Is it where famous photographs have been taken? Why do we come, from a diversity of cultures around the world, to a place that is irrefutably spiritual and inspiring, and want to have the same experience that everyone else has? If the trading post sold postcards of the canyon filled with smoke, would visitors demand frequent fires?

Eventually some kind person finally asks me a question about the fires. There are three fires burning on the North Rim. I point out the various smoke columns.

"These fires were started by lightning," I explain.

There are raised eyebrows when I say the first ignition was in July. It is almost October. My audience has been hooked. I will get at least five minutes with them under the reddening skies to lecture on the role of fire in the ecosystem. If my teenagers were here, they would be rolling their eyes. I am a bit passionate about my work.

"These fires are being allowed to burn under a strategy we call *Wildland Fire Use*. During the past century, our knee-jerk reaction was to put every fire out as soon as it began, or at least try to," I tell my captive listeners.

I talk about how that century of fire exclusion led to unnaturally crowded forest conditions. I can tell from their faces that this is not a new message. Following last summer's horrific fire season that included burning over four hundred homes in Los Alamos, public awareness of poor forest health conditions is high. I detect an anxiousness in their manner; they want to believe this error can be corrected.

I explain that in the areas where the fires are burning, there is a recent history of prescribed and natural burns. Some acres are now being burned for the second or third time this past decade. The more opportunities fire has to burn in these woods when fuel conditions are not extremely dry, the better prepared these forests are to survive the more catastrophic fires that occur under extreme weather conditions.

Before fires were excluded, they burned through the forest at irregular intervals. In ponderosa pine forests, those intervals averaged every three to fifteen years. For individual trees, the intervals were more sporadic with a single tree typically showing fire scars ranging from a series of three or four annual fires to periods of twenty-five or thirty years without a fire. Most of these fires were low-intensity blazes that moved quickly through the grassy forest, killing the youngest trees or occasional thick clumps of saplings. Ponderosa pine seedlings need several fire-free years to grow large enough to resist fires in order to survive. Fires provided a natural check on the number of trees that would become established.

Today we are trying to restore that natural process. When lightning struck on the Walhalla Plateau on the fifteenth of July, we paid attention, but we did not rush out to be firefighting heroes. Taking into consideration the area's fuels, the projected weather conditions, and the absence of resources threatened, park managers decided to allow the Vista Fire to run its natural course. This was a conditional decision as long as the burning conditions remained favorable, air quality standards were not exceeded, and the fire remained within a designated area. The Vista Fire crept around for ten weeks before a week of hot, dry weather changed the burning conditions. The fire slipped down into the canyon where it wasn't welcome, and generated smoke columns that rivaled the famed canyon for enormity. The Vista Fire was awarded full wildfire status, and crews were mobilized into action to put it to bed. Less than a week later, the fire was contained, having burned 3,658 acres in its eleven-week lifetime.

Meanwhile, two neighboring fires continue to burn on the North Rim. Lightning ignited the Swamp Ridge Fire on August 17 and the nearby Tower Fire twelve days later. Each time a fire started, park officials thought carefully about the decision to put the fire out or to let it burn its natural course. When the Vista Fire reached wildfire (suppression) status, these fires also exhibited increased fire activity. For a few days, managers closely monitored the Swamp Ridge Fire, and even took measures to secure a few of its flanks as it reached the edge of its designated area. The Tower Fire, being in the middle of a large "okay-to-burn" area, continued to expand its edges. Tonight, the two fires combined have burned over 4,500 acres. I explain to my now-tiring tourists that we consider these acres an "accomplishment" rather than a tragedy.

With the lesson drawing to a close, I answer pressing questions of bathroom locations and lodging options. I saunter back into the crowd, elbowing my way to the "best spot" to watch the ever-reddening skies. To the people around me, I murmur that the sunset is so spectacular because of smoke particles from fires burning on the North Rim. No one seems to take the bait.

Ignoring the crowd around me, I contemplate those early explorers who chanced upon this large ditch rather unexpectedly. Although asphalt and concrete walkways and black chain-link fences dominate my immediate environment, I am feeling solidarity with those early travelers. My canyon is filling with smoke as the sun goes down, and so was theirs. Fire is finally back as a part of the natural ecosystem.

THE PERFECT FIRE ON POWELL PLATEAU
August 2003

When fire researcher Stephen Pyne dubbed last year's Rodeo-Chediski Fire in west-central Arizona as "The Perfect Fire," I was a bit unsettled. He was referencing Sebastian Junger's book *The Perfect Storm*, which inspired a movie by the same name. The Perfect Storm refers to a meteorological phenomenon of uncommon weather conditions that combine to produce the most violent storm. Still, Rodeo-Chediski was anything but perfect if one applies the common meaning of the word. It was human-caused. It burned more acres than any fire ever recorded in Arizona. It destroyed over four hundred homes. It required the evacuation of ten communities along the Mogollon Rim. It is awfully hard to employ the word "perfect" in describing this disaster.

This summer I worked on a fire much closer to "perfect." The Powell Fire was in a remote region on the North Rim of the Grand Canyon. On June 15, lightning struck on the far northeast corner of Powell Plateau.

"It could not have started at a more convenient location," explained Jim Kitchen, the park's assistant fire management officer.

With prevailing southwest winds, and less flammable vegetation to the northeast that prevented fire spreading that way, the Powell Fire spent most of its life as a backing fire burning into the wind. This kept flame lengths low and allowed for light-intensity burning that slowly spread across the plateau over the next few weeks. The fire was recently declared out on August 20 and had burned approximately 3,800 acres.

One of the perfect conditions for this fire can be attributed to the geography of Powell Plateau itself. The plateau is separated from the main North Rim by Muav Saddle. Although a trail crosses the plateau, there is no road access. There is no history of grazing or logging, and very little fire suppression. As a result, the Powell Plateau supports what forest ecologists claim is more akin to the natural forest that evolved under a natural fire regime. Large ponderosa pines tower over a carpet of grasses. Due to regular burning (Powell Plateau last burned in three fires in the mid-1980s), there is little buildup of branches, logs, and other debris that firefighters see as "excessive fuel."

Another vote for perfect status was the lack of threat to lives and property. The historic cabin on Muav Saddle, built for Teddy Roosevelt's lion-hunting trips, was covered with protective wrap as a precaution if fire burned that direction. With closures to the area and no need for immediate access to the flames, no lives were threatened; no accidents occurred.

Twenty miles away, a thousand feet lower, and a gaping chasm between my location and the smoke columns, I was engaged in storytelling about the fire. One piece of the perfect story is the commitment to fire management practiced by the Grand Canyon park staff. All the i's are dotted, all the t's are crossed, and the plans are in place that identify conditions when fires are allowed to burn their natural courses. Called a *wildland fire use strategy*, park firefighters dispatched to wildfires now ask the critical question: Should we even try to put this fire out?

I like the concept of redefining the perfect fire. Forests across the Southwest should burn more like the Powell Fire and less like the Rodeo-Chediski Fire.

BURNING PILES
December 2006

On a full-moon night I drive out along Highway 260 east of the town of McNary to check on the day's burn project. Flames flicker among the piles that extend well beyond sight of the road. Turning off the engine and headlights, I stand in the cold night marveling at the moonlight filtering through the recently thinned forest canopies and illuminating a light layer of snow.

Fire in the forest tonight is invited and welcomed. This winter season burning is reducing fuels generated where crews recently thinned trees. Consequently, this forest has a slimmer chance of being destroyed by wildfire in coming dry seasons.

The history of agency-ignited, prescribed burning on the Fort Apache Reservation stretches back to the 1950s and 1960s, even before other agencies recognized the importance of fire. Now, a new chapter begins in the ongoing story of people, fire, and forests. After a two-year break, a new prescribed burning program is in place. The new program is a cooperative effort between the White Mountain Apache Tribe (WMAT) and the BIA Fort Apache Agency (FTA) Fire Management Program. With new personnel in key positions, and following all national standards and qualifications, fire is reclaiming a role as a management tool in the forested lands of the White Mountain Apache Tribe. This fall all projects involved burning piles of slash—limbs, branches, and small boles—from thinning and logging projects.

Many of the slash piles we are burning this year are adjacent to homes. The pile-burns complete fuel reduction projects, making homes in the forest safer from the threat of catastrophic fires. Piles are also

Piles of thinning slash are burned in the winter with snow on the ground. Courtesy of Dan Ware.

burned in areas thinned under other forest management activities designed to improve forest health and harvest wood products. Burning conditions are defined by an approved plan. If weather and fuel conditions are not within specified ranges, no burning is conducted. Burn units are bordered by roads or other fire breaks. Firefighters monitor burning and insure the fire remains confined to project areas.

Piles are ignited opposite of the wind direction so flames generate less heat. Usually the maximum flame height is six to ten feet above the pile and lasts less than thirty minutes. Piles may burn for several hours and smoke for a few days. Most of the time, about 90 percent of the pile is consumed in the fire, leaving a few blackened larger logs.

Generally, the fire is confined to slash but sometimes the fire creeps away from the pile, burning pine needles or grasses. Flame lengths are usually less than six inches. Although the top layer of needles may be blackened, this type of fire does not provide the same cleansing benefit of a broadcast burn.

Since burning piles have compacted material, they generate large amounts of smoke. Although this smoke is minor compared to a wildfire, smoke management is still a major focus of our burning program. The Arizona Department of Environmental Quality approves burning plans for federal and state land management agencies in order to coordinate the amount of smoke generated by agency burning. The White Mountain Apache Tribe provides the state information on our burning plans each day so tribal smoke contributions can be factored in the regional air-sheds.

Tribal staff monitor air quality sensors and have predetermined levels that will trigger shutting down ignition operations. If weather conditions are not favorable for dissipating smoke, operations are terminated until the weather changes. All burning plans are posted on a local information line and website (http://www.593info.org/) to keep residents—especially those with health concerns—informed.

With the two-year break in the burning program, sixty thousand acres of treatment areas had piles that needed burning. Agency and tribal staff treated about fifteen thousand acres during this season. For these acres, fire managers will be less concerned about wildfires generating intense heat.

I will long remember that moonlit night, standing in the snow, watching the flames dance in the forest. Through our efforts to thin trees, burn piles, and manage brush, we are honoring the role that fire plays in our landscape. Standing there, I thought about the term *firefighter,* and struggled for another way to define my colleagues and myself. Although we do not shy away from battling fire when conditions are extreme and fires are destroying resources, the title only hints at a portion of our jobs. The Confederated Salish-Kootenai Tribes in Montana have a native word for a person who burns, and I wonder if our language will develop a similar job title.

BURNING QUESTIONS
October 2007

I slip into a crowded room of colleagues who have gathered to work on the prescribed burn plan. The room hums with energy as team members exchange ideas. I am awed by the experience in the room as burn bosses, experienced fire technicians, seasoned foresters, and other specialists lean over laptops and clipboards. Our assembled group includes representatives from local, regional, and national offices. We bounce ideas off each other as the document takes shape.

During a break I am on the phone with a friend, and upon learning how I am spending the day, she replies how pleased she is that prescribed burns are so well planned and executed.

"Sure they are," I reply, "and it's akin to herding cats."

Later in the afternoon I am assigned to the Goals and Objectives group. Our job is to explain why we are burning. For a while we are stumped on defining the outcomes. If we bring fire to the forest there will be changes. However, we cannot predict exactly where these changes will occur. At different fire intensities, there will be different impacts. With knowledge of weather and fuel conditions, we have a reasonable handle on predicting fire intensity as long as there are no unanticipated or unexpected deviations in these conditions.

In order to kill excess young trees and leave open forests similar to forests that existed a century ago, the fire needs to be hotter than the low, creeping flames often associated with prescribed burning. Fire burns in chaotic patterns regardless of whether it is a wildfire or a prescribed fire. On the ground we can observe these patterns in different intensities—we talk about the fire "fingering" as it leaves unburned patches, or "torching out" when isolated trees or tree groups burn without burning the forest around them.

I am reminded of lessons learned from a lifetime of watching the Rio Grande and other river systems. Each spring the river floods or, at least, it floods in places where water flow is not regulated by dams. One cannot predict which sandbar will be washed out in the flood, but one can predict, based on the snowpack and rate of melt, approximately what percentage of sandbars may be washed away and reformed.

Fires, like floods, are disturbance forces. If we encourage a fire to burn through a forest under certain conditions, some trees may be killed. With drier conditions, fire burns hotter and tree mortality is greater. Therefore, by identifying what is acceptable in terms of size and number of trees lost, we can select a "prescription" that matches the outcomes we are trying to achieve. We may not be able to predict exactly which pockets of trees will blow out, but we can tailor our firing techniques to protect specific areas, including cultural sites or sensitive soils.

I drift to another writing group. For the smoke management section, we insure that communications are clearly outlined for coordinating our activities with neighboring agencies. We determine how to keep the public informed of which days we plan to burn. We also plan how to shut down the burning if smoke particulates exceed acceptable levels.

In two days of concentrated effort, a solid draft of the broadcast burning plan is completed. Over the next week, missing information and additional input will be added and the plan will be finalized. By the end of the month, weather permitting, we will be in the field with drip torches and hopes that everything goes according to plan.

SEATs take no back seat
in air tanker business
May 2003

As a twenty-year veteran firefighter, I was skeptical when I first heard about single-engine airplanes dumping fire retardant on fires. I wondered how small planes could be as effective as large military bombers. A visit to the Single Engine Air Tanker (SEAT) base at the Las Vegas (New Mexico) Municipal Airport convinced me these small planes are the answer to problems presented by the current aging large air tanker fleet.

The SEAT used for firefighting is the largest single-engine plane in the world with a wingspan sixty feet across. The Air Tractor AT-802, built in Olney, Texas, can carry eight hundred gallons in its hopper. Unlike the large air tankers, the Air Tractor's versatile storage area can switch between loads of water, retardant, or another firefighting liquid known as wet water, which reduces surface tension. Typically the plane's first load is water, which can either be dropped on the fire if the reported fire is found, or dumped elsewhere without sacrificing an expensive load

Single Engine Air Tanker (SEAT) on the tarmac at Las Vegas
Municipal Airport. SEATs provide air support for firefighting
by accurately delivering various fire retardants to wildfires.
Photo by author.

of slurry. When the plane isn't being used on fires, the hopper can also
be loaded with seed, fertilizer, or any other aerial applications.

The larger bombers carry two to three thousand gallons of retardant, which is loaded on the planes from permanently placed vats at
designated air tanker bases. Depending on the model, these planes can
drop their retardant in one pass or in several separate loads. In New
Mexico the three air tanker bases are in Albuquerque, Alamogordo, and
Silver City. SEATs, on the other hand, are loaded from easily transported
mixing tanks mounted on a trailer. Any airstrip, or even stretch of highway, can be set up to refuel and reload the small planes in the time it
takes to drive to the location. Therefore, by placing the SEAT operation
closer to the fire, the SEAT has a significantly faster turnaround time
between loads.

The plane is also plumbed for rapid turnaround and can be refueled
and reloaded with the engine still running. The average "pit-stop" time

is between three and five minutes. Louie Casaus, Las Vegas district forester and a wildfire incident commander, described being on the ground on a recent fire utilizing the SEAT.

"It would seem just a matter of minutes since the plane left, before we'd hear it coming back again. It was just amazing."

Casaus and other incident commanders have been especially impressed with the pinpoint accuracy of the retardant drops. Armed with built-in global positioning system equipment, the plane's state-of-the-art technology provides precision guidance. This ability to lay the retardant exactly in needed locations actually reduces the amount of overall retardant needed to fight the fire, providing one more cost-saving measure in the operation.

State-of-the-art technology is apparent in various safety measures built into the plane as well, including excellent pilot visibility, a rugged airframe, and features that make the plane crash-worthy. Pilot Dan Rinner of Aztec, New Mexico, recently had an incident that might have proven fatal in a different craft. After dropping a retardant load his plane hit the treetops, but he was able to fly the plane back to the airport and make a safe landing. Although the plane sustained damage, the pilot escaped injury. The Clovis-based company Dan works for, Aero Tech Inc., brought in a replacement plane and the SEAT operation was only temporarily out of service.

"Safety is the primary focus of our operation," explains retired army ranger Harry Weeks. A certified "SEAT manager," Weeks is the official agency employee responsible for the safety and use of the aircraft. The aircraft does not fly without a SEAT manager on the ground to supervise the operation and a certified crash/rescue unit on call at the airstrip. At the Las Vegas Municipal Airport, this service is contracted from the Las Vegas Fire Department. The City of Las Vegas supports the SEAT operation with the services of the city's Public Water Works as well.

In addition to the Las Vegas location, the New Mexico State Forestry Division also sponsors a SEAT operation based out of Ruidoso in cooperation with the Village of Ruidoso. Aero Tech Inc. has the contract for that operation as well, offering a truly New Mexican solution toward addressing the national issue of air tanker availability.

SOUTHWEST FIRE FIGHTERS
July 2007

It is approaching nine p.m. and excited chatter wafts through a tangle of fire gear strewn out along the Fire Management warehouse dock. Fort Apache Crews 11 and 12 are repacking their two-week packs and organizing their field gear into day packs.

"I still need two more squad bosses." The speaker is Victoria Burnette, and she is the SWFF (pronounced "Swift") coordinator for the White Mountain Apache Tribe.

I mentally go through a list of fire leadership staff in our department. We already have employees in Oregon, Utah, and Arizona, and these crews are heading for Nevada. I make a few more cell phone calls.

The Southwest Fire Fighters (SWFF) are the backbone of our firefighting operations in Arizona and New Mexico. Classified as "emergency" firefighters, these folks only get paid when they are assigned to a fire incident. The twenty-person "hand-line" crews are sponsored by a wildland firefighting agency such as a local Bureau of Indian Affairs office or Forest Service Ranger District.

Each crew consists of a crew representative, who handles the administrative aspects of keeping firefighters productively working on the fire line; a crew boss, who is in charge of the crew; three squad bosses, who each supervise five other firefighters; and fifteen firefighters. Only six of these firefighters can be "rookies" who have not yet worked on fires actively burning. Among the more experienced firefighters, a few need to be cross-trained as sawyers.

Many rural communities throughout Arizona and New Mexico have organized SWFF crews, but the majority of the crews come from the area's reservations. On Fort Apache Reservation, where 60 percent of Apache adults are unemployed, getting SWFF crews organized and dispatched to fires is an important and critical job. For many, the only income they will earn all year will come from this seasonal work.

Each spring prospective firefighters take physical fitness tests, medical exams, and drug tests, and get training to ensure they qualify for the fire season. Their experience and training is logged in national databases, and anyone who does not meet set standards is not allowed to participate.

The warehouse manager is distributing gear and lunches and making sure the crew boss has the right number of first aid kits and other essential crew gear. I talk to some other squad bosses and get leads on who else might be available. We send runners to see if we can find someone with the right qualifications. Since the crew won't be going out until five a.m. the next day, someone who is taking a mandatory day off might be eligible to join this group. Eventually we complete the manifest, a formal listing of the crew members.

I gather the crew and go over the mandatory safety briefing. We work through a list of behavioral dos and don'ts based on past experiences and common sense. The crew bosses will establish a strong regimen of discipline. Participating on a fire crew is similar to being on a short-term military assignment. The consequences of breaking the rules are serious and can result in a lifelong ban from participating in the program, in addition to any legal implications.

I remind the Apache crews that their people have a long tradition of understanding fire, a tradition that goes back before there were federal agencies and Meals-Ready-to-Eat. Despite all of our attention to safety standards and guidelines, they do risk their lives. They are part of a long line of organized Apache crews who have traversed the country over the past five decades fighting fires. I am honored to have the opportunity to send them on their way.

The firefighters pack up and head home to catch a few hours' sleep before the bus departs. As the warehouse dock empties out, I consult with the dispatchers, Victoria, and my notes. Tomorrow there will be another crew request, and we are already trying to line up the next set of squad bosses.

WHO PAYS THE BILL?
April 1989

If you have not heard by now, New Mexico is gearing up for one of its worst fire seasons. The reason is simple: it is dry. No rain, low humidities, below normal snowpacks, and no promising weather forecasts.

Not only are the forests dry, the grasslands, roadsides, and even the two-by-fours in your home are drier than usual. Despite major efforts to caution the public on fire use, there will be fires this summer. You may be wondering who will fight them.

Fire responsibilities come in two broad categories: structures and wildland. Of course cities have fire departments, but outside city boundaries, the New Mexico Fire Marshall's Office, and under its direction the rural fire departments, arc responsible for structural fires. Wildland fires are handled by a multitude of agencies including the rural fire departments.

Beyond quick, safe suppression, one issue firefighters are concerned with is "who will pay the bill?" Provided no one can be held responsible for the fire, the agency that manages the land where the fire originated picks up the tab. This means that if the fire is on national forest lands, the United States Forest Service foots the bill. If the fire is on a reservation, the bill goes to the Bureau of Indian Affairs. In New Mexico, the agency with the largest area of wildland fire suppression responsibility is the New Mexico State Forestry Division. State Forestry is responsible for wildland firefighting on all state and private lands.

The wildland fire near Raven Road, south of Tijeras, last week was a State Forestry fire. Of course there were green Forest Service trucks and red county fire department engines out there with the white State Forestry rigs. New Mexico is a leader nationwide in maintaining a multiagency approach to fire management.

Joint powers, mutual-aid, and initial attack agreements are much more than bureaucratic papers cluttering the halls of government. The state is divided into logical areas for initial attack where the closest unit responds when a wildland fire occurs. The Raven Fire was in Bernalillo County Fire District 11 and the wildland initial attack zone for the Sandia Ranger Station, Cibola National Forest in Tijeras.

Once the fire escapes initial attack, or after twenty-four hours has gone by, the agency responsible for the fire takes control.

So if the green Forest Service trucks were at the fire because of initial attack responsibilities, what about the county fire department vehicles? First, fire departments were on scene to protect structures (remember, that is their primary responsibility), and second, those fire departments fight wildland fires all the time under agreement with the State Forestry Division. Although the Raven Fire occurred within the boundaries of Bernalillo County District 11, the adjacent fire districts have mutual-aid agreements and were there to help out as well.

Although State Forestry has the greatest number of fires and the largest area of responsibility, it is the smallest natural resources agency in the state with wildland firefighting responsibilities. For example, State Forestry's Bernalillo District has three full-time employees to cover six million acres in eight counties. Therefore, State Forestry relies on the rural and municipal fire departments to help them handle the job.

In exchange for fighting wildland fires, State Forestry provides fire districts with training and pays them for the forest fires they fight.

All of this cooperation is the result of hours of planning and meeting and pages of signed agreements. However, on the fire ground, the cooperation works well. Nationally, New Mexico is viewed as one of the leaders in cooperation between local, state, and federal resource agencies engaged in wildfire suppression. Perhaps because our state is large, our population is relatively small, and our people regularly celebrate our diversity, we are in a position to show the nation how to coordinate firefighting relationships.

 ## ADDRESSING THE WILDLAND URBAN INTERFACE
March 1991

On May 24, 1989, a missile fired from Kirkland Air Force Base in Albuquerque, New Mexico, ignited what was to be the six-hundred-acre Coyote Fire. About the same time, several miles to the south, a house fire near Raven Road ignited the surrounding forest and threatened several nearby structures. As the smoke plumes rose and merged, the confusion surrounding the fires increased.

Initially, county engines were battling fire burning from tree to tree with structural firefighting techniques. Meanwhile wildland firefighters were puzzling over flames threatening propane tanks. Radio frequencies buzzed with confusion as firefighters tried to find quick ways to communicate with each other on separate channels. Traffic jams developed on roads congested with emergency vehicles going in and evacuating residents coming out.

Although only the original home that ignited the Raven Fire was lost, firefighters found that they had clearly stretched their levels of expertise.

"We had been hearing about the wildland-urban interface concerns for years," District Fire Management Officer Louie Casaus said, "but until the Raven Fire, we just didn't understand the practical applications."

The Sandia and Manzano mountains lie on the eastern edge of Albuquerque. Former city dwellers have been moving into the East Mountain area at rapidly increasing rates over the past two decades. This situation follows a national trend of exponentially greater numbers of residences in formerly wild lands. Natural resource managers have dubbed this situation "the wildland urban interface" and are challenged with protecting both habitat and newcomers.

The Bernalillo District is one of six field offices for the New Mexico Forestry and Resources Conservation Division. Division responsibilities include fighting forest fires on all state and private lands and providing technical forestry advice to private landowners. The district's four employees are responsible for over six million acres in eight counties, including the four counties containing the mountainous suburbs next to Albuquerque.

The Coyote and Raven fires raised the public consciousness about the effects of human development in the forests and provided the impetus for a new organization to address fire management concerns. By the end of the year, the East Mountain Interagency Fire Protection Association (EMIFPA) was created to help address wildfire threats in the East Mountain communities.

EMIFPA is composed of thirteen county fire departments, two wildland firefighting agencies, and four local county sheriff departments. The goal of the organization is to facilitate cooperation on wildland fires, especially where homes and lives are at stake. The organization has actively taken on three main program areas: training, public information, and communication.

In the past year and a half, EMIFPA sponsored six trainings on wildland firefighting techniques and using the Incident Command System (ICS). ICS is a national management strategy originally developed for wildland firefighting but applicable in emergencies of all kinds.

The highlight of these trainings was "Operation Mockingbird." Initial attack on a mock fire was made by a helitack crew, with tanker and helicopter drops following. Trainees implemented the Incident Command System, and proceeded to deal with simulated escaped fire, injuries, evacuations, and flame-involved structures. After the exercise, firefighters critiqued the event. For many volunteers this was their first experience applying ICS to wildland firefighting.

The EMIFPA public information program has several objectives. In addition to letting the public know about the organization's programs, the goal is to educate homeowners, builders, and developers on ways to reduce loss of life and property.

A flyer depicting fifteen correct household practices to reduce wildland fire threat was published in the spring of 1990 and distributed to area residents. Agencies also sponsored school programs to emphasize fire prevention. Currently the organization is developing a plan to notify area residents and visitors of high fire dangers through the use of red flags and fire danger rating billboards.

The primary hurdle to get over for the communications group was to provide association members access to common radio frequencies. An important result has been several mutual-aid agreements that legally allow the entities in EMIFPA to cooperate. Due to these agreements, any wildland firefighting agency can access personnel and equipment from a county fire department through the State Forestry Division. The ultimate communication goal is to set aside a frequency that can be used on any ICS event.

The short fire season of 1990 provided successful tests of the new organization: Firefighters from various agencies worked together smoothly on two fires on the Cibola National Forest. Although neither fire directly threatened structures, the Forest Service used the improved access to personnel and equipment from the county fire departments. Although EMIFPA was originally developed to address wildland fires, the organization has provided the environment to manage other disasters, including hazardous material spills and rescue operations.

Postscript: This article was written in 1991, but EMIFPA is still active and setting standards for the development of innovative training, public outreach, and community collaboration.

FIRE IN THE BOSQUE
July 2003

Early in my professional career, I cut my firefighting teeth down in the bosque. At that time (the mid- and late 1980s) no one paid much attention to fires in these cottonwood forests alongside the Rio Grande. Volunteer fire departments were happy to turn over the fire when we would show up in our State Forestry fire engine. Our district included six large New Mexico counties, so we fought plenty of fires in the mountain forests as well, but bosque fires always signaled the beginning of our fire season. These fires also broke all the rules of what we knew about fighting fire in the higher elevations.

When I pursued a master's degree in the 1990s, I knew I wanted to study fire ecology and assumed I would look at some aspect of fire in ponderosa pine ecosystems. However, Dr. Cliff Crawford at the University of New Mexico encouraged me to develop an understanding of the role of fire in the bosque.

Now with recent fires that threatened Albuquerque communities, I've been fielding many questions about bosque fire ecology. Unlike our upland forests, fire is not a beneficial part of this ecosystem. Fire provides a major threat to the survival of the cottonwood forest along the Rio Grande. Human influence created volatile conditions, and I think solutions need to be human-engineered as well.

In prehistoric times, with regular flood pulses from spring mountain runoff, the river shifted and meandered throughout the floodplain, generating a mosaic of wetlands, forest clumps, grassy meadows, and willow thickets. Fires may have moved into the bosque from adjacent grasslands, and early Native Americans may have burned portions of bosque to drive game into the open. Generally, few fires occurred due to high moisture in potential fuels and rapid litter decomposition. Fires were probably not large-scale events. Regular flooding over the river's banks helped woody debris decompose rapidly, and during most years kept conditions relatively moist. Fires probably burned at a lighter intensity than recent fires.

Many factors contribute to the hotter fires we have today. Upstream dams restrict overbank flooding, slowing litter decomposition rates. The river has been relegated to defined channels by levees, which has led to long, narrow, continuous stands of forests. Compared with pre-historic conditions, there has been a dramatic decrease in wetlands and lakes that may have provided regular fuel breaks. The addition of exotic shrub species such as salt cedar and Russian olive also provides more vertical fuel ladders and continuous mid-story fuels. More people visiting the bosque provides increased sources of ignition. Taken together, these factors result in a more intense fire regime in today's cottonwood forest.

In 1995, I took a careful look at a fire database compiled by New Mexico State Forestry to learn about bosque fires from the past decade's statistics. Of the recorded ignition sources, humans were responsible for starting 98 percent of all bosque fires. Also, the number and sizes of fires were increasing. In 1996, a large bosque fire occurred at Bosque del Apache, which generated more public awareness and agency interest in public education. When I repeated the analysis in 2000, I found that the number of fires annually had dropped in half in 1996 and held steady each year after that—a result I attribute to increased fire prevention and awareness programs.

My research focused on the mortality of cottonwoods from fire. Top-kill of cottonwood trees ranged from 50 percent in the lowest fire severity areas to 100 percent where fire severity was most intense. Due to accumulating limbs, dead trees, dried grasses, and other fuels, bosque fires now burn much hotter and longer than the conditions under which cottonwoods evolved. In some areas, the stumps and roots of cottonwoods do resprout, but they are often out-competed by non-native shrubs and trees. In general, cottonwood forests cannot survive in today's fire environment.

The arrangement of the bosque in long, narrow bands against a levee-confined river is not natural, and neither are fuel conditions, recent changes in ground water hydrology, or other disruptions of ecological processes including the changing role of fire. If we want to avoid life- and property-threatening fires, we need to take a different approach to managing the river and its adjacent forests. We need to restore conditions that mirror a healthy ecosystem. In the long run, we need to honor the natural hydrological processes and restore a river that experiences flood pulses and has its own water allocations. Immediately we need to address the rapidly building fuel conditions in the bosque.

OKLAHOMA FIRE RESPONSE
February 2006

Often when working in the vast ponderosa pine forests of the Southwest, my co-workers are surprised when they learn I earned my undergraduate forestry degree in Oklahoma. Despite the eastern pines and central cross-timbers, the Sooner State doesn't immediately conjure up images of forests. Most years Oklahoma doesn't conjure up images of forest fires, either. However, since November, the state has been a literal hotbed of wildland fire activity.

Recording a little under a half-million scorched acres burned in just over two thousand fires since November 5, 2005, Oklahoma is experiencing one of its worst fire seasons in the state's history. I was dispatched to my old stomping grounds as one of thousands of firefighters from over thirty-five states who spent time this winter chasing brush and grass fires around the state.

When I arrived at the Incident Command Post in Shawnee, Oklahoma, I was greeted by Mark Bays, a former college classmate who is the urban forester with the Oklahoma Forestry Division. Among Mark's many accomplishments is nursing back to health an elm tree that survived the 1995 blast that brought down the Alfred P. Murrah Building in Oklahoma City. Mark was now part of a team led by Oklahoma Forestry Division employees determined to survive another catastrophic event in recent Oklahoma history.

The division's main objective is to support the scattered network of rural fire departments battling fires that often number more than twenty each day. In a sustained effort that has lasted for several months, firefighters from across the country bring engines, dozers, air tankers, and other tools to assist with blazes that generally are extinguished the same day they start. Burning in grass and brush, these fires blacken thousands of acres daily and have, this winter, destroyed over two hundred homes. On my fifth day in Oklahoma I witnessed three homes consumed by fire.

"We were getting national media attention at the end of December and in early January," information officer Michelle Finch explained, "but once their attention was distracted by mine accidents, the media haven't really come back to us."

The Forestry Division and their extended support represent only a portion of firefighters committed to the Oklahoma effort. The Bureau of Indian Affairs (BIA) carries responsibility on fires impacting the checkerboard pattern of Indian lands. The BIA also headquarters their fire response at the Shawnee Incident Command Post to ensure coordinated efforts within the state.

Coordination is the key word, as the first (and often last) firefighters on the fires are from local fire departments. My experience on the ground with these departments was extremely varied. Some departments had state-of-the-art, vehicle-mounted laptops that conjured satellite-furnished images of the area. Meanwhile, other departments were operating ancient federal excess firefighting equipment from the 1950s and 1960s. I even met a team of ranch hands who were staffing a fire engine they had built just the week before in response to a fire that had threatened their local horse ranch.

When I left Oklahoma, there had been a few days of icy sleet and snow. The fire behavior specialist didn't expect the reprieve to last any more than a week before fire activity would pick up again. With fires this year already burning in Texas, Oklahoma, Arizona, New Mexico, and California, and very little snow or moisture in the high country, fire managers are preparing for an early and intense wildfire season throughout the Southwest. We expect most fires this spring and early summer will be started by people. Perhaps we can learn a lesson from the winter fires of Oklahoma and pass the word for everyone to be especially careful this year with any ignition sources.

FAREWELL TO MY FIRE BOOTS
April 2006

For the past three years while working for a tribe, I have lived on the reservation. I have great friends and neighbors. I live within walking distance of my office. I can work long hours without having to face a late-night commute on highways patrolled by large wildlife.

The downside is that my home is broken into frequently. In fact, fourteen times in thirty-two months. I try to stay upbeat about this insult. I often joke about how humbling this job is, including curing me of owning material possessions.

I try to console myself with far-fetched rationalizations. Like the time my camping equipment was stolen, I tried to imagine that whoever ended up owning my winter expedition-grade North Face tent probably needed a good home for their children. When two of my guitars were taken, I decided some budding musicians would not only make it big someday but they would look me up and compensate me for the instruments that started their career.

The weekend my deceased grandfather's tools disappeared I was crushed. I tried joking about it but that greasy box of ancient wrenches, screwdrivers, and hammers included memories that no one else would recognize or cherish. I felt the same way when my earrings and necklaces vanished. No one else would know that my grandmother wore that turquoise or that my great aunt gave me those earrings.

Of course, I have lost my CDs and DVDs, and I sincerely hope the thief has developed an appreciation for my eclectic collection of folk music and musicals.

The local police have told me that the burglars are probably local drug users looking for stuff to sell to support their addictions. Regularly people come to my door trying to sell me things—appliances, CDs, DVDs, jewelry, tools. After making sure none of it is my own stuff, I inquire if these things are stolen. I am always assured they are not. Then the seller quickly moves on his way.

Initially, with early break-ins, the thieves helped themselves to whatever beer was in the refrigerator, or wine or liquor bottles in the cabinet. My housemate set out water-filled gin bottles, but within a week of the theft of these decoys our home was ransacked. The perpetrators left graffiti on the walls and appliances. Now I refuse to keep any alcohol in my house because I do not want to have that added bonus available to any unwelcome intruder.

Each time I am burglarized, the thief takes a bag to carry the loot. When I moved to the reservation, I was rich in extra daypacks and travel bags, but now I only have a few I keep with me.

I guess I should have anticipated one of my more recent losses, but I was tired. After returning from a fire assignment in Oklahoma, I dropped my fire pack on my living room floor and then headed off to work. When I returned, the kitchen window was broken and my fire pack was gone. The thief had politely left my dirty laundry on the floor, but kept my recently rebuilt twenty-year-old White's fire-fighting boots.

A colleague from Montana was sympathetic when I told my tale.

"Wow, they stole your Whites!" he exclaimed. "That's like stealing your soul."

"Worse," I corrected, "it's like stealing two soles!"

In college, I always dreamed of owning a pair of these custom-built Cadillacs of the fire boot world. Then I fought fires in a pair of Red Wings and suffered the insult of not owning White's. Once I was out of school and working, I found rent, groceries, and diapers higher on the priority list than getting ideal boots.

In 1986 I received the Outstanding Tree Farm Inspector award from the New Mexico Tree Farm Committee for my forestry work with private landowners. The prize was a pair of the custom boots. Since then the boots have been my steady companions through decades of firefighting. During fire season, they accompany me everywhere I go. In airports during the summer, I am the one holding up the security lines while I unlace and lace up my stylish footwear.

Despite spending hundreds of hours rubbing them with Neat's foot oil, the soles had become slick and the uppers were sporting wear. This past winter, I sent them in for new soles and uppers. The $200 refurbishing job seemed cheap compared to the $380 cost for a new pair. I thought I would be able to spend at least a few more decades in them chasing fires. Now perhaps some other firefighter will benefit, but I cannot help hoping he gets awful blisters.

Speaking of blisters, I was so distraught about the loss of my boots I did what any normal woman would do: I got a pedicure. This time instead of insisting on preserving my calluses built up over three decades of active hiking and firefighting, I passively let the attendant remove them. I was defeated and throwing in the towel.

Of course that is not an option. I am a firefighter. I have already started wearing another pair of boots. However, while most foresters are stressing over drought index charts and the dire possibilities of large fires on the landscape this season, I am worrying about the dire possibilities of large blisters on my feet.

10

ALASKA ADVENTURES

June 2006

There are many ways I could have come to Nenana, Alaska—barge, train, plane, canoe, parachute—but I came the most conventional way: by rental car. Nenana has a special magnetism that attracts a plethora of goods and people. The small village an hour southwest of Fairbanks on the George Parks Highway lies at the confluence of the Nenana River and the broad Tanana River. Railroad tracks partially encircle the town and frequently host freight and passenger trains, the former providing interface with barges on the Tanana. An airstrip at the south end of the town offers the fourth major form of transportation in and out of the community.

My first night in Alaska, I stopped in Nenana to catch a few hours of sleep by the side of the road. I had flown into Fairbanks on Friday and was heading toward Denali National Park. The main purpose of my Alaskan visit was to attend the thirtieth annual Intertribal Timber Symposium in Fairbanks. I arranged to spend the weekends on either side of the workshop exploring the Last Frontier.

After rafting on the Nenana River and hiking in Denali National Park, I rendezvoused back in Fairbanks with my staff. The Tanana Chiefs Council headquartered in Fairbanks was sponsoring the native-focused national forestry gathering. On Wednesday during the conference, our staff broke in two groups. While a small group of renegades took the day off to visit Denali National Park, most of our group participated in the conference-hosted field trip. After a morning of learning about black spruce, white spruce, and birch-aspen forest ecology, Nenana tribal leaders set out a beautiful lunch with tables on the Tanana River beach. Tribal children entertained us with traditional dancing and singing.

At our next forest stop above the town, we noticed a plume of smoke in the valley below. As the speakers explained how global warming was increasing forest insect and fire disturbances in boreal forests, we watched the smoke column grow. My Denali-bound employees called in to report that their attempts to travel were thwarted by a closed highway, tall flames, and smokejumpers coming out of the sky.

Despite the excitement of watching the fire develop, my staff members were preoccupied with the conference. On Thursday, five White Mountain Apache Tribal Forestry employees presented papers relating

Mary in Alaska, Tanana River and smoke column from Parks Highway Fire in background. Courtesy Tee Voight.

to our work in Arizona. This was their first opportunity to speak at a national conference. With well-crafted PowerPoint presentations and hours of practice and coordination, the speeches drew wonderful evaluations and generated thoughtful discussions.

Still we found ourselves awake through the bright, near-summer-solstice Alaskan night, mesmerized by the smoke column, now quite visible from Fairbanks. When I took my staff to the airport the next morning, one of them asked me to go by the Alaska Fire Center and purchase a fire sweatshirt for her.

That afternoon I wandered into the Parks Highway Fire Information Center that was still hastily being organized. Recognizing the chaotic rush that comes in the first days of a fire incident, I quickly volunteered to answer phones. In an attempt to gain credibility, I whipped out my current "Red Card" identifying me as a Type 2 Information Officer. Recognized nationally by all interagency wildland firefighting agencies, the "Red Card" is carried by trained and registered firefighters and outlines the carrier's experience and qualifications.

The staff there looked at me in awe. Although other information officers were en route from other parts of Alaska and the Lower 48, the current needs were immediate. A house had already burned near Nenana and the whole town was threatened. A voluntary evacuation was in place and the Alaskan Railroad was bussing passengers rather than risk running the train through the middle of a fast-moving wildfire. Rather than volunteer for an afternoon, they wanted me to sign up and stay for a fire assignment. After a few calls to my home unit in Arizona, I was officially one of the 551 firefighters who would respond to the incident.

That evening in Nenana, I attended a large community meeting and got my first briefing on the fire. Just as the university professors two days earlier had described, the homogenous stands of black spruce were burning intensely and fire was spreading rapidly. One home and some cabins had already burned. More were threatened. People with smoke-related health concerns were encouraged to leave the area.

Tom Kurth, the incident commander, explained that the airstrip on the south end of town would provide a good fuel break to help firefighters defend the actual town area, but the outlying home sites were still quite vulnerable. Many residents were evacuating. That night the town lost power and another home burned.

I spent the next nine days working out of Nenana at the Incident Command Post. The operation was set up in a student dormitory, currently empty of students who summer in their bush-village homes. My co-workers marveled at how unique it was to have an Alaskan wildfire anywhere near a highway. Alaskan information officers are accustomed to less immediate media and public access, so my Lower 48 wisdom came in handy. The days were full, as changing winds threatened additional

Birch burning in 40 mph winds by the side of the road during
the Parks Highway Fire near Nenana, Alaska in 2006.
Courtesy of Bruce Swaim.

communities along the Parks Highway. I had a chance to learn about
firefighting techniques utilizing trains, helicopters, river access, and
slopping through the muskeg.

As I came to know residents and firefighters, my enchantment with
Nenana grew. Although I found myself fantasizing about moving to the
Great Land of Adventure, I was needed back in Arizona where fires were
also burning. My planned week in Alaska had stretched past two weeks
and I now had lifelong friends all over the state. As I finished my assignment, I finally made the right connections to buy the sweatshirt I had
originally been tasked with finding.

REMEMBERING SAM TOBIAS
October 2000

Late afternoon on May 11, 2000, ten miles south of Cloudcroft, New Mexico, a tree fell across a power line, sparking a fire in the surrounding forest. Call it luck, or call it premonition, but as preparations were being made for a flight to check out this new start, both available air attack supervisors hopped into the observation plane. The standard protocol only called for one.

The country down south near Weed and Sacramento, communities southeast of Cloudcroft, is a wild place. It is one of those populated places that defies rural addressing. It is a mountain paradise where an independent soul can build a home from scratch, live an unencumbered lifestyle, avoid government intervention, praise God, and carry a gun.

Forests of pine, fir, and—now remember Storm King Mountain—Gambel oak lay between these people and the rapidly growing fire heading their way. Folks were scattered up canyons, on mountaintops, on hillsides, in side canyons throughout a relatively large area. Many of the—for lack of a more accurate word—"roads" were impassable. Chief Gene Green of the Cloudcroft Police Department had assumed the command of the evacuation process.

Pushed by the wind, a wall of flame was racing across the landscape. By the time the fire reached the outskirts of the small hub of Weed, it had traveled approximately twelve miles in five hours.

Gene Green told me later that the evacuation would never have gone so smooth or have been so effective without those "Angels in the Sky." Working as a team, Bob Peña was in the back seat with the maps and the best local knowledge, and Sam Tobias was up front handling the radio. In a calm and friendly voice, Sam directed the ground force of law enforcement officers and volunteer firefighters through the maze of wooded wildlands until every person was located and given the opportunity to evacuate. Sixty-four homes were destroyed, but no one died that night on the Scott Able Fire.

My Type 2 Incident Management Team was initially assigned the fire, and I was the lead information officer (IO). As the smoke was clearing, and my team was completing a line around one side of the fire, we were replaced by a varsity squad, a Type 1 team from California. This team was more qualified to handle the complexities of lost homes, but because of my local knowledge, I was asked to stay on the fire to assist the new information officers when my team demobilized.

I expected the upcoming days would consist of escorting media to the fire line, running information to stores and cafes that served incredible pies, and visiting the Red Cross station and the Weed Cafe to be showered with support actually intended for firefighters on the line. For a day I enjoyed this lifestyle.

On Tuesday, May 15, Maria Garcia and I were facilitating a television interview with some board members of the Sky Ridge Church Camp. The camp, and the neighboring subdivision, which included many cabins owned by church members, had been annihilated by the fire. As the reporter was interviewing the camp director, my radio started to squelch so I backed away to cause less of a disturbance. The dispatcher was trying to make contact with a plane. After a few repeated attempts, the dispatcher reported a possible accident.

Our own situation was heating up. The relative humidity was dropping, and fire activity was picking up in the canyons around us. I explained it was time to escort our guests out of the forest. I continued to monitor the radio for news of the accident. The incident air attack supervisor kept saying it was not one of our aircraft.

Once we had safely escorted our wards out of the fire area, we headed for the Weed Cafe. We learned from the deputy sheriff that it was indeed our aircraft. Later I learned that the definition the California-based air operations staff had for "our" included only those aircraft assigned explicitly to the incident. The plane that had crashed was hosted by the Lincoln National Forest, and that day Sam Tobias was on board as the aerial observer. Sam Tobias's mission had been to fly the whole forest looking for new starts, in addition to offering observations to the Scott Able fire.

In the ensuing days, I was pulled into the tragedy of the deaths of Sam Tobias and Leo Kuponen. I did not know either man, and although I had met Sam once, he had never given me one of those bear hugs he was known for. Leo was a contract pilot from California. Sam was well loved by the Lincoln National Forest staff, and so our small team of information officers stepped in to support the Lincoln Forest staff, run interference for the family with the media, and assist with the memorial service.

With the media focused on the Cerro Grande Fire in Los Alamos, the story of Sam Tobias, the angel in the sky who made possible the safe and timely evacuation during the Scott Able Fire, has not been told much. There is another little-known final-days-of-Sam-Tobias story as well. On the night of May 7, Jose Martinez, the Lincoln Forest supervisor, called Sam and asked him if he would consider going up to the Cerro Grande Fire to help out as an information officer. Sam turned down the new opportunity and said he would stick to what he knew, Air Attack.

What if Sam had gone to Los Alamos? Would we have had fatalities at Scott Able on the night of May 11? I asked his widow, Jackie, and she assured me Sam was not interested in being an information officer. He said that he belonged in the sky helping firefighters. Sam, Leo, and the many other firefighters and pilots who have died on wildfires are truly heroes whose lives were dedicated to saving others.

THOUGHTS ON FIRE AND MORTALITY
April 1993

Friday morning. Driving home from the elementary school. My mind is busy organizing the day. The radio disc jockey suddenly catches my attention: "The Forest Service's prescribed fire in the Jemez Mountains blew out of control yesterday leaving one firefighter dead."

There is no further news. I turn off the radio.

Quiet.

Solemn.

Overwhelmed, actually.

It is not my fire. A few days ago I was laughing along with some of my friends about why we were not on the fire.

"Nobody invited me."

"I even begged to go and got told 'no.'"

We wished we were there. We were concerned about the wind, the weather, and the size of the burn.

"Do you really think they should be doing sixteen thousand acres all at once?"

It was not our show, but we wanted some part of it. We had pride and admiration for those firefighters on it. We had a shared belief that they were making history. Prescribed fire needs to have a major role in the management of our forests.

I call my friend Jean Szymanski, who works in Public Affairs for the United States Forest Service. She asks me to explain to her once again (so she can tell the public) why we chose to work with fire, which has proven time and again to be such a deadly force.

I write the following letter to grapple with the issue.

August 22, 1993

Dear Jean,

I called you this morning, my friend, to share in this tragedy. A firefighter is dead. We all feel the emptiness. We do not have a name. We do not have a face. We each have our individual worries as we think of all the names and faces who may have been involved in this accident. But the sadness is the same. Someone from our community of firefighters has died. Someone has given his or her life for . . . that is the hard question that you have asked me to address.

If it were me who had died, I would not think the death was senseless or unnecessary. I can only put a value on my own life though. I cannot put a value on another's person's life. If it were me who had suggested the project, had spearheaded the effort, had pushed and argued for this controlled burn, I would be devastated. Maybe that is why I feel so bad now. If I had been in the position to push and argue and plan this burn, I would have done it. These days I always seem to be pushing and arguing for burning to play a major role in the ecosystem. I was proud of the Santa Fe National Forest's decision to do this one.

Hindsight. No one thought this control burn would end up this way. Of course the Forest Service would not have started that burn if they thought someone would be killed.

Then why did someone die? As far as the specifics are concerned, that awaits investigation. I can only address the general question of whether we should be doing controlled burns when there is a proven chance of losing a life.

You had heard the argument that there would be a loss of individual animals in this fire, but the burn would improve wildlife habitat. The individual life would be sacrificed, but overall wildlife populations would be better off. An ethical dilemma. Do we sacrifice animals today for the benefit of their kind in the future? A difficult question, but in lighting the fire, one that had been answered "yes."

An objective of this particular burn, and many prescribed burns in general, is to reduce the chances of a catastrophic fire that will certainly occur (the only question is when) if forest conditions are not altered. An obviously absurd argument could be made that we would have a greater chance of losing many more firefighters in this predicted firestorm than the one life lost yesterday. We value human life far too greatly to find any comfort in this parallel argument.

Perhaps military commanders have made decisions to "sacrifice" human life for overall gain for the good of the whole. Firefighters do not do that. The number one rule in firefighting, and extend that to fire setting, is to provide for safety first. Firefighting involves an overall mindset—both individually and as a unit—to constantly monitor the fire's behavior, predict what the fire may do, and act accordingly to provide for safety of firefighters.

Hindsight. What happened in the Jemez Mountains? We are so shocked, concerned and sad. Why did the federal government set that fire?

Jean, as a forester whose strongest interest is in forest ecology, it is my opinion that our forests in the Southwest are in trouble. It is not from devastating logging that plagues other parts of this country. On the contrary, we have too many trees. Our hundred-year history of fire suppression has left us with a legacy of cramped, crowded, cluttered forests.

For example, in a recent northern Arizona study, researchers determined land that had up to 851 trees per acre growing on it today, may have had as few as 23 trees per acre in presettlement times.

Prior to the settlement of the Southwest by folks of

European descent, fire played a regular and necessary role in the dynamic forest cycle. C. F. Cooper described fire's role in the establishment and development of presettlement ponderosa pine forests in a paper published in 1961. Fire made it possible for ponderosa pine trees to germinate and get started by preparing seed beds of exposed mineral soil. Fire thinned young trees so those remaining would not experience severe competition and would grow into large mature individuals. Regular recurring fires recycled nutrients from dead plant material to components of soil that could be used by living plant material. Less often, fire assisted in catastrophic removal of tree cover that started the cycle all over again.

Cooper was not the first forester to notice the importance of fire. Even Gifford Pinchot, America's first forester and one of wildfire's biggest foes, recognized the presence of fire in natural ecosystems. Pinchot, however, believed that wildfire and human use of the forest could not coexist. Were the early foresters and settlers who initiated and pioneered the firefighting system wrong to fight fire so aggressively?

In hindsight, I think so. The unhealthy state of our forests today is a result of complex ecological and political situations, but primary among them is the lack of frequent fires on the landscape.

Hindsight. Hard to blame our ancestors for not predicting the long-term effects of fire exclusion on the forests, especially when we know how devastating fire can be. Fire's destructiveness is what gives fire its bad rap. Fire's destructiveness reared its ugly head yesterday when it claimed another life.

In my churning gut that has been unsettled since I heard yesterday afternoon's shocking news, I don't know if prescribed fire is worth the risk. In my aching heart, that so dearly loves the Southwestern forests and our Southwestern people, I want to see a healthy forest and a healthy people harmoniously coexisting. In my professional mind that strongly advocates the benefits of fire in the ecosystem, I am convinced we must continue to promote a role of fire in our forests.

In the next few months, and even years, many specific questions will be addressed regarding Thursday's tragedy. Lessons will be learned. Questions will be answered. Policy will be made. Overall we as a collective people will struggle once more to determine how we view and how we use fire in the forests.

Fire is neither a foe nor a friend. Fire is a natural force. As a forester, fire is, for me, a tool—a tool for helping the forests become and stay healthy. I have other tools, too, such as logging and thinning. The challenge of managing our forests to be and remain healthy ecosystems is going to require careful thoughts and observations, extensive knowledge and comprehension, and finally a complete set of tools and capabilities.

The impact of our society on our forests is immense, as is the impact of our forests on our society. Our appetite for wood for homes and woodlands for home sites is enormous. As are our needs for water, food, and mental health our forests provide.

I do not know the specific details that led to Thursday's tragedy. I do know that in general we must find a role for fire in our forests. If someday, I am killed in a control burn, I hope my family, friends, and colleagues will find some solace in my belief that fire does indeed need to be in our forests. If I exist in some form beyond that moment, I will be expecting my community to learn the lessons the incident offers, and to move forward in the quest for healthy forests and healthy communities.

CHAPTER TWO

Forestry

Summer 1995

Fresh burn areas draw all kinds of curious animals, and foresters are among the crowd. From the years of mopping up forest fires— spending the last few days on assignment putting out any smoking log or duff that is near the control line—I have witnessed many animals that find fresh-burned ground fascinating. The elk come in and browse on the needles of remaining saplings as if they are discovering a smoke-flavored delicacy. The raptors fly around, hoping to catch some rodent emerging from the safety of its burrow but no longer into a world that offers immediate camouflage. The bears saunter through, turning over rocks and logs and generally just seeming to look around.

When we see so many bears after a fire, we often debate whether it's because bears are attracted to burn areas, or because bears are always this close in the woods, but until the brush has burned away, they are just hidden from our view.

Therefore, I should not have been so surprised that afternoon, when marking trees on Buddy Elkins's ranch outside of Grants, to hear three sharp whistles coming from the drainage below me.

As a homeschooling parent and a consulting forester, I often have my kids work with me. In this instance, my work was to mark leave trees on a private salvage sale after a major wildfire. The work required me to evaluate every tree in the area, which meant continually moving up and down the slope.

Aspen stand in fall. North Rim, Grand Canyon National Park. Photo by author.

My seven-year-old twins preferred playing in the drainage bottom while I worked the hillsides marking trees that had the best chance of postfire survival. We all had whistles, and throughout the day we would communicate. One whistle was a simple question, "everything is fine, but where are you?" This was answered with a single whistle. Every ten to twenty minutes, we would signal each other. I would also leave my gallon paint cans with the kids, and tie in with them in person each time I emptied the quart-size paint gun I carried with me.

The two-whistle call was more serious in nature. It meant come here as soon as you can, though it is not an emergency. Usually the kids used this call to signal they were ready for lunch, or that they needed a jacket from the car, or some other pressing reason to ask Mom to set down her paint can for a while.

The three-whistle call was a real emergency, and up until this day, we had never used it. When I heard it, I immediately came crashing down the hillside in the direction of the kids. As soon as I spotted Roland, he was waving his arms at me to stop.

Between us there was a large black bear that was fixed on something behind the kids. It only took a second to realize it was a bear cub. I hollered at the bear to let her know I was behind her and to distract her from my children. Then I told the twins to start moving slowly up the drainage toward our car, away from the bears.

Mama Bear must have had the same idea, because she growled at her cub and the little guy started moving down the drainage. In less than a minute, I was reunited with my cubs, and she was reunited with hers.

I'm not sure what the bear family did the rest of the day, but we broke camp and headed home. I left the kids with their father and finished the marking job alone.

I STARTED WRITING *The Forester's Log* TO SHARE MY LOVE FOR FORESTS and my passion for my chosen profession. Most people do not understand what foresters do. If month by month I could share a piece my life, I might make a small dent in the way our society treats our forests and woodlands.

At the heart of forestry is a respect for the forest as a living, complex, and changing ecosystem. Some critics have trouble acknowledging the forest as dynamic and responsive to both treatment and lack of treatment. We as foresters gear our management activities toward working within the parameters of each ecosystem. This requires keen observation and understanding. We can holistically provide forest products without upsetting ecological balance.

Prior to European settlement, fire was a major force in shaping the forests of North America. With the absence of fire, young tree establishment went unchecked resulting in more stems per acre, smaller individual trees, and stagnated and overgrown forests.

Poor logging practices in the past also contributed to current forest conditions in the Southwest. Prior to the 1970s, few regulations addressed logging practices and often the trees harvested were the largest and best trees available. As a result, throughout much of the Southwest, densely spaced, small-diameter trees dominate our second-growth forests.

Today, however, logging can be an important tool in creating healthy forests. When logging is approached with silvicultural objectives, what can be a destructive force becomes a creative force. Silviculture is the art and science of harvesting trees to develop future healthy forests. In writing *The Forester's Log*, I wanted to interpret silvicultural principles to a wide audience.

In the twenty-five years since I received my undergraduate degree in forestry, there have been many significant changes. The climate has gone from wet to dry, cool to hot. Society has spread out into the forests, both physically and philosophically. Our profession has realigned from being product oriented to being protection oriented.

These writings under the heading of "Forestry" span this time frame, and come from experiences in state, tribal, federal, and private forest management. As an introduction to forestry, they barely scratch the surface. First, they only tell of one forester's experiences, but also this collection is only a small example of many stories that come from twenty-five years of working in the woods.

2 RED BELT OF 1984
August 1986

When Philmont Scout Ranch seasonal staff members arrived in northern New Mexico in the summer of 1984, they found acres of brown trees. The conclusion that these trees were dying, although inaccurate, was a devastating idea. The trees were suffering from a condition called red belt.

Red belt occurs in conifer or needle-bearing trees when temperatures fluctuate rapidly during winter months. Environmental conditions that cause red belt may occur over a broad geographic area, be confined to a narrow elevation zone, or even be restricted to a few trees in a small area. Often this damage occurs in sharply defined bands or belts, which inspire the descriptive name.

When a layer of warm air is trapped between colder air below and above it, the air mass is known as an inversion. At night, colder air flows down the slopes into the valley, and the warm layer rises. The trees along these slopes are first exposed to warm, drying winds, and then to cold air. When the ground is still frozen, the needles on the trees experience tissue damage by the rapidly changing temperatures. The needles turn red overnight.

Often only parts of the tree's canopy are affected. All evergreen trees, including ponderosa pine, Douglas-fir, white fir, blue spruce, junipers, and pinyon are susceptible to this abiotic disease. Red belt only affects the needles of the trees. The severity of injury depends on the size and health of the trees. Small and unhealthy trees have a harder time recovering, and red belt makes them more susceptible to other tree diseases including dwarf mistletoe and root rot. Bark beetles are also attracted to trees in distress.

The red belt incident impacting Philmont occurred during an unusual atmospheric condition covering much of New Mexico in late December of 1983. Red belt resulting from this "Christmas Day inversion" occurred from Raton as far south as Capitan in south-central New Mexico. The Forest Pest Management section of the U.S.D.A. Forest Service estimated the total affected area as 63,000 acres including 11,250 acres on Philmont Scout Ranch.

By the end of the summer, most of the brown needles had dropped off the trees, and many trees had fresh green growth. As Philmont's seasonal staff headed back to their homes and colleges, they had learned a lesson in forest resiliency. If only all forest insect and disease outbreaks were so easy to recover from!

CIRCLE A THINNING
February 1987

Jack-straw tree trunks lay crisscross on the forest floor like an enormous game of pick-up sticks. Normally I'd have no trouble seeing where to place my big black White's smokejumper boots. Today, not only is there a foot of snow blanketing the mess, but I have developed a large belly where a set of twins are cooking. My boss, Fred Rossbach, is skipping through the woods ahead of me. He keeps looking back at me struggling though the icy slash. He shakes his head and asks again if I am okay.

We are counting trees. More specifically we are only counting trees on our sample plots that are systematically spaced on a grid throughout the blackjack pine thinning project. By conducting a post-project inventory, we can approve payment for the landowner, Alice Woolf. The project, partially funded by a federal cost-share program, involves cutting trees to improve her forest's vigor and growth rate.

Alice Woolf bought the Circle A Ranch when her kids were small, and now, along with occasional help from family that includes full-grown grandchildren, she operates a quaint hostel outside of Cuba, New Mexico.

Alice is one of many private landowners in New Mexico who are taking the initiative to keep their forests healthy through thinning. Like vegetables growing in a garden, trees need ample room to maximize their growth. When too many trees are too close together in the forest, they grow slowly.

Foresters use an increment borer to measure the growth rates in trees. The borer extracts a core of wood. The growth rings are easily discerned because of the way trees grow. In the spring, growth is rapid, and new cells are large and light in color. After about the first three weeks, the tree adds cells much more slowly. These summer wood cells are dense and dark and form the tree rings.

When the forest is too thick and trees are not growing well, the rings are tight and close together. Once thinned, the trees put on more wood, and thus wider rings, until they grow large enough to fully occupy the site again. At this point, the trees will need another thinning. When the trees are young and small, the land can support more trees on each acre. As trees get larger, they need more room to grow, and fewer big trees occupy the same space. With each entry, each thinning project harvests more valuable products. Since large trees produce high-value products, landowners can maximize the potential of their land by actively thinning every twenty to forty years.

Fred and I flounder in the snow until all our plot data is collected. The contractors have cut enough trees to bring the forest into compliance with the program guidelines. The federal government will pay Alice a cost-share to help shoulder the cost of this precommercial thinning.

We stumble into Alice's cozy kitchen with the news, and are greeted with hot tea and friendly kitties. Despite being in the midst of chores, Alice is wearing beautiful southwestern jewelry and a perpetual smile. She sits us down to tell us about the forest. She admits that at first she hated the idea of cutting any tree. Now she realizes how important the thinning is for the health of the remaining trees.

She embraces her role as steward of the forest. Not only is a healthy forest important to her children and grandchildren, but to all of the guests and friends that come to the ranch. She is excited about the twins that I am carrying, and insists they grow up loving her forest. We start to plan her next thinning project.

BETTY JANE CURRY:
AN AMERICAN TREE FARMER
November 1987

Deep in the mountains along the winding, gravel road between Jemez Springs and Cuba, a big green and white sign that reads "Tree Farm" hangs by a gate. Scattered throughout the country, similar placards indicate members of the American Tree Farm System. Behind each sign is a story about a family or person dedicated to forest management on their private lands. Behind this one is the story of the Curry family, particularly their matriarch, Betty Jane Curry.

The Currys' land, Sombrio Ranch, Inc., consists of four separate parcels: Wolf Canyon, Turkey Canyon, the Walker Place, and the Curry Place. Nestled in the Nacimiento Mountains of central New Mexico, the ranch has been in the Curry family since 1910. Ponderosa pine–dominated hillsides surround valleys of open meadows. Stands of aspen and mixed conifers blanket the north slopes.

Sombrio Ranch activities include running cattle, renting out a recreation home, growing and harvesting wood products (timber, vigas, posts, and fuelwood), growing blue spruce for nursery stock, and hunting. Although the property has only been certified as a tree farm since April 1984, the family has managed the forest throughout their ownership.

"We bought stocks in Weyerhauser for our children," Mrs. Curry told me one day. "Each year we received a beautiful annual report. One year we read about the Tree Farm Program." Jack Curry, Betty Jane's late husband, had sent off for information on how to join the program fifteen to twenty years earlier, but his request had not been answered.

For the uninitiated, the term *tree farm* conjures up images of perfectly manicured trees spaced uniformly in rows. For the vast majority of certified tree farms, this is far from reality. Most tree farms are well-managed forests that are natural, diverse, and brimming with plants and wildlife. This is true of most of the Currys' land. They do, however, have two small plantations that resemble the stereotypic misconception of a tree farm.

In the early 1970s, the family planted blue spruce seedlings behind their home to create a college fund for grandchildren. A few years after establishing the first plantation, the family planted several hundred more spruce in the Turkey Canyon meadow.

The Currys' contact with New Mexico State Forestry began in 1972 with the second spruce-planting project. Fifteen years later my job is to provide technical forestry support to any private landowner in our six-county district who desires professional forestry advice. The Currys are now selling the spruce trees, which are now six to twelve feet high, as nursery balled stock.

Mrs. Curry and her daughter, Peggy Ohler, are active in all aspects of running the ranch. In the late 1970s Betty Jane and Peggy did ten acres of thinning on their own. "Boy, we learned a lot from thinning ourselves,"

Mrs. Curry confided to me. "I guess we didn't really know what we were doing then, and the forester had the hardest time with us."

The notes are there in the file. The thinning just barely passed inspection. I marvel at how far the Currys' understanding of forest ecology has come. Last spring I was marking leave trees on the pole/post/firewood sale in Turkey Canyon. The goal was to paint marks on the best trees that we did not want to be cut out of the stand. By cutting the poor-quality trees now, the best trees are left to develop into future saw timber. As I marked, my constant companions Betty Jane and Peggy would often point out better leave trees.

The Turkey Canyon project illustrates the Currys' commitment to sound forestry and their interactions with State Forestry. Their conservation heritage might be best illustrated from grandson Jason Ohler's perspective. Peggy, despite being in the late term of her pregnancy, came to the woods in the February snow with her mom and the foresters to discuss the potential wood product sale. Jason was born in April, and by May he was in the woods in a pouch on his mother's chest while she was marking timber and helping with the inventory. Meanwhile, Mrs. Curry spent each day tallying and providing insight and inspiration.

In August, the women, along with six-month-old Jason, held a Show-Me Tour for interested fuelwood buyers to view the harvest area. Mrs. Curry auctioned off the wood to the highest bidder. Afterward, she and the cutter signed a contract she had prepared. Contract provisions included discouraging further erosion by placing branches and tree tops, known as slash, in the arroyos.

Recent limitations in timber harvesting on national forests have forced the closure of dozens of family-operated small sawmills in the state. Mrs. Curry responded by making two small sales available to Young's Sawmill. Over the past seventy years, the property has been harvested several times by the Hernandez-Young family.

"We cut this area in the forties," Mrs. Curry recounted. "I couldn't get out here as often as I wanted because the kids were just babies."

"We did a good job, though," Walter Hernandez added from his seat on a log from where he was supervising the current harvesting. His son and grandson do the work now, and Walter, unable to walk without his cane, reminisces about the work of the past.

"We sure left you some pretty good seed trees," he added. Looking around the site, this is evident. The majority of the trees are approximately forty years old and growing vigorously. Today we are removing many of the seed trees that are dead or dying. By saving the best trees then, the next generation of trees has excellent form, and now the Hernandez family is cutting high-quality timber.

Conservation and working with nature are important concepts for the Currys. They schedule thinning and harvesting activities in late summer and fall to reduce the possibility of bark beetle outbreaks. While foresters are willing to give log landings and skid trails time to revegetate naturally, Mrs. Curry is out spreading grass seed *just to help it along*. Mrs. Curry consults with the Soil Conservation Service, and often uses logging slash to reduce erosion and stabilize gullies on her property.

We are looking into a gully feeding into Telephone Canyon. Much like the gullies all over New Mexico, the gully formed as a result of the same poor land use a century earlier that lead to the field of conservation.

"Look here, Peggy." Betty Jane is pointing down into the arroyo. "Look how much silt that rock dam we built has caught."

The women are excited with the progress, and they start planning their next dam to raise the base of the arroyo up another notch.

"When did you build that dam?" I ask.

They look at each other, mumble a few "let's-see-now's," and I get the impression that rehabilitating arroyos takes a long, long time.

Betty Jane recently stepped down as chairperson for the Cuba Soil and Water Conservation District. Within moments of her resignation, she was volunteering to be the board's secretary. The board has planted a demonstration windbreak, hosted Holistic Resource Management courses, and provided a long slate of conservation activities for the Cuba community.

In April I went to a Cuba Soil and Water Conservation Board meeting to give a fifteen-minute presentation on forestry. The meeting started at 6:30 p.m. and did not end until midnight. Throughout the long evening, enthusiasm and energy for conservation never waned. The board remained focused and accomplishments were many. When it was my turn to present, there were so many questions on forestry that my short talk stretched to forty-five minutes.

"You know, the Rio Puerco Basin used to be known as the Bread Basket of the Southwest," Walter Hernandez explained. "And it is a semi-dry desert today! How did it get that way? Well, they cut all the trees."

For Betty Jane and the board, watershed restoration includes reforestation.

Cuba, New Mexico, is the hub of the Rio Puerco Basin, and also the site of the annual Rio Puerco Basin Fair each August. As a Fair Board member, Mrs. Curry, with Peggy's help, publishes a bulletin of over a hundred pages of rules and information for participants.

Another publishing task the mother-daughter combination tackles is *The Cuba News*. Each month the Penistaja Homemaker's Extension Club in the Cuba area publishes the twenty-two-year-old paper. Betty Jane types each issue, and Peggy does the artwork.

Three days a week, Betty Jane delivers mail to her remote neighborhood. I was twelve years old and attending Rancho del Chaparral, a nearby Girl Scout camp, the first time Mrs. Curry had an impact on my life. While I was at camp experiencing the love for nature that would later lead to a career in forestry, Mrs. Curry was delivering letters from home and friends that made the stay that much more enjoyable. I asked my mom what the address line "Curry's Route" meant on my camp address.

"Oh, that's probably the name of the mail carrier," Mother replied with maternal wisdom.

Mrs. Curry is also a member of the local search and rescue group and collects weather information daily as a volunteer for the National Weather Service.

The New Mexico Tree Farm Committee selected Betty Jane Curry for the New Mexico Outstanding Tree Farmer this spring. Besides winning a nice chainsaw, the award entitles the recipient to a three-year term on the New Mexico Tree Farm Committee.

Knowing Betty Jane's busy schedule, I approached this aspect of the award cautiously.

"If you have the time," I started, but Betty Jane cut straight to the point.

"If it is worthwhile, I can make the time."

After attending her first meeting she enthusiastically accepted the appointment.

There are other green and white Tree Farm signs scattered all over the country. Behind each of these signs in a story about people loving the land they live on.

3 WILDLIFE INSPIRES
BACKYARD TREE FARMERS
January 1990

The arrival of an unprecedented number of black bears in Albuquerque and surrounding communities triggered concern for the effect of urban sprawl into adjacent forests. Human populations in the Sandia Mountains, like many other forests and fields surrounding our nation's urban centers, have greatly increased over the past two decades. A primary motivation is the desire to live closer to nature. Along with fresh clean air, quiet stillness, and starlit nights, the forests' newest residents are often looking for regular encounters with wildlife. The frustrating paradox is that as people in these areas increase, wildlife populations are reduced.

In New Mexico, the Backyard Tree Farm Program is providing the technical bridge to help landowners of small parcels manage their land to reduce their impact on the ecosystem. In addition to growing and maintaining healthy forests and reducing soil erosion, providing for wildlife habitat is a primary interest for Backyard Tree Farmers.

"People generally are most interested in attracting birds," county extension agent Curtis Smith explains. "Hummingbird feeders certainly top the list of things people do for wildlife."

Any hummingbird in the Sandia Mountains will testify that Bob Cooper's certified Tree Farm in Las Huertas Canyon is the place to be if you are small and have rapid wing action.

"We've seen eight varieties of hummingbirds here," Bob explained. "That's the largest number of species seen in any one place in New Mexico."

The Coopers spend twelve dollars per week in sugar to keep over a dozen half-gallon feeders on their porch in operation.

The New Mexico Backyard Tree Farm program was initiated last summer on a Tree Farm tour of the Cooper-Ellis Ranch. As the group watched scores of winged creatures sip quarts of sugar water, they made plans to build western bluebird houses, plant trees and shrubs, arrange more tours, and form a network to keep the forests healthy and green.

Traditionally, Tree Farmers are landowners with at least ten acres of properly managed forest land who are recognized in a program sponsored by the American Forest Council. The new program targets property owners with fewer than ten acres.

The New Mexico Tree Farm Committee is the primary sponsor of the Backyard Tree Farm Program. The technical cosponsors include the Soil Conservation Service (now the Natural Resources Conservation Service), the New Mexico Forestry and Resources Conservation Division (now the State Forestry Division), and the New Mexico Cooperative Extension Service. These agencies provide land management advice for private landowners.

As acreages are subdivided, the numbers of homeowners expecting services from these agencies expands exponentially. Through the Backyard Tree Farm Program, the technical cosponsors serve more people.

Since Backyard Tree Farmers generally own small parcels of land, single trees often take on special significance. Each year after the yuletide season, Haskell and Marie Wright tie their Christmas tree to a pole supporting a birdhouse. Even as it dries and browns, the tree's limbs provide shelter for birds foraging at a nearby feeder.

Backyard Tree Farmer Dan Shaw is a wildlife education consultant for the New Mexico Department of Game and Fish. He holds seminars on improving backyard wildlife habitat.

"Here in the arid Southwest, the key to wildlife habitat is providing water," Dan says.

Although water may be a key ingredient to the enhancement of wildlife habitat, Backyard Tree Farmers Don and Carol Bush point to another important aspect for wildlife to thrive.

"Let's face it, these critters need space. We can forget having wildlife if the mountain is completely divided into two-acre lots."

The Bushes own a hundred acres, and like many of the other larger landowners in the area, taxes for the property are jeopardizing their ability to maintain a wildlife preserve.

Master Gardener and Pioneer Tree Farmer Judy Dane emphasizes using native plants to keep wildlife happy. She has a greenhouse for starting native wildflowers such as penstemons. Judy recommends the New Mexico State Forestry's seedling program to her neighbors to get native shrubs and trees established.

New Mexico Tree Farm Committee chairman Pat Wester's land is in the Manzano Mountains, a southern extension of the Sandias. Pat's not going to get left out of the wildlife enhancement picture. He recently built a squirrel feeder that provides a cute chair for the squirrel to sit on while it munches blue corn on the cob.

Backyard Tree Farm chairman Jack Henley will be quick to point out that not all wildlife encounters are desirable. Jack spent years establishing pine trees on his 160-acre grassland spread east of the Sandias. This winter, jackrabbits gnawed the bark off several well-established trees. Jack discovered the trespass during a Backyard Tree Farm tour so he at least had an understanding support group to acknowledge his loss.

For the twenty-five-dollar membership fee, Backyard Tree Farmers receive the *American Tree Farmer* magazine and information about caring for their backyards. The program is presently in a few states, but can be added by state Tree Farm committees wherever there is sufficient interest.

Postscript 2008: The Sandia/Manzano Backyard Tree Farm Program is still active and the only remaining chapter in the American Tree Farm System.

4 AN ARGUMENT FOR KEEPING THE BACA RANCH PRIVATE
June 1997

Managing for biodiversity, which is maximizing the number of species a landscape can support, is a major goal of many forestry activities these days. When an ecosystem supports a wider array of species, it has higher biodiversity.

Every animal and plant has requirements—food, water, habitat—and those requirements vary among species as each animal or plant claims its niche in the environment. As land managers, our job is to protect all habitats in order to provide wide diversity on the landscape. When changes occur that reduce habitats, then we risk losing species.

As stated by Aldo Leopold, "A thing is right when it tends to preserve the integrity, stability, and beauty of the biotic community. It is wrong when it tends otherwise."

If land managers were omniscient, all-knowing, we would never

Elk in fog at the Valles Caldera National Preserve.
Courtesy of David Lewis.

make decisions that would lead to species loss or habitat degradation. However, many of our "mistakes" are realized in hindsight. One of our saving graces is the diversity in land management philosophies. Not only is biodiversity important, but diversity in management approaches is equally important in providing resiliency to the greater ecosystem.

Landowner objectives drive activities on the ground. Historically, the Park Service has lost biodiversity when trying to preserve habitats but not allowing natural disturbances such as fire. The Forest Service has lost biodiversity when applying practices under a multiple-use strategy that had some flawed impact not readily apparent. Generally, by splitting land management among multiple philosophies, we tend not to make the same mistakes at the same time over all the landscape.

The Jemez Mountains provide an excellent example for this point. Major landowners in the Jemez include the Santa Fe National Forest, the Bandelier National Monument, Los Alamos National Labs, several pueblos including Santa Clara, Jemez, and Santo Domingo, and right in the middle of this, a large private ranch we simply call "The Baca."

The Baca is a hallowed piece of ground. I am extremely lucky to have an intimate knowledge of this landscape. As the timber management officer on the Bernalillo District, New Mexico State Forestry, I spent many days on the Baca Ranch developing forest management prescriptions, fighting forest fires, regulating timber sales, and conducting tours to share the lessons of the land.

I know the Baca Ranch, not as a pristine wilderness, but as a healthy and resilient landscape that has seen both good and bad management practices. The Baca is also sacred ground, honored by many peoples as a source of connection with the earth. On the Baca, one does not separate mankind from the ecology of the system.

The value of private ownership of this large ranch contributes to the health of the Jemez Mountain ecosystem. However, many people are excited about the potential sale of the Baca Ranch to the United States government. Since potential massive subdivisions would greatly impact the integrity of the landscape, perhaps federal ownership is the lesser of the evils. However, for the sake of preserving the ownership diversity, I would rather see the land remain a private ranch.

Postscript: The federal government did buy the Baca Ranch in 2000, but created the Valles Caldera National Preserve managed as a trust with objectives unlike any of the other government agencies managing land in the Jemez Mountains. Hopefully this designation will continue to provide land management diversity to the greater Jemez Mountain ecosystem.

5 THIS YEAR, GET A PATRIOTIC CHRISTMAS TREE
November 2001

This Christmas season do your patriotic duty, and cut down your own Christmas tree. A serious problem facing our country is an excess of trees. Small trees. Christmas tree–size trees. What we admire as festive holiday decorations are seen as ladder fuels when left cluttering our forest. If we all went to the woods to cut a Christmas tree, with improving forest health as our overriding motto, think of the safer forests we would have next year when fire season rolls around!

Here's the game plan to start a Christmas tree revolution.

First, prominently display an American flag while engaged in your tree-cutting outing. Remember, this is a patriotic endeavor! Your mission will be more effective if you can convince others to follow your lead. The American flag just might attract enough attention to explain your intentions. Once you have an audience, educate them on their civic duty.

You might start with the battle cry "REMEMBER LOS ALAMOS!" For those of you who don't remember Los Alamos, I am referring to the Cerro Grande Fire in May of 2000 that burned over 43,000 acres and destroyed 239 residential dwellings in a northern New Mexico community. The real culprit in that disaster was the condition of the forest once it was burning—a severe case of "too many trees." Since that fire and the ensuing severe fire season that followed throughout the West, Congress has responded with almost three billion dollars for the National Fire Plan. Although communities, government agencies, and industries aimed at using small trees have hit the ground in full force trying to address this problem, it won't be solved in one fell swoop. It took over a century of fire exclusion to build up the excess trees and fuel in the forest; it may take decades of hard work to return the forest to health.

It may also take a Christmas tree revolution.

If your potential recruits still don't get the patriotic tie-in, point out that hundreds of military troops were involved in fighting fires in 2000, and that those same troops might be otherwise preoccupied when our country faces its next brutal fire season.

The next step is to find an area to cut the tree. Regardless of our noble, all-American intentions to save the forest, we still have to follow the laws that govern the age-old of tradition of Christmas tree cutting. An obvious choice is to cut trees on public lands. Each land management agency has its own approach to okaying this operation. The U.S.D.A. Forest Service administers their tree-cutting programs at the district level. This requires making some phone calls and perhaps a visit to a district office to get the proper paper work and pay the appropriate fee. In New Mexico, if you cut a tree on private land, you need to have written permission of the landowner in your possession when you cut and transport the tree. If you are the landowner, you need proof of that fact such as a tax bill or a copy of the deed. Nobody ever said that doing your patriotic duty was going to be easy.

Once you've loaded your briefcase with the proper documentation, it's time to head to the woods. Dress warmly, pack a big lunch complete with a thermos of hot chocolate, and don't forget to bring a saw and a rope to tie the tree to the top of your car.

The next step is to select the perfect Christmas tree, and considering our patriotic mission, this may take on a wholly new definition. For those of you familiar with Christmas television specials, we are talking "Charlie Brown" trees here. Remember, you are trying to improve the forest, which may mean taking out the trees that are growing too close together.

When trees grow too close together, they become somewhat lopsided. They certainly don't have the bushy elegance of a plantation-grown tree, but they usually do have this elegance on at least one side. The solution to this is to cut two or three of these less perfect trees and lash them together for the ideal tree. (Did I fail to suggest you buy more than one permit? Hopefully you have read ahead and are already prepared.)

In the Southwest, we have several species that make excellent Christmas trees. At lower elevations, which are usually easier to access in the winter, the tree of choice is the state tree, the two-needled pinyon. A few New Mexicans will opt for junipers, but most of us natives have such severe allergies, just the word "juniper" is enough to throw us into a sneezing fit. In the woods, the juniper pollen won't come out on the tree until January or February, but bring the tree indoors where it is warmer, and the tree thinks it is spring. Now if one only cuts female trees that don't produce the pollen . . .

In the ponderosa pine and mixed conifer forests, the ideal Christmas trees are Douglas-fir and white fir. These species have soft needles, and are generally the "ladder fuels" within the pine forests that need to be removed. If you desire a spiny-needled tree that will keep the kids and pets away, you might look for a blue spruce, usually found in cold drainages. Most people shy away from ponderosa pine trees in their living rooms. The branches are sparse, the needles are long, and even a robust pine sapling has "Charlie Brown" written all over it. However, if a ponderosa pine is the tree that needs to leave the forest, remember you are doing your patriotic duty.

The ecology of the high-elevation spruce-fir forests is somewhat different, and you will stay out of more snowdrifts and achieve your patriotic duty more completely by cutting trees at lower elevations.

Once you have your tree(s) home, there are a few things to keep in mind. Remember we justified this operation as removing potential "fuel" from the forest. Well, you just took that fuel into your house. Be sure to keep the tree trunk sitting in water always, and monitor the tree closely for signs of drying out. If it is losing too many needles, toss the tree out. A well-cared-for cut tree should last several weeks, but don't take any chances if you think it is dry. Besides, you could always double your patriotic duty and go cut another one.

Maybe you want to buy a tree. You can still do the patriotic thing by buying a locally cut tree from our own forests and avoiding those less-than-fresh plantation specimens from the West Coast. Just be sure to ask the tree seller if forest health drove their selection process. (Yes, they will think you are totally nuts this year, but once our revolution takes hold there may even be a "certified-ecologically sound" tag attached in future years.)

Finally, and this is a matter of personal preference, consider flying a flag at the top of the tree (maybe the angel could hold it?). Once again, this is to offer your guests an opportunity to politely ask why you have three trees lashed together in your living room with a flag on top. Just explain you have done your patriotic duty this year, and be sure to tell them how they can do theirs by joining the Christmas tree revolution.

GREEN SIDE UP, OKAY?
December 2001

"Green side up, okay?"

That's the bottom line when it comes to tree planting. The roots go in the ground, and the "green" part of the plant is above the ground. Years ago I worked for a state agency that distributed tree seedlings throughout New Mexico. Each year, we would spend days dispensing tree-planting advice while handing out seedlings to landowners. We'd start out passionate, and our first few customers would get a one-on-one extensive course in tree planting. By the end of the day, we'd simply stare at the last customer and say "Green side up, okay?"

On the surface, tree planting is a rather simple task, until you ask a forester for advice. We tend to get bogged down in the details. Yet, outside of manipulating the weather, there are plenty of tips and tricks to help trees survive and grow.

Personally I am somewhat humbled by the whole potential of tree planting. If the six-inch pine seedling that little ol' five-foot-six me puts in the ground today survives, it will outweigh me by thousands of pounds, outlive me by hundreds of years, and outgrow me by tens of feet.

Successful tree growing consists of selecting the right tree species for the soil, aspect, and climate; placing the tree in the right location; handling and planting the seedling carefully; controlling weeds, rodents, and other damaging agents; providing critical moisture for the tree to get started; and waiting for the tree to grow. In our "instant" society sometimes the last activity becomes the hardest. Of course one solution is to plant bigger trees, but bigger trees are more expensive to acquire and plant, and less likely to survive.

In the mountains of New Mexico, the traditional time for tree planting is in the spring. It's best to plant while the trees are dormant, but, where soil is likely to freeze, not to plant in the fall when they could be susceptible to frost heaving through the winter. Anytime, however, is good to start planning a planting project. The state forestry agency or county extension agent is a good place to get free advice.

As a consulting forester, I usually give out tree-planting advice at my kids' basketball games or in the checkout line of the grocery store.

I first ask the questioner to tell me about the site and why they want to plant trees there.

The most important piece of the tree-planting equation is location. In many places, we already have too many trees. We aren't doing anyone any favors to go out there and plant more. However, there are places where tree planting is appropriate. Nothing is more rewarding, and perhaps more tiring, than spending a day putting tree seedlings in the ground in an abandoned bean field or a burn site. Talk to someone who just planted a hundred trees and they will tell you that tree planting is hard work; find someone who did that task ten years ago, and they will add a postscript: tree planting is rewarding work, too.

In a world of continually complex issues, anyone can plant a tree and make a lasting, positive environmental statement. Perhaps because I am a forester, I think everybody needs a tree-planting hobby. Of course, if everybody were planting trees, I'd end up answering a multitude of questions. By the end of each day, I'd pick up the phone and simply say, "Green side up, okay?"

CREATING COTTONWOODS
February 2007

While wandering in the tall cottonwood-dominated bosque along the middle Rio Grande, I came across an open area that had recently burned. Young trees, all about six feet tall with a plastic band wrapped around the base, dominated the setting. As I walked into an opening by the river, I found an array of bright orange wire flags. Next to each marker was a mound of sand surrounding a deep, circular hole four inches in diameter.

As odd as this situation sounds, I knew exactly what was going on. I had stumbled onto an area where cottonwood trees would soon be growing as a result of much human intervention and effort.

The cottonwood tree is a central feature of these woodlands that grow beside rivers of the American Southwest. The tree is remarkably beautiful—large, spreading branches, rich green leaves that turn to golden yellow in the fall, and deeply furrowed gray bark that wraps around what can, with time, become humongous trunks.

Fossil evidence of cottonwoods dates back over a million years, and the story of cottonwoods along rivers is a beautiful tale of interaction with the elements. For hundreds of thousands of years, cottonwoods have grown along rivers without any human help. To understand why augers are needed today to grow cottonwoods, it helps to understand the natural rhythms that have been disrupted.

Start in March, with cottonwood catkins. While many species of trees produce both male and female flowers, cottonwood trees are dioecious, meaning that individuals are either male or female. The bright red, pollen-producing flowers on the male trees are arranged on a string or catkin. The female flowers also grow in catkins, but are less conspicuous in early spring. By May these female flowers have transformed into strings of marble-size fruits, or tetones.

In late May or early June, timed to coincide with floodwaters from snowmelt in the mountains, these tetones burst forth with millions of "cotton" seed. The filaments surrounding the seed allow for wind dispersion. Some communities have passed ordinances requiring planting of "cottonless" cottonwood only. Essentially, these regulations promote the increased establishment of "male" cottonwoods leading to the proliferation of allergy-producing pollen. Ask any allergy sufferer and they would rather have cotton in their yard any day!

The distribution of cottonwood seed is not what is broken. Cottonwood trees are still in sync with melting snow. The breakdown in the establishment of new cottonwood trees today is in the next steps. In order to grow, a seed must land on bare, wet soil exposed to direct sunlight. In upper watersheds of unregulated rivers such as the Jemez River in Jemez Canyon, these ideal cottonwood nursery sites develop during spring runoff. As a result, multiple age classes of trees can be found along unregulated rivers.

However, with dams, levees, and the impoundment of spring runoff for agriculture and flood control, bare, wet soil in the open is hard to find in today's regulated floodplains. These microsites are limited to frequently flooded low sandbars within the river channel.

The next challenge for the small cottonwood seedling is to "keep its feet in the water." The cottonwood is a water-loving, water-thriving tree. To stay alive, it must have roots in the water table. Since the water table drops through the summer, the seedling must grow roots at a rate that keeps pace with the declining water level. Again, the hydrology in the "regulated river" is often disconnected from natural cycles, and cottonwood seedlings die out when water levels drop faster than roots can grow.

Once rooted in the water table, the final step in cottonwood survival is avoiding floods that can sweep the young seedlings away. When rivers freely move across the floodplain, cottonwood trees survive in places where the river channel shifts away from the newly established stands.

With human alterations to the river, natural cottonwood recruitment has severely declined in the last half century. The last major recruitment of cottonwood seedlings along the Rio Grande below Cochiti Dam was just before the dam was completed in the early 1970s. Most young cottonwoods found in the bosque now are "pole plantings."

Plantation-grown cottonwood poles are about three inches in diameter and fourteen to twenty feet tall. The pole is planted in a hole dug to a level where the water table is known to exist year-round. By placing the end of the pole in standing water, it sprouts roots. Providing some other agent (such as beavers) does not remove or kill the tree, this is now the surest way to establish new cottonwoods.

Walking through this piece of Albuquerque bosque, it was easy to read the landscape and recognize the work involved to reestablish cottonwood trees in a recent burn. The young trees with the plastic bands were poles planted in previous years. The plastic wrap provides protection from nibbling rabbits and beavers. The recently dug holes will soon be populated with new poles. The wire flags made it easy to find where the auger had dug the holes. With a bit of imagination, it is easy to envision the future forest of large spreading limbs, and trees with trunks that will take two or three people linking arms to encircle each one.

SURVIVOR TREE SYMMETRY
August 2007

In the predawn dark I am drawn toward what might be the perfect tree. As I climb cement steps, I admire the off-center symmetry of the tree's dark silhouette. Leafy branches spread like a misshapen umbrella radiating from the center of a tiled plaza. I circle the tree, marveling at its

This American elm, known as the Survivor Tree, sustained
major damage in 1995 at the Oklahoma City bombing.
Now it is a central feature of the Oklahoma City Memorial.
Courtesy of Helen Robertson.

good health, then move to the railing to gaze out over the dark reflecting
pond that stretches across this downtown Oklahoma City block.

On April 19, 1995, this American elm survived the bombing of the
Alfred P. Murrah Federal Building. Located in a parking lot across the
street from the blast, the tree was severely damaged; its branches riddled
with residue. In the aftermath of the tragedy, the tree became a symbol
of surviving, of moving on. Now a national icon, the Survivor Tree of
the Oklahoma City Memorial not only bears witness to the tragedy of
1995, but as small black birds dart in and out of its lofty foliage, reminds
me that each day requires its own survival skills.

On May 20 my father had a major stroke and survived. The stroke affected the left hemisphere of his brain. Along with other brain injury–related challenges, he is unable to move his right-side extremities. His speech and communication center is severely impaired. However, in the past ten weeks, Dad has made remarkable, though slow, progress. His efforts seem to mirror the amount of attention and concern that his friends and family have directed toward him. Therefore, I have tried to spend as much time as I can in Oklahoma this summer.

When possible, I come downtown to visit the tree. The lopsided canopy reminds me of Dad's lopsided smile. There are more parallel observations.

Neither was in great shape before the defining moment of their tragedies. Dad fit almost every risk category for people prone to have a stroke. The tree was in a parking lot, with asphalt plastered up to the trunk on all sides. Yet, each was uniquely loved for many qualities.

Though the elm looked like any other shade tree in a parking lot, it is one of the few American elms to have escaped death by Dutch elm disease. Once a prevalent tree throughout the eastern United States, American elms are now few and far between due to this imported malady. Although Dad might have resembled any other seventy-five-year-old white male with white hair and a beard, he, too, is unique. As one friend kindly put it, "Your dad is a rare breed, just like John Wayne, gonna get back on the horse even if he's been shot in the gut. One of those guys who will never back down, and never give up."

My college classmate from the Oklahoma State University Forestry Department is now the state's urban forester. After the attack, Mark Bays oversaw the treatment of the tree through the recovery process and memorial construction. While in Oklahoma, I found Mark and asked about the project. He described the aeration and watering system under the plaza that provides an optimum environment for root health. He grimaced at the initial trimming the elm underwent before he became involved in the project.

"The memorial team was great," Mark confided. "They took every suggestion I made and did everything I recommended. Other projects have sought my advice since then on how to rescue trees in difficult situations, but they fail to follow through with the recommendations and their success is marginal."

Dad's in the same boat of needing to follow the advice of experts.

When he does everything his physical therapist, occupational therapist, speech therapist, doctors, nurses, and caseworkers recommend, his progress is impressive. When he tells them all he'd rather stay in bed, he slips backward.

The bench by the bus stop is decorated with silhouettes of the tree, but the shape is odd, with a branch sticking up like the feather on a Hollywood Indian brave. I ask Mark about the odd shape, and he explains that right after the bombing the silhouette did include a branch that towered over the rest of the tree.

"The branch is still there," Mark explains, "but the rest of the tree has now grown up around it." We smile, we are foresters. The fact that trees grow and change is what makes our jobs so interesting.

I think about a nurse at the hospital early in the summer. She said our father, who was rather nonresponsive and had feeding tubes and IV lines sustaining him, would never get any better. Six weeks later he was eating solid food, saying whole sentences, and propelling himself down the hall in a wheelchair.

I love the changes Dad's made, and each day he adds a new surprise.

"Be sure to keep the Civil Engineering books," he mutters one evening as I explain that we are selling some of his things that were in the house he rented. I pay close attention; this is the first sentence that has made sense in a few minutes of his attempts to communicate. "I will need those books to work again."

Next to the Survivor Tree, a plaque reads: *The spirit of this city and this nation will not be defeated: our deeply rooted faith sustains us.*

I stand beneath the tree's lofty branches, overlooking the foggy downtown skyline in the early morning light. Dad's spirit will not be defeated either. I stretch my arms out toward the sunrise, mimicking tree branches, and find a deeply rooted faith that will sustain me through this trial.

6 LIVING IN A LOG HOME
January 2008

I did not play with dollhouses with frilly curtains, pink-papered walls, and miniature matched furniture sets as a girl. Instead I spent hours constructing toy homes for my plastic cowboys and farm animals from the warm red logs, the sleek white window frames, and the rough green roofing strips of my Lincoln Log set.

This past fall when I attempted to turn my log home's roof green, I finally completed the life-size version of my childhood retreats.

Sane people would hammer down a new layer of asphalt shingles during the warm summer months, but wildland firefighters do home improvement projects in the dead of winter. At least that was the excuse my comrades and I were clinging to all Thanksgiving weekend as we wobbled around on my roof, heavily bundled, occasionally sweeping off snow to lay the next row of shingles.

The following week, the wind blew. Not the usual winter gales, but one of those freak wind events that herald disaster. Up in the mountains hundreds of trees blew down. On my roof hundreds of shingles blew off and spread all over my neighborhood.

In central New Mexico, prevailing winds come from the southwest. The southwest quarter of the roof was stripped down to an old layer of red shingles, exposing the only section of the roof that had leaked in the first place.

Indoors, the southwest corner of my log cabin also bears watermarks along the bare log walls. Occasionally, horizontally delivered precipitation, both rain and snow, is pummeled through miniscule gaps in the chinking and cracks of the Engelmann spruce logs. Only the south and west walls of my three-bedroom, two-bath cabin have exposed logs. The north and east walls are reinforced with extra insulation and siding. I am reluctant, however, to completely cover the memories represented by the logs that create my home.

A thick three-ring binder stuffed with papers documents the house construction project. A hand-drawn map identifies the origin of these beetle-killed, spruce logs in the Manti-La Sal Mountains of southeast Utah. Harvested by his son, the timbers were milled into double-tongue-and-groove logs in 1989 by my friend Bob Applegate at his Regina, New Mexico, sawmill.

As a state-employed forester, I frequently visited the small mill to scale logs cut from private timber sales. Log scaling is a skill that calculates the volume of wood in board feet. One board foot is equivalent to a one-inch-thick board that is a foot wide and a foot long. Since landowners are paid for the trees cut on their property in terms of volume, my job required that I visit the mills regularly to measure sample loads of logs.

I was always pestering Bob Applegate for house logs so I could build a cabin on my newly acquired property. One day, while eating lunch with Bob and his wife, Alice, Bob gave me some solemn news.

"You need to order logs for your cabin soon if you want me to mill them." Bob explained that he had been diagnosed with cancer, and he was willing to cut my logs between chemotherapy treatments.

My logs were among the last orders he filled.

The house contains fifteen thousand board feet of wood, twice the wood used to construct a similar-size conventional home. Trees are renewable resources, unlike other construction materials such as insulation, stucco, brick, and sheetrock.

Sitting in my kitchen, in the southwest corner of the house, listening to wind, I enjoy the warmth of the wood that surrounds me, and honor the memories and challenges of creating my own life-size "Lincoln Log" home.

7 FORESTER'S CONFESSION
December 2002

The tiles were recently replaced on the front facade of a tile showroom in north Albuquerque. Each time I drove by the large building adjacent to the interstate and noticed the three tiles missing from the grandly decorated exterior, I would chuckle. "Great advertising," I would muse, then realize this was the pot calling the kettle black. Their business is tiles, my business is trees, and in my own yard I have some dead trees.

When I built my log cabin years ago, one of the first things I did was plant trees on the property. My lot, nestled squarely in the middle of the pinyon-juniper woodland, had more than enough trees growing on the site. Yet, instead of the short-stature pinyon and juniper that graced my view, I wanted pine, white fir, and even blue spruce trees. If I could not build a cabin in the forest, I thought I could bring the forest to the cabin.

I might have been more successful if I were a horticulturist instead of a forester. To keep trees alive in this lowland environment they must be coddled. Tended. Landscaped. Cared for. It goes against my professional sensibilities to allocate precious water during a drought to nurturing trees. Instead, I created microsites to utilize existing moisture to the fullest extent. My best success was a six-inch pine seedling my toddlers and I planted at the corner of my office building where the pitched roof dumped harvests of rainfall. When it rained.

My efforts first started failing in 1996, when my budding orchard bit the dust. I installed a drip system in 1990 when I planted the young, catalog-ordered grafts. Over the years the system had deteriorated. As a wildland firefighter, I am not home much during droughts because that is also when fires occur. That drought year I wasn't paying attention. Fortunately, my generous neighbors are more successful orchard tenders, so I am never without fruit. I justified my failure with the orchard mumbling that I was more interested in native ecosystems and the fruit trees just weren't meant to grow here. Besides, I had this really nice ponderosa pine tree growing next to my office that was taller than the kids who helped plant it.

In 2000 I lost the last of the white firs. A fellow firefighter gave them to me when I moved in. He had been growing them for years at his ranch near Cuba, New Mexico, as possible Christmas or landscape trees. They were almost three feet tall when we transplanted several to my place. Although I lost one the first year, it seemed the mulch and drip irrigation were allowing them to hang on. However, through the years, only one tree adapted to living in the woodland. Then came another drought year, and another failed drip system.

The irrigation system failed because I was unwilling to turn the water on. My well is marginal, and I feared the well would go dry for our domestic needs if I spent precious water keeping trees alive. Besides, I had this really nice pine tree growing next to my office that was as tall as me.

This past summer of 2002 the drought gods descended once again. When I arrived home from two weeks on a fire, my beloved pine tree next to the office was sporting some brown needles. All day I wrestled with the dilemma of whether to water in a drought. Almost on an impulse, I turned on the garden hose, hoping to salvage my last effort. Not wanting to admit my decision, I immediately forgot the deed.

A few days later there was no water at my tap. The thousand-gallon tank that collects the meager water my well produces was empty. All my fears of the drought were well founded; my well had gone dry. I left for a weekend excursion, promising to face life without water when I returned. Sunday night, coming back tired and dirty, I was delighted to find my reservoir replenished. I turned the water back on to the house, and wondered how the well had been able to pump a thousand gallons when I thought it had gone dry. Did I have a water leak somewhere? Then I remembered the tree.

I raced out to my office and was immediately thwarted by the quagmire. At least a thousand gallons of water had dripped from the end of the garden hose over the last week. The ground around my office and my tree had the consistency of gelatin. As I shut the water off, I knew I had killed my tree. The ponderosa pine growing by my office that was now several feet taller than me would never survive this drastic overwatering.

I miss the missing tiles on the facade of the Albuquerque showroom. It was a nice reminder that I am not the only one with a blemish on my reputation. I won't be planting any replacement trees. It has taken over a decade, but I've learned to accept that my log cabin is in the woodlands, not the forest.

CUTTING THROUGH THE
TANGLE OF PRIVATE TIMBER SALES
February 2003

Recently some friends asked me to help with a timber sale on their forest land. I had assisted with logging their property in the late 1980s. The opportunity to work on the same piece of land two cutting cycles in a row is a forester's dream. I knew my worth when I took a look at a proposed *Forest Harvest Practice Plan* given them by a mill bidding on their timber. The cutting prescriptions were completely counter to my friends' objectives. They knew to bring in a professional forester, but I shudder to think how many other private timber sales have occurred under the "boiler plate" format that plan proposed.

First, let me go on the record: I like logging. Although that may shock the people who know of my passion for trees, I see logging as a tool we can use to achieve healthier forests. As a forester, I use logging to carefully sculpt the forest into better habitat for wildlife, a safer place for residents, and a more vigorous environment for trees. However, applying logging as a tool for improving forest health takes humility—a willingness to be particularly observant of the results, to admit mistakes, and to adjust future actions based on these lessons. Each time a forest is logged, there is opportunity to make the forest an overall healthier ecosystem. Thus, the chance for a forester to work on the same property two cutting cycles in a row creates the opportunity to apply lessons learned and make that landscape resonate.

My friends' main reason for cutting trees is to improve their forests' resistance to catastrophic wildfires. They have lived in the mountains all of their lives. They are concerned with recent drought conditions. Since they have actively managed their forests over the years through thinning and previous timber sales, many trees on their property are large enough to have commercial value. In their case, logging is a viable tool for thinning their forests.

The economic incentives of logging make the tool work, but they are not what should drive a timber sale. The logger or mill may want to log an area in the most efficient method to maximize their profit. The forester, representing the landowner, wants to have an area logged in a method that leaves the remaining forest in better condition than before the logging.

In New Mexico, private landowners cutting commercial timber on twenty-five acres or more in a calendar year are required to get an approved harvest permit from the State Forestry Division. The landowner is required to submit a written plan detailing the land management objectives and the methods of harvest that will be used to meet those objectives. In this case, the soliciting sawmill proposed a plan that would maximize dollars, but minimize the opportunity to meet landowner objectives.

For example, one cutting prescription described a forest that is "primarily second growth ponderosa pine with a few larger mature trees." Their plan suggests, "Removal of the larger, mature trees will reduce the fire danger." Actually, the small trees are the more imminent threat in wildfire situations. Older, larger ponderosa pines have thicker bark to resist fire damage. Their branches are generally well above the forest floor and do not offer the same fuel ladders as branches of smaller trees that can turn low-intensity surface fires into raging crown fires. Cutting the larger mature trees and leaving the young, denser second growth will only add extra slash to an already volatile situation.

For another tract, the mill's proposed plan suggests "thinning from above" which is a euphemism for taking the larger trees. The line I thought was most atrocious from this faulted plan followed a description of a timbered area where ponderosa pine is scattered and small. Their suggestion was to limit removal to the oldest and most accessible trees, exactly the trees that should be left in the forest to meet the landowners' goals.

With years of accumulated drought effects, we are poised for a major bark beetle outbreak in the pine. Since timber slash provides an excellent breeding ground for bark beetles, typical slash treatments may not be adequate this year to control such risks. A harvest plan needs to address these issues.

Timber harvesting will be a good tool to improve my friends' forest conditions, if they can find the right operator willing to put forest health as the first priority. At least they should know what company they do not want cutting their trees.

DIVINING HEALTHY FORESTS
September 2002

When I was a freshman forestry undergraduate, a wizened professor tried to explain to us eager, know-it-all eighteen- and nineteen-year-olds that forestry was both an art and a science. Blah, blah, blah. It was the seventies, and we knew we were going to save the earth. We were products of the "Earth Day" generation and our lives would be devoted to caring for the forests. Give us four years of accumulated semester hours, unleash us to the woods, and everyone would live happily ever after in a magical wonderland.

The professor droned on about the value of experience, the complexity of ecosystems, and the importance of recognizing what you do not know. Blah, blah, blah. We wanted it laid out in black and white. We wanted him to get past the introduction and tell us in crisp, clear, concise lessons just what we needed to know to be keepers of the forest. Yet he withheld such a simplistic outlook. He insisted we become artists inspired by science and scientists inspired by art. He made us look beneath the surface and divine what we wanted when we asked to manage healthy forests. By the end of the semester, we no longer craved the black and white but had found fascination in the multitudes of gray.

Twenty-five years later, the forests are no wonderland. We are far from living happily ever after as we face unprecedented, unhealthy forest conditions. In recent dry summers we have watched our dreams literally go up in smoke. We have spent decades trying to apply our craft, to address increasingly dense forest conditions in the face of an almost hostile political climate opposed to any forest management. Then the weather changed. Dry years: 1996, 2000, and 2002, each year escalating the severity of the conditions in the forest. There is no joy in saying "we told you so." What minor elation comes in finally getting our message across is dulled by the pain of witnessing abnormally catastrophic fires ripping through the countryside.

In the wake of public opinion turning toward taking action in the woods, I am concerned about a different form of destruction ripping through the countryside. This is a simplistic, one-size-fits-all dogma that the solution is simply to remove more trees. I am reminded of the professor of freshmen forestry students who refused to let us see the world in black and white. We are selling our forest communities short when we do not recognize the various hues of gray. Forest management is both an art and a science that demands every bit of experience, every minor observation, and every thoughtful insight to each action we take on the ground.

We need to act quickly and decisively to address the dense, fuel-laden forests, but it is much more complicated than racing to the woods with our chainsaws. We need to work with the ecosystem, apply our knowledge, understand the nuances of each situation. For example, much of the research on fuels treatment has been done in the vicinity of Flagstaff, Arizona, in close proximity to a research station and a university. The dominant plant association there is ponderosa pine/ Arizona fescue. This is a forest community that grows trees and grass. It is possible to remove many trees and create grassy fuel breaks in this type. If we take the cookbook approach pioneered there and apply it to a different forest, say a ponderosa pine/Gambel oak plant association in Los Alamos, New Mexico, the result could be disastrous. Instead of creating a safety zone, we would create the kind of shrub brush field that was responsible for fourteen deaths in 1994 on Storm King Mountain in Colorado. There are at least thirty different plant associations that support ponderosa pine forests, and understanding the implications of working with this diversity is only a part of the knowledge we need to apply as we go to the woods to create healthy forests.

Perhaps we had to "dumb down" the message to a simple mantra of "remove trees" in order to get the support of politicians and media moguls in search of sound bites. Let's hope though, that as we go to the woods with chainsaws, we are going well informed, with a well-designed plan of action that will truly help us restore health to the forests of the Southwest. Whether we are homeowners or foresters, contractors or government employees, let's make sure we are applying art and science to our actions.

 ## A COMMON VISION FOR JEMEZ MOUNTAIN ELK
April 2003

In 1998 in the small town of Bernalillo, New Mexico, a handful of people met one late fall day to talk about a large mammal population in the mountains northwest of town. This group included an employee each from the Forest Service and the New Mexico Department of Game and Fish and some folks representing the Northern New Mexico Livestock Association, the Rocky Mountain Elk Foundation, and the New Mexico Council of Outfitters and Guides. They agreed that elk are a focal point for the Jemez Mountains. There needed to be more coordination and cooperation among all of the people, agencies, and organizations that impacted and were impacted by elk.

The Jemez Mountains Seeking Common Ground Project emerged from this small gathering and represents over forty agencies, tribes, organizations, and interests. Privately funded, primarily through grants from the Rocky Mountain Elk Foundation and the National Fish and Wildlife Foundation, this group has met for the past four years to seriously address the issues of forest and elk management. Recently they published a *Strategy for Adaptive Management of Elk in the Jemez Mountains.*

Wild and majestic, elk are an important natural resource in New

Elk are an essential component of the Jemez ecosystem.
Courtesy of David Lewis.

Mexico. However, as elk populations have grown and their presence on public and private lands becomes more dominant, elk management has become increasingly necessary, incrementally political, and incredibly controversial. Elk have become unwelcome guests in farmers' alfalfa fields, obtrusive hazards on forested highways, and destructive browsers when concentrated in specific areas. On the other hand, the opportunity to view and enjoy elk in the wild is valued by most Jemez Mountain visitors and residents.

Hunters appreciate healthy populations, and in some public access hunting areas, too few elk are a problem. With many divergent and sometimes opposing approaches to managing these animals, it is imperative for all interested parties to work together to develop a strategy for elk management in the Jemez Mountains.

Elk are integrally linked to the whole ecosystem. Elk can modify the habitat in ways that are clear and dramatic. To understand elk, we must understand where they live. To manage this land, our focus must extend to all parts of that ecosystem, and not concentrate on any one species. We must include ourselves and recognize the social and political concerns that shape our thinking and our range of potential actions. Thus, Seeking Common Ground's objective is to develop strategies for supporting a healthy ecosystem and for addressing social concerns regarding elk.

The group's belief is that "what is healthy for the overall system" will determine "what is healthy for the elk population." The Jemez Mountains are a beautiful collection of diverse vegetative and faunal communities that exist upon an equally diverse landscape. Lay upon this many human cultures, agencies, interests, and people who interact daily with the Jemez Mountains, and the complexity intensifies.

The *Strategy* provides a starting point—a trailhead to the path where practical and effective land practices serve both elk and people. The document is dynamic, and strategies will change in response to monitoring and adapting practices based on experience.

The vision is for a healthy and viable elk population with a balanced distribution throughout the Jemez Mountains that minimizes elk damage to other resources.

DYING PINYONS
August 2002

There is an epidemic of dying trees throughout the pinyon-juniper woodlands of the Southwest. If you conduct a casual windshield inventory of brown trees, you will rapidly lose count. Most of these dead or dying trees are pinyon pine, but a number of junipers are dying as well.

Dead pinyons first started showing up in significant numbers during the drought of 1996. In 2000 many more trees turned brown. Neither of these years compare to the extent of mortality we are witnessing now two years later. Still, I have remained relatively calm, and almost pleased to witness this death in the forest.

The frequent causes of mortality are bark beetles (*Ips*) or twig beetles (*Pityophthorus*). The argument can be made that drought, not the insects, is accountable for this heavy tree mortality because related drought stress makes these trees more susceptible to insect outbreaks. Perhaps drought should not take the major rap for this mortality, either. The real culprit is the conditions of the woodlands, which, over most of the pinyon-juniper range, is crowded with too many trees.

It is becoming a familiar tale. Due to a long history of excluding fire, we have too many trees in the forests. This summer, however, it has been fascinating to watch the combination of drought and insect outbreaks bring some balance to the forest woodland. As a resident of the pinyon-juniper belt, I have, for years, been watching and waiting for this phenomenon.

In my neighborhood many pinyon are relatively young trees. Although large "grandfather" size pinyon are scattered throughout the hillsides, a good number of our neighborhood trees would qualify as Christmas trees. Here, as well as many other areas in the Southwest, large numbers of pinyons died during a multiyear drought in the 1950s. Many of today's trees have become established since then.

Julio Betancourt, a Tucson-based scientist with the U.S. Geological Survey, suggests that the drought of the fifties significantly disrupted the pinyon-juniper woodland, causing changes in nutrient and carbon cycling and shifting boundaries of vegetation communities that had been stable for thousands of years. In many places in the Southwest, he and his colleagues have demonstrated shifts in tree occurrence as much as 330 feet (100 meters) upslope. Now, fifty years later, drought is taking another stab at reducing the pinyon population.

A friend recently showed me a pair of aerial photos of a mesa near the Jemez Mountains from 1935 and 1998. In the 1935 photo, there are clearly fewer trees. The telling observation was the white halos around each tree in both photos. My friend had been out ground-truthing the photos and confirmed my suspicion that each of the trees is surrounded by bare soil. The tree roots dominate available moisture and make it difficult for grasses or other plants to grow. The scary observation was the immense increase in bare ground in the 1998 photo due to an increase in tree density. Not only does more bare soil mean less grass and habitat for wildlife ranging from insects to browsers, but bare soil is also subject to erosion.

Soil development in the pinyon-juniper woodlands is slow due to the semiarid conditions. In fact, much of the soil in these regions developed 10,000 to 100,000 years ago when wetter climates supported mixed conifer forests. The soil that washes off the hill slopes during our monsoon storms is, at least from a human time perspective, irreplaceable. Therefore, it is easy to get concerned about increased numbers of trees.

Grass roots do a better job of holding surface soil than trees because their roots are generally more fibrous and shallow. When grasses are reduced and surface runoff washes away soil, remaining plants are left on pedestals. The height of pedestals provides a good gauge of how many inches of soil have been lost. Fuel-wood cutting, thinning and chipping, and burning can reduce the density of trees on the landscape, and, if grass seed is in the soil bank, create conditions for more grass reestablishment. If we do nothing to address the unnatural conditions we have created in the woodlands, we can be sure that nature will make an adjustment. The trouble is we might not like the results.

Nature seems to be speaking up now in the form of drought-induced bark beetle attacks. The jury is still out on the impacts this will have in the woodlands. There are significant changes going on this summer. Pinyon may be "edited" out of the ecosystem in some drainages and draws where the bark beetle populations explode. The occurrence of pinyon trees could even shift by hundreds of feet in elevation. Extra fuel from dead and dying trees may accelerate fire behavior and expand fire spread. Perhaps, the reduction in trees will allow grasses and other plants to establish and hold the soil on the site.

We have front-row seats to this performance. When asked if I am concerned about the number of dying trees in our woodlands, I cannot respond with a definitive "yes" or "no." Rather, I find the phenomenon fascinating.

OBSERVATIONS OF A DYING PINYON TREE
October 2003

Like many southwestern woodlands, the woods behind my log cabin have experienced a dramatic increase in dead and dying pinyon trees. As a forester, I see the impact of this beetle epidemic on a landscape scale and contemplate the implications of this major dieback on long-term forest health. As a middle-age woman struggling to stay in shape, my contemplations focus on individual trees that line the path behind my house where I walk or run several times a week. This morning I discovered that the first tree from my informal study has fallen to the ground.

I noticed this young pinyon pine soon after I moved into my home in 1989. It was three feet tall and growing close to the trail. It had a perfect symmetrical shape, and since it would eventually block the trail if it reached adulthood, I started fantasizing about taking it home some year for our Yuletide celebrations. It needed some height, and besides it marked the half-mile point from my doorstep, so it was safe from my saw for a while.

The summer of 1996 my Christmas fantasies were dashed when its needles started to turn brown. The tree was then about five feet tall. Upon close examination, I found the pitch balls indicative of a bark beetle attack, but essentially I chalked the fatality up to drought stress that had attracted the beetle activity. Unable to enjoy the tree fancied up with ornaments and tinsel, I delighted in an opportunity to informally study the death of a small pinyon pine.

We foresters pride ourselves on our ability to read the landscape. We like to kick at a stump and estimate how long it has been since the tree was cut. When we look at a snag (our four-letter word for a dead standing tree), we notice the size of the remaining limbs, the amount of bark that is sloughing off, the color of the exposed wood beneath the bark, and depending on the species and our guess at the mechanism of death, we muse about how long ago the tree died.

By observing this one small dying pinyon, I could improve my estimates at aging pinyon death. When I started my study, I had no idea how handy my learning would serve me, as we have seen major diebacks of pinyons in 2000, 2002, and an even greater number now in 2003. Based on my totally nonscientific sample size of one, I find myself now walking through woodlands assigning death dates to fading pinyon snags.

The first year, brown needles clung to the stems, and I could not help but worry about the flammability of such air-dried tinder should a fire come through. This fear is especially keen this year for landscapes such as the woods southeast of Santa Fe, where brown crowns dominate, closely touching and stretching for miles.

The needles began to drop the second year, although a few held on giving the snag a rather forlorn expression. By year three, the needles were all piled at the base, adding to surface fuels should that anticipated wildfire burn through. At this point, the ends of the stems began to break off, but still the stem-end diameters were tinier than my littlest finger.

In other places pinyon needles and stems have been stripped from the tree in a single hailstorm, so clearly rates can vary.

Four years following the death of my subject, we saw the next widescale recruitment of dying pinyons. By this point the stems on my tree were getting stubbier, but still they did not reach little finger size until year six, in 2002, when even more of my tree's neighbors were beginning to fade and turn brown.

Now, this autumn, seven years since its death, my study specimen has fallen to the ground. The base, approximately four inches in diameter, shows the rotted roots and shallow pit of a natural tumble, although I wonder if another traveler along the trail may have given it a push. I know from years of tree observations not to expect every dead pinyon to fall over in seven years. Larger diameter trees may take longer and factors such as soil moisture may affect the rate of root decay.

Generally, though, I think ahead to 2010 and imagine a more open and grassy woodland throughout the Southwest. I wonder if in 2050, people will have forgotten this major pinyon dieback, much like we had forgotten the pinyon population decrease during the drought of the 1950s. Since the way we manage our pinyon-juniper woodlands can either contribute to or reduce the impacts of catastrophic dieback, I hope the lessons will linger longer.

Meanwhile, I'll be watching a small, dead pinyon log and hopefully live long enough to know when the last limb decays into the ground.

PINING FOR PINYON
September 2006

Last week approximately a hundred and fifty foresters and range managers convened in Albuquerque to focus on pinyon-juniper woodlands. The conference was a joint meeting of the Society of American Foresters and the Society for Range Management. It wasn't the first time a conference had been held to learn about the short-stature trees. As one speaker pointed out, six previous workshops stemming from 1975 to 1997 had generated 272 articles and over 1,600 pages of proceedings. Of course, this was before pinyon trees started dying by the millions.

Fifty-four million dead pinyons in New Mexico, one speaker suggested. That would be 100 million dead trees throughout the pinyon's (three different species) range in the United States, which takes in the bulk of New Mexico, Arizona, Colorado, Utah, and Nevada. That's only about 15 percent of existing trees, another speaker optimistically offered. Tell that to someone in Santa Fe, Abiquiu, Prescott, or any other die-off hotspot where at least to the untrained eye, almost every pinyon seems to have taken a hit. The tree counters have interesting data. No size class is immune. The deaths of small, little, medium, large, and granddaddy trees seems to follow classic J-shaped population curves indicating that all age classes are experiencing the same ratio of mortality.

Throughout the three-day conference, the esteemed presenters found various areas of disagreement. Everyone agrees that pinyon trees died during the 1950s drought, but whether this current die-off event is much larger is debatable. Bark beetles are universally blamed as the primary causal agent of the tree deaths; however, opinions varied on whether drought conditions weakened the trees and made them vulnerable to beetle outbreaks. Some feel recent dry periods are part of normal weather fluctuations while others feel global warming is a key part of the equation.

Overall, there were few tears shed for the trees that had died. The general consensus is that, in the absence of regular fires burning across the landscape as in presettlement times, pinyon and juniper trees have been increasing in our woodlands and grasslands. The trees intercept and transpire rainwater that would have otherwise entered into groundwater, streams, and springs. In addition grasses and wildflowers are more likely to flourish where tree numbers have decreased. When these plants grow beneath trees, soils are less likely to erode. A study at Bandelier National Monument illuminates this situation. On a 1/10 hectare plot in dense woodland, over one thousand potsherds were found in soil that had eroded from just one storm event.

The final conference day focused on thinning woodlands and utilizing wood products. In addition to using pinyon and juniper firewood to heat homes via traditional woodstoves, power plants burning woody biomass produce far less pollution than coal-burning plants. Not only is energy a marketable commodity, but energy credits gained by creating less pollution can be marketed to companies and countries to meet worldwide air-quality guidelines. A Mountainair businessman also shared challenges of creating new products utilizing pinyon and juniper wood fibers.

Pinyon-Juniper woodlands cover approximately one-quarter of New Mexico and over one-eighth of Arizona. These lands provide water, forage for livestock and wildlife, wood products, and recently a vast number of home sites. Clearly, with awareness and knowledge, foresters and range managers are better prepared to care for this important and seemingly fragile ecosystem.

HABITAT TYPING
August 2006

The pinyon pine/mountain mahogany (PIED/CEMO) woodland behind the Jemez Ranger Station is somewhat tricky to key out this year with the lush response of forbs and grasses due to the recent rains.

The forest up by Oscar's Grave near Alpine is either blue spruce/dryspike sedge (PIPU/CAFO) or possibly blue spruce/Arizona fescue (PIPU/FEAR). This explains the sporadic response of the aspen sprouting despite the nine-foot-tall elk fence.

The ponderosa pine/black sagebrush (PIPO/ARNO) stand by Tres Piedras is similar to ponderosa pine/big sagebrush (PIPO/ARTR2), but the sagebrush that dominates this swale is much smaller in stature. Planted with ponderosa pine years ago, our group discusses whether the trees belong or are encroaching in a natural meadow.

Outside of McNary, the fuel reduction treatment in the ponderosa pine/Gambel oak (PIPO/QUGA) stand may result in a brush field of more volatile fuels than the original overstocked pine forest.

These are a few of the observations made during two week-long Habitat Typing Workshops held this summer in Arizona and New Mexico.

Habitat typing, also known as identifying plant associations, is an important skill set for natural resource managers working in woodlands or forests. Managers can be more precise when they can classify the

Steve Boyer and David Lawrence, Forest Service silvicuturists, discuss recent tree removal at the Monument Canyon Research Natural Area in the Jemez Mountains during a habitat typing class. Photo by author.

forest into distinct plant associations. For example, a ponderosa pine forest can, with the right books and training, be identified as one of forty or so habitat types that support ponderosa pine forests. Knowing the type allows managers to compare, contrast, and predict the responses of plants to various activities such as burning, thinning, and logging.

Habitat types are named for the most shade-tolerant tree the site can support and an understory plant that best represents the site. Ideally this indicator plant thrives in the specific plant association but does poorly in other places. Frequently, though, the community is named for a dominant plant in the understory. Plant associations have names such as *pinyon pine-mountain mahogany,* which when using scientific names for plants would be *Pinus edulis/Cercocarpus montanus.* Since habitat types were originally developed for government workers, and government workers are famed for creating acronyms, the name is often shortened to unintelligible but pronounced monikers by using the first two letters of both genus and species for each plant, thus PIED/CEMO.

Knowing the habitat type provides specific information not apparent to a casual observer. For example, many people consider the ponderosa pine forest on the Mogollon Rim in central Arizona as the largest homogenous stand of ponderosa pine. Actually, the forest is a mix of many types. The ponderosa pine/screwleaf muhly (PIPO/MUVI) type is wetter than a ponderosa pine/screwleaf muhly–Arizona fescue (PIPO/ MUVI-FEAR) stand, which is still moister than a ponderosa pine/ Arizona fescue (PIPO/FEAR) forest. Near the edges of this vast pine stand, ponderosa/blue grama (PIPO/BOGR) is even drier. It is hardly homogenous at all!

Habitat typing was developed in the Pacific Northwest in the 1960s, and plant associations have been classified in all of the western states. The first comprehensive plant association classification of southwestern forests was completed in the 1980s. In the mid-1980s, Will Moir and Milo Larson from the Forest Service's Southwest Regional Office held eight week-long workshops to introduce the new system to natural resource managers. I attended one of these trainings and then held a similar session for my colleagues. Soon I was teaching courses as a contractor with the Forest Service. In the mid-1990s, I helped edit the regional Plant Association guides into a two-volume set, one for forests and one for woodlands.

Since 1991, I have facilitated over thirty week-long trainings involving about six hundred resource managers throughout Arizona and New Mexico. Each course includes five days in the woods, full of spirited discussion and learning, and visits to a plethora of plant communities from the woodlands to the spruce-fir alpine transition. I end each week excited about forests, and I hope the participants have one more tool to promote forest health across the landscape.

10   WHITE MOUNTAIN
STEWARDSHIP PROGRAM
September 2007

There is a buzz about cutting trees in the forests of the east-central Arizona White Mountains, but it is not coming from chainsaws. Chainsaws are too inefficient for this operation. This is a story about efficiency and the government. This story is about the White Mountain Stewardship program on the Apache-Sitgreaves National Forest.

"We're out here at least twice a month giving tours about this project," explains Apache-Sitgreaves National Forest supervisor Elaine Zieroth. The group she is addressing on this day includes tribal forestry leaders from across the West. Many tribes are interested in this newest way of doing business with the Forest Service: via the Stewardship Contract. Well into the third year of a ten-year contract, the White Mountain Stewardship Program is an ideal model of efficient action, both in the woods and in the offices.

The Stewardship Contract combines removing commercial wood products with acquiring forest treatment services. Before Stewardship Contracting, these were separate projects. A timber sale focused on removing commercial wood products from the forest. A thinning contract focused on removing small non commercial trees in order to leave healthier forests. The Stewardship Contract pulls the two practices under one entry, and forest health and wildfire protection objectives drive what happens in the woods. The commercial aspects of the operation offset the costs of getting the acres treated.

Our tour stops at a landing in the woods east of Show Low, Arizona. The stand consists of ponderosa pine trees, with smaller oaks and junipers growing underneath the pine. The seasoned foresters in our group suggest that most of the pine trees appear to have started growing around 1919, an optimal year for ponderosa pine establishment in the American Southwest. The fire managers point out how the dense patches of oak and juniper provide fuel ladders that make the stand (before the treatment) susceptible to crown fires. The ecologists note that the blue grama grass and juniper trees indicate this is a dry site for the pine, and not one of the more productive timber stands.

As we compare the meager deck of saw logs with the huge pile of small diameter poles, it is clear that this forest could not be thinned by cutting only commercial wood products. Even though the small trees will be chipped and used to make wood pellets, the cost of handling the trees to take them out of the woods is greater than the value of the wood fiber going into the pellet mill.

Dwayne Walker has plenty to grin about as he addresses the group. A local White Mountain resident, Walker is one of the principal owners of Future Forests LLC, the company that has the ten-year contract to treat 150,000 acres of the Apache-Sitgreaves National Forest. Dwayne's resources include machines called fellerbunchers, forwarders, and skidders that munch and crunch their way across the landscape transforming hundreds of thousands of tons of green biomass into wood products.

Left in the woods, this material is referred to by firefighters as fuel. Folks in the White Mountains are especially conscientious of fire threats since the 2002 Rodeo-Chediski Fire scorched almost a half-million acres of the region and burned hundreds of homes. One of the reasons the White Mountain Stewardship Project is successful is because of widespread support by area residents.

"The White Mountain Stewardship Project didn't just happen overnight," explains Molly Pitts, the executive director of the Northern Arizona Wood Products Association, an organization that represents over fifty companies and individuals whose livelihood is dependent on forest products. "It has taken over a decade of trust building between all kinds of community members to back this kind of effort."

Walker offers that his books have been audited three times this year to insure that his costs are commensurate with the payment he receives for the work accomplished. A sixteen-member citizen monitoring board meets monthly to insure social, economic, and environmental objectives are met by the project.

The White Mountain Stewardship Project is crafted to address local issues and concerns. However, as the first large Forest Service Stewardship program, there are plenty of lessons for other regions to study and perhaps emulate. Our particular tour group looks forward to building long-term relationships that involve tribes in the management of national forests. As each community defines how the concept of stewardship contracting will play out in their forests, there is new hope for combining the concepts of "efficiency" and "government" throughout the West.

IN DEFENSE OF INFORMED,
INTUITIVE FORESTRY
February 2008

Winter months are traditional training times for foresters, and this year I attended a fire ecology conference that was inspirational, informative, and, in some ways, disturbing. Over the next weeks or months, I will assimilate new information and add to my tool bag new concepts, language, and approaches that will enable me to make better decisions for the land I am honored to manage.

The meeting attendance was skewed toward those who work in university and administrative settings. Those of us who work in the woods were underrepresented. Personally, I had no travel funds, so I mooched off friends, slept on the couch, and remembered my college days when increased knowledge came at the price of personal comfort.

Foresters have a long tradition of relying on intuition to guide management decisions. However, at this conference, use of intuition was being criticized as "seat-of-the-pants" forestry. The implication was that foresters were ignoring research that would guide them to a different course of action.

Clearly, reliance on both science and intuition has led to poor but widespread and accepted dogma within the profession. For many decades, fire in the forest was considered unhealthy and was controlled as much as possible. Today's forest health issues are now attributed to this misguided policy of fire exclusion. With hindsight, we are critical of our profession for embracing extensive fire suppression and keeping fire out of the forest.

Historically, researchers and practitioners who embraced burning were often ridiculed and removed from their positions. Yet, a few foresters stuck to their unpopular convictions that fire belonged on the landscape. Today these individuals are heralded as heroes.

When science fails to provide meaningful guidance, foresters are still faced with daily management challenges. Since research does not provide all the answers, foresters must continue to hone and use their intuition.

The informed, intuitive forester bases her decisions on three major sources: academic learning, lessons from adaptive management, and intuition.

This stand of stately old trees on the Valles Caldera National Preserve has been dubbed the History Stand, in respect for the centuries these trees have lived. Courtesy of David Lewis.

Academic training begins with a college education but requires continual updates such as attending conferences, reading papers, and conducting detailed literature reviews when faced with a new challenge. One might also lump the vast body of guiding principles and procedures under the background information that forms the foundations of the forester's decision-making process.

Adaptive management, in simple terms, is applying lessons learned from observing past actions. In practice, this requires careful monitoring, analysis, and an institutional willingness to immediately adapt on-the-ground activities based on feedback.

While adaptive management is grounded in the institution, intuition is grounded in the individual. Intuition is developed over time and combines past knowledge and experiences with thoughtful analysis and common sense. When I am making decisions in the field on where to place the boundaries for cutting or planting blocks, or fire lines to hold a burn, intuition informs my decisions at critical moments.

It is poor management when foresters do not stay current or monitor their activities, but foresters need the right to rely on intuition to make decisions. The term "seat-of-the-pants" forest management can be reserved for sloppy practitioners, while "informed, intuitive" forest management applies when good forestry is being practiced.

The challenge lies in recognizing the difference. Humans tend to focus on the next day or week. Ecosystems operate on the scale of decades or centuries. It may take forty years to acknowledge the wisdom contained in an intuitive decision made today.

LOGGING IN ON FORESTRY
July 2006

"Captain's log, star date . . . ," a popular television show from my youth would start out each week—and hence my inspiration to call my writing a "log." Later, in the late 1980s when I started writing a column as a professional forester, a colleague suggested *The Forester's Log* as the title. Appropriate enough, since one of our tools as foresters charged with the job of looking out for the health of our forests is logging.

I write *The Forester's Log* each month because I love forests and I like sharing the efforts that my colleagues and I make each day toward trying to keep our forests healthy. I make less than minimum wage on the project. My monthly column is a labor of love—love of forests and love of people who love forests.

Therefore I was a bit shocked when one of my editors forwarded a letter regarding the column that started with:

> The wildlife in my care is sacred to me, as are the trees they call
> home. Many animals left orphaned come from trees that have been
> cut down. Why then, is there a section in your periodical called
> Forester's Log? I find it contradictory to our goals when many
> species depend on a forest for their survival.

The forests in my care are sacred to me. I dedicate my life to caring for forests and all of the plants and animals (including us) that depend on healthy forests for survival. However, for forests to be healthy, trees need room to grow. Like thinning carrots growing in a garden, some trees need to be cut out of the forest so the forest can continue to be healthy. One part of a forester's job is identifying those situations and then overseeing the process to insure the environment receives the best protection during these operations.

I think about the idea of orphaned animals. Don't we all agree that the greatest threat to wildlife is habitat loss? On the Rodeo-Chediski burn, where I currently focus most of my professional energy, the only forests that survived the 2002 catastrophic fire event are the forests that had been logged, thinned, burned, or some combination of these activities. These projects were planned and overseen by foresters. After the fire, the same foresters lamented that they had not had the funding to apply similar management activities throughout the entire area. If they had, we would not be facing the vast regions of eroded hillsides where all the trees were killed. Not only have animals been displaced, but hundreds of thousands of tons of soil have washed off the hill slopes jeopardizing the potential of reestablishing the animal homes that were destroyed in the fire.

I read on:

> Regardless of how well intentioned this forester may be, with logging comes road building, soil erosion, and degradation of streams and rivers.

Foresters do many other projects that support wildlife and tree health. Still, logging is one of the tools in our toolbox, and I feel compelled to offer some explanation. On timber sales I have worked on, one of my jobs as forester is to insure "best management practices" are being used to protect streams and rivers and prevent soil erosion. Often, because we have a logging operation in an area, we have an opportunity to address existing problems with roads or drainages that are causing soil erosion and water quality problems. Roads in forests are used for much more than logging. However, with today's logging operations, by the end of the project more roads have generally been closed than opened.

And according to the National Geographic (Sept. '04) the clearing
of forests and the burning of fossil fuels are said to be a major cause
of global warming. Forests are the world's lungs. The ecological
functions of forests can't be underestimated. Their destruction
causes species extinctions and loss of biological diversity.

Indeed, forests are the planet's lungs. When those lungs are seared
by catastrophic wildfires that release massive particulates and gases to
blanket the atmosphere, they produce a large contribution to global
warming. If the forests are healthy, managed woodlands, when fire
occurs the burn is not as catastrophic and may even contribute to the
health of the forest.

Most clearing of forests in our country, and perhaps the world, is
done by people moving into that habitat. When forests are designated
as part of the timber production land base, they are dedicated to being
kept as "forests." Even when clearcutting is utilized (which is much less
common today than it was in the past), the area is planted right away,
and young, growing trees actually work as more efficient "lungs" in producing oxygen and taking in carbon dioxide.

Regular readers of my column know that my work in the last few
years has included supervising the planting of over a million trees. We
know our society is dependent on trees; that's why we dedicate our lives
to looking out for them.

Even dead and dying trees are vital to an ecosystem. The USDA
says dead and dying trees provide homes to over 400 species of
birds, mammals, and amphibians. The agency urges us to leave
these trees standing.

Exactly. This is why when foresters write the prescription that guides
timber sales, dead and dying trees are designated to be left in the woods.
This column is dedicated to helping readers understand these things.
Clearing the path for human habitation rarely leaves dead and dying
trees for other animals' use.

With all due respect to its author, please replace Forester's Log with
a more animal friendly article. Thank you.

With all due respect to this letter's author, the reason I write *The Forester's Log* is to show that foresters are truly concerned about wildlife, water, trees, plants, and the complex biological and ecological functions that occur within our forests. We are concerned about habitat, without which wildlife cannot live. I think the motto of the New Mexico Share with Wildlife Program expresses this philosophy: Helping Wildlife Where It Counts, Where Wildlife Lives.

The letter writer is not alone in her misconceptions about forestry, foresters, and even the role of "logging" in our forests. Like all professions, forestry is always evolving. Our understanding of forests and forest ecosystems has changed through the years. Just as today's doctors cringe at treatments their predecessors prescribed decades ago, today's foresters are often strong critics of past practices. Our professional society tracks our continuing education credits, and certification is dependent on keeping current with knowledge in our field. Patients do not expect their doctors to prescribe treatments that have been proven detrimental, but some people assume that today's foresters are continuing to make the same mistakes from previous decades. Where foresters in the 1960s and 1970s were focused on "board feet," today's decisions are based on values such as "preserving biodiversity" or "restoring ecosystem functions." In this context, in some places, trees need to be cut to thin the forest or create a mosaic of habitats when the natural role of fire has been absent. Logging is a useful tool, and wood products are required by our society.

When I call my column *The Forester's Log*, I like the image of a log heading out of the woods to build a home, provide some paper, or be a renewable source of energy that creates one-tenth of the pollution as coal generation. I like the image of the forest that supplied that log being more vital, healthy, and providing a complex array of homes to the diversity of wildlife and plant life that inhabit it. Yet it is the double meaning of the word that inspires me. Here is my "log," just like Captain Kirk's. A few brief words to document what is going on in my world.

CHAPTER THREE

Burn Area Recovery

Autumn 2004

Having driven the Ford Expedition over five miles of rough, rocky, mountain road, I was surprised to reach the helispot before the hospital's helicopter.

My employee was lying on the ground, surrounded by a circle of caring and excited people.

"Mary, we can't find a pulse."

When the call first came across the radio, I had immediately headed for the helispot location where staff members were taking our unconscious bee-sting victim. Having medical training they did not, I adjusted her airway. Her body shook with a deep involuntary breath. Yanking off her boots, I found a weak pulse in her ankle. Her gasping breaths were sporadic. The welcome thwacking of the helicopter's rotor-blades coming over the hillside interrupted my decision on whether to start rescue breathing.

Within moments the helicopter landed. After we loaded the patient and the craft was gone, we formed a tight circle of people offering prayers and sharing our experience. Despite the tree planter's allergic reaction to the beesting, the response of her co-workers had probably saved her life. I was standing amid a group of heroes.

When the incident occurred, Bryan Antonio had been in charge of the unit. His cool head set the tone for the team's response.

Our patient had been working with Adam Henry and Anthony Quay, tribal contractors who were participating in our first "Tree

Despite severe fire activity during the 2002 Rodeo-Chediski fire, beauty still abounds near Limestone Lookout Tower on the Fort Apache Indian Reservation. Courtesy of Daniel Kessay.

Planting Camp." After accidentally disturbing a nest of ground bees, she had been reaching for her EpiPen when she lost consciousness. Carried by those who have a known allergy to bee and wasp stings, the device delivers a dose of epinephrine to counter allergic reactions. When the men tried to administer the drug, the lifesaving liquid spurted out before the needle had pierced her skin.

Nearby, co-worker Franklin Lewis recognized the emergency. Despite the angry bees flying around, he offered his own EpiPen to help the fallen victim.

Meanwhile, Daniel Kessay, the camp's operations chief, was down in our base camp on the radio walking Bryan through our operations plan and instructing him to the closest predetermined location for a helispot. Daniel then contacted the dispatcher back in Whiteriver to order a Life Flight, and provided the GPS coordinates so the team could rendezvous with the helicopter.

Norman Skidmore, one of our seasoned crew leaders, knew the procedures to assist the helicopter and prepared the landing field and gave hand signals to the pilot.

From the prepared, detailed operation plan which included first-aid directions, helispot locations, radio frequencies, and a command structure; to fast-acting field first aid; to general level-headedness of people—both employees and contractors—involved, the incident had flowed in a textbook manner.

Days later, Bryan told me that for years he had rehearsed in his head how he would handle an emergency if he was ever in such a situation. Clearly his practice resulted in a well-honed performance.

Once our huddle parted, I picked up one of her relatives and headed to the hospital.

Rushing into the emergency room an hour later, I found my employee sitting in bed with a grin on her face.

"Where are my boots and my pack?" she asked, indicating that she was ready to go back to work.

I AM NOT SURE HOW I CAME TO BE "MAMA BAER," BUT IT WAS A ROLE I cherished. A forester from the Fort Apache Agency first contacted me about the job. The White Mountain Apache Tribe had contracted the implementation of the Burn Area Emergency Response (BAER) program from the Bureau of Indian Affairs. The tribe needed to hire an implementation leader to coordinate emergency response activities. They had already hired and fired one colleague.

I adamantly refused to consider the position. Having worked on the Rodeo-Chediski Fire the previous season, I had a vague idea of the enormity of the project. After that initial refusal, I found I could not sleep, or if I did, I dreamed of crown-dancers on burned-out landscapes. A month later I called back and learned that the position was still vacant, and the urgency for a director was intense. When I arrived to discuss accepting the job, there was little negotiation. By afternoon I was calling prospective employees from a pool of hundreds of applicants and putting together my first group of forty workers to install log erosion barriers.

Through the years my staff varied between forty and a hundred, and I had oversight of hundreds of others working as contractors. With an always chaotic pace, the opportunity was exhilarating.

In addition to providing direction for the Tribal Forestry workers assigned to the fire rehabilitation, I also coordinated with other tribal departments—wildlife, hydrology, land operations, utilities, and the police department—working on BAER projects.

As a white woman working with predominately Native Americans, I was targeted early on for an "Apache" name. Although I was called other names, the one I like the most means Mama Bear. When circumstances threaten my "cubs," like my namesake, I am ready to stand and fight.

REHABBING THE RODEO-CHEDISKI FIRE
January 2004

Several months ago I was hired by the White Mountain Apache Tribe for a job that seems akin to "Mission: Impossible." My assignment is to coordinate efforts rehabilitating the Rodeo-Chediski Fire. The fire, actually two separate fires that joined together, burned over 467,000 acres in June and July of 2002. Both starts occurred on the Fort Apache Indian Reservation in Arizona, involving 277,000 acres of tribal lands. Over 160,000 of these acres were classified as "high or moderate severity" meaning the trees were all killed and the fire effects were catastrophic.

In my new job I work with hundreds of people who are involved with day-to-day recovery activities. This past year we built a hundred miles of fence, planted 650,000 pine seedlings, cleaned and cleaned again hundreds of clogged culverts, dropped thousands of tons of hay from helicopters to mulch hillsides, placed tens of thousands of logs along the contour to capture eroding soil, and that's just the short list.

At times, it seems our efforts are almost heroic, but when faced with the daunting expanse of burned-out drainage, next to burned-out drainage, next to burned-out drainage . . . I wonder if any human action can atone for the drastic impact this fire has inflicted on the landscape. Then I am confronted by outstanding arrays of wildflowers, none of which we seeded, that carpeted the canyons during this summer's monsoons. I find myself perched on the edge of a roadway carved away by raging floodwaters, marveling at the magnitude of the valley floor to sustain this increase of water. In this new landscape, our road is in the wrong place. I crawl through acres of thorny New Mexico locust shrubs that have almost magically returned to carpet hillsides. It is clear nature is the major force in this forest recovery and not our feeble efforts.

There are so many lessons to learn here. One of the obvious observations is the pattern of burn severity. Where the forest had been recently treated by timber sales, thinning projects, and/or prescribed burns, the fire intensity was less severe. There are still green trees and the soil is not washing off the hill slopes. These are the acres I do not lose sleep over. These are the acres where fire indeed seems to be a natural force in harmony with the landscape. If there was any doubt about the value of forest management in reducing catastrophic fire effects, the Rodeo-Chediski burn lays those concerns to rest.

We are facing an unprecedented challenge. Never before has so severe a fire burned so vast a forest in the Southwest. Yet, if forest conditions throughout the West are not drastically altered, our burn is indicative of fires to come. If we achieve nothing else, at least we can witness the role of nature in recovery and reestablishment of an ecosystem, an ecosystem that may or may not resemble the one that existed before.

It is an honor to have a role in this journey. I serve a people who are keenly connected to the land. We are a team of dedicated people—tribal members, tribal leaders, and tribal and agency employees. We have diverse backgrounds, multiple talents, and varying perspectives, but we share the challenge of giving our best effort to this healing process.

My goal is to share the story of this effort in this monthly *Forester's Log* column. Throughout the West, as the drought continues and forests continue to accumulate fuel, we will continue to have landscape-size, catastrophic fires in our forests. Burn area rehabilitation is becoming a major focus of forest management. We need to share the lessons the land has to offer.

2 MIXING IN MEXICO
October 2003

The terraced landscape stretches before me: undulating hills with occasional lone, tall pine trees, a plantation of tree seedlings with this year's shoots stretching beyond a foot's growth, and miles and miles of trenches that follow contours in rows roughly thirty feet apart. The El Huerfano Fire occurred five years earlier in 1998. Our guides are animated when they recount the fire. They speak of helicopters, scores of firefighters, long-term drought conditions, and extreme fire behavior never witnessed before. It is a similar story line to the fires in my home states of New Mexico and Arizona, but I am in a foreign country.

I am keenly aware of my alien status because I cannot follow the conversation. My poor Spanish can get me to the baño, order a cerveza, and pick up a café a llevar. I cannot get the gist of the intention or science behind the ditches. The bilingual members of our party try to translate. Community members of the local ejido who work for $10.50 a day have dug these trenches by hand. These men have spent four years digging, and they are funded for another eight. The trenches are a half-meter deep, a half-meter wide, and every three or four meters there is a half-meter-wide break (perhaps a bridge for wildlife, I muse). The ditches are designed to keep water on site. With a twinkle in his eye, one of the Mexican foresters explains to us Americans that they would not want the water to get to Texas. There is a paper from a university that can answer my more technical questions.

I am standing in this burn, in the Sierra Madres, near San Juanito, Chihuahua, with a group of approximately eighty foresters. Half of us are from the Southwest Society of the Society of American Foresters, a section of the national professional organization that includes New Mexico and Arizona. The rest are professional foresters from the Sección Chihuahua, Asociación Mexicana de Profesionales Forestales. Every two years the two sections meet for a conference, and the conferences alternate between Mexico and the United States.

This year's theme includes wildfire restoration, and as a newly hired coordinator of rehabilitation efforts for a large burn in Arizona, I am eager to exchange ideas. My Mexican colleagues do not disappoint. They offer a fresh viewpoint to similar problems, as do the other forty

Contour ditches, planted trees, and check dams are some of the activities Mexican foresters are applying on the El Huerfano burn in the Sierra Taramuhara in Chihuahua, Mexico. Photo by author.

foresters who have made the trip with me from El Paso. We travel in a chartered bus, and the conference is held in the city of Chihuahua and the town of Creel, with field trips from the latter.

We buy trinkets from the Tarahumara natives, and we sip tequila in the bars at night. We marvel at the multiple species of pine and oak, and we sit through technical sessions that, even with the advent of PowerPoint, are still the bane of professional meetings.

At one such session, there is a strong exchange of emotion and cultural values. The title of the presentation is "Proyecto para el Approvechamiento Turístico de El Divisadero, Barrancas del Cobre Chihuahua." A director of tourism outlines grandiose plans for developing the Copper Canyon country and improving the standard of living for the native people.

I am proud of my colleagues when the question/answer session focuses on lack of involvement of the Tarahumara people in developing the plan. "They may not know what they want, but they will learn," the tourism director explains, inferring that this model is obviously a benefit to the local people. I am hoping something has been lost in the translation.

It is the pot calling the kettle black. In the American Southwest we have a long history of impressing our *concept* of development onto native peoples with disastrous results to their cultures. Currently we are in a sensitive mode, attempting to recover what has been lost. We urge our Mexican comrades not to make the same mistakes. Although I leave skeptical our message has been heard, I am proud these government and academic foresters, generally a conservative group, made such a vocal objection.

Overall, the conference exceeds my expectations. I can return to Arizona, still puzzling about the watershed restoration trenches and wondering if our own treatments will seem as strange to my new Mexican friends when they come to the next reunion in Tucson in 2005.

GATHERING THE BAER CLAN
June 2004

Rodeo-Chediski. Biscuit. Hayman. Cerro Grande. Grand Prix-Old. Aspen. Bobcat. Coal Seam. Missionary Ridge. Grizzly Gulch. 8th Street. Trap & Skeet. Hot Creek. Trail Creek. Rattle Complex.

Big fires. Large, hot, destructive fires. Burns upon the land that clearly transcend the range of natural variability. With the advent of these increasingly severe, intense, broad-scale wildfires, a new breed of land manager is emerging. Burn Area Emergency Response (BAER) Implementation Leaders met in Denver to discuss techniques to stabilize and rehabilitate the land. Commonly called the BAER Team, these folks follow on the heels of firefighters to provide emergency stabilization actions after catastrophic wildfires.

When Ben Nuvamsa, a Hopi tribal member and the superintendent of the Fort Apache Agency in east-central Arizona, addressed the group, he offered them a new identity.

"At first I felt a stranger here among so many white people," he explained to the crowded room, "but then I realized I was among family. I am BEAR clan, and you are BAER clan, too."

Bureau of Land Management. Bureau of Indian Affairs. Bureau of Reclamation. Forest Service. Natural Resources Conservation Service. National Park Service. U.S. Fish & Wildlife Service. U.S. Army Corps of Engineers. Tribal Governments. State Governments. County Governments. City Governments.

Wildfires show no preference for political boundaries. No one seems exempt from the roulette of wildfire ignition in this western-states-wide, multiyear drought. Many at the Denver clan gathering, until quite recently, had no career aspirations that included rehabilitating burns until they found their own ward facing such a challenge.

After communities and agencies suppress a huge and devastating wildfire, these people face yet another potentially more devastating disaster from flash flooding and erosion when the next rains pound bare and blackened hillsides. When storm events that would previously barely raise stream levels become the equivalent of one-hundred-year floods, and several of these occur in a span of weeks, the results can be detrimental.

Conference participants viewed multiple slides of mudslides wiping out highways, torrents washing out bridge supports, houses, although heroically saved by brave firefighters weeks earlier, filling with mud or being battered to pieces by moving boulders.

Hydrologists. Soil Scientists. Foresters. Engineers. Botanists. Wildlife Biologists. Range Conservationists. Environmental Planners. Geologists. Archeologists. Administrators. Managers. Ranchers. Technicians. Cowboys.

With diverse backgrounds of varied experience and education, the clan is tasked with daily challenges. In forest and rangelands, rills become gullies, gullies grow to canyons, soil loss is measured in feet, and the resulting sediments clog downstream reservoirs. Where fire intensity was hottest, seed sources are often vaporized and soil chemistry is altered, creating water-repellent coatings that prevent rainfall from soaking into the ground.

Regardless of background, BAER Implementation Leaders quickly become generalists, mastering the mechanics of coordinating dozers and excavators in one breath while honing the ecological details of monitoring vegetation recovery in the next. Conference topics raced from "applying seed" to "removing culverts" to "capturing wild horses" to "spraying hydro-mulch" to "tracking budgets."

Aerial seeding. Aerial straw mulching. Hydro-mulching. Log erosion barriers. Wattles. Check-dams. Contour felling. Low water crossings. Culvert cleaning. Sediment basin clearing. Bank & channel stabilization. Fencing. Feral horse removal. Imprinting. Range drilling.

The overall objective is to stabilize the slopes, staving off excessive erosion and massive flooding. The approaches are as diverse as the varied ecosystems where they are used. A practice that works well on one fire may fail miserably on the next. Other actions work all the time but may be too costly to justify in every instance.

The conference participants spent a day touring the 2002 Hayman Burn. Local resource managers shared the lessons they learned participating in stabilizing one of Denver's key watersheds.

On large fires a team of experts—the BAER Assessment Team— dictates the first round of land prescriptions. Only assembled for a few weeks, the team addresses immediate concerns and writes a plan that outlines projects to implement.

The job of completing these projects and deciding what else needs to be done falls on the shoulders of the implementation leader. Often a lonely responsibility, implementation leaders can now lay claim to "Clan" membership, and enjoy the benefit of shared lessons and experiences.

LAYING A LOG EROSION BARRIER LEGACY
February 2004

It seems a simple idea, these log erosion barriers. In a landscape of black tree skeletons and bare ground that loses tons of soil with each storm event, use what is there to do what makes sense. Fall dead, standing trees along the contour. Make sure they form a seal with the ground they lay on. Anchor them because moving water across the denuded landscape is forceful enough to shift thousand-pound stems.

When the rain comes, and soil is gathered by surface flow, these prone logs will slow the runoff. Give the water a chance to soak into the ground. Deposit a shelf of sediment on the uphill side of the log.

Rob the downstream reservoir of a tiny bit of choking silt, misplaced soil a hundred thousand years in the making. Actually, there is nothing simple about it.

I am convinced it is all about technique, this careful placement of burned logs on a burned landscape. Just skew the log a few degrees off the contour, and instead of creating healing plateaus of arrested soil, water is channeled into rills that grow to gullies and cause more harm than good.

When I first came to the White Mountain Apache tribal lands last summer, I gathered up a handful of tribal members, the "leadership" of what would expand into a small army of BAER crew members. We spent a day examining the log erosion barriers (LEBs) that had been installed in previous burns on this Arizona reservation. I explained to my new employees that this was their land, and their chance to make a difference. There were guidelines about how many logs would be needed for the steepness of the slope, but the best guide they would have would be their own intuition. I asked them to read the landscape, to observe what the upcoming monsoons would teach them about their practice. This wasn't just a job but a chance to help the land heal and mend from the largest, hottest forest fire to occur in the Southwest.

Five months later and the crews have nearly completed the two thousand acres and spent the money prescribed by our guiding plan, yet we have treated less than two percent of the severely burned landscape. Mild as the winter has been, the crew has shifted to lower elevations to avoid frozen ground. Since our burn area stretches from pinyon-juniper woodlands to mixed conifer, it is not a difficult task to find lower-elevation acres that need attention.

We are on a hill slope above Cibecue, one of the larger communities impacted by the fire. After months of working behind the "feller-buncher"—a logging machine that fells the trees and arranges them on the contour—the crew has convinced me they are ready to drop the trees themselves. This is the second day of their operation that includes directional felling. I am there to insure that our safety protocols are in place and to assure myself they are up to the task.

The BAER crews have the discipline of fire crews, and have adopted the same guidelines for safe operations in high-risk environments. We discuss the challenges of the task, the difficulty of determining what is actually perpendicular to a slope with multiple angles, or the challenge of cutting down a dead, rotting, leaning tree so it will fall exactly where you want it. We acknowledge the necessity of being constantly alert and constantly aware. The workers are dedicated and careful in their actions.

It occurs to me that I am just beginning to understand the Apache approach to the land. Although I have been told that the Apache way is to let the land heal itself, no one seems opposed to helping burned logs to the ground in a way that will keep some of the soil on the hillside. I recall the tribal chairman explaining that the Apache word for "land" also means "mind," and for me, it is hard to separate this healing task from the people that are doing it.

SHE RAN CALLING "GODIŁTŁA'"
March 2004

When some people have a midlife crisis, they dream of owning fancy sports cars. My midlife daydream is a horse. Not just any horse, and certainly, similar to the fantasy sports cars of my peers, not a practical horse. No, I fantasize about owning a wild horse captured in the Rodeo-Chediski Burn on the White Mountain Apache tribal lands in east-central Arizona. It's something of an office joke that I am afraid has the potential to go a bit too far.

In order to allow the vegetation in the burn area to recover, we try to keep browsing and grazing to a minimum. The area is excluded from livestock grazing for at least two years—longer if our plant surveys show we need to extend the furlough—and we try to keep the feral horse and maverick cattle populations in check. Feral horses have a long history of running wild in these woods.

Horses released by early settlers and historic road construction operations were occasionally lost and never recovered. Over the last century a wild population of horses has expanded on the reservation. Apaches hold high regard for horses and often tolerate large herds. In fact, the feral horse population had grown so large it was affecting vegetation years before the burn occurred.

Vegetation is the key to holding an ecosystem together. If too

My first picture of Godi, freshly captured, and hungry.
Photo by author.

much plant tissue is removed too often, plants are no longer able to
bind soil, protect hillsides, and assist water in soaking into the ground.
Fortunately, the tribal range program had already taken action. In 1998
they trapped 700 feral horses and 130 maverick cattle from the same
area that burned four years later. If all these animals were here following
the burn, the vegetation would have a slim chance of recovering. This
would impact soil loss, water infiltration, and a host of other ecological
recovery processes.

Although some horses died during the fires, the majority of the rem-
nant herd survived the flames and was poised to threaten vegetation
recovery if left unchecked. Once again the tribal range program stepped
up to the plate and, since the burn, has captured sixty-one feral horses
and thirty maverick cattle.

Eighteen months later, Godi is happy in Placitas. Godi is my mascot for the progress the land was making as well. Photo by author.

Captured horses with brands are turned over to the appropriate live-stock association responsible for managing the land. The captured feral horses must be sold off reservation to ensure that they do not escape and find their way back into the burn. I make sure the cowboys get paid for the horses removed. Here's where the trouble starts.

One day I just happened to mention that I would love to own a white and blue paint I saw months ago . . . and now the cowboys are chasing it down, aiming to please. I've tried to explain this possibility of me bring-ing home a wild horse to my friends and family as a simple midlife crisis. My kids are horrified. My friends laugh.

"Will you call him 'Wildfire'?" one friend asks, referring to a Michael Murphy song popular in our youth.

"Well, since the horse is clearly Apache," I ponder, "I guess I'll call him 'Godiłtła'—an Apache word that loosely translates to 'forest fire.'"

Like most midlifers, my daydream is totally impractical. I currently live on the reservation involved in a job that consumes all the hours a day has to offer . . . I have no time for a horse that would not be allowed to return to this land. However, when I think that most of these wild ponies bound for the livestock auctions have uncertain futures, I hope someone will be there to offer them a home that honors their wildfire heritage.

STREAM SENSE
April 2004

I am standing in a gaping wound in the landscape. The trickle of greenish orange liquid gathered around my mud-caked boots seems insignificant. It is hard to believe this same stream has cut a gully that is, at places, thirty feet wide and seven feet deep. Standing upright near the head of the cut, I am eye-level with what was, only months earlier, ground level. It is this rapidly degrading watercourse that has focused our attention today.

I gaze up at my colleague standing in the streambed where this drastic cut begins. Our mentor, Alvin Medina, a research ecologist with the U.S. Forest Service's Rocky Mountain Research Station in Flagstaff, stands off to the side.

"Larry is standing on the answer," he instructs us.

A tribal member and contractor with the tribe's watershed department, I have sometimes thought that Larry Ethelbah *is* the answer—at least to questions on how to move rocks around streambeds to protect roads, cultural sites, and other sensitive landscape features.

Our patient teacher wants us to understand the natural processes that held this stream together before the fire occurred. When asked what I see, I state the obvious. "Larry is standing on a lens of coarse gravel," I reply, pointing to a layer of rocks exposed by the cut. I hope I am demonstrating how quickly tree-focused foresters can grasp new fields of study.

Bingo. For the moment, this rock lens is keeping the soil from unraveling below. It is a hardened spot in a streambed affectionately termed a "nick point." Nick points can be rock, root, or buried wood. They affect everything above and below them. When you lose a nick point, you lose the integrity of the stream system.

Medina is a master reader of streambeds. He escorts us farther up the drainage, encouraging us to see through his eyes. The goal is to understand the natural rhythm of the stream course. There are patterns of pools and riffles that have developed over the centuries. They alter with changes in slope and substrate. We are instructed to observe and interpret what we see. Although solutions are apparent on each site, they vary from stream course to stream course.

Once we understand nature's patterns we can emulate the geometric arrangement we see. By mimicking patterns of rock size, arrangement, and spacing, we can nurture the damaged watercourse back to stability. What took hundreds or thousands of years for nature to arrange, a handful of caring, observant people can pull back together in a matter of days. At least our instructor seems to think so.

There are some guidelines for this work. We should avoid metal, such as wire baskets of rocks (known as gabions) or steel girders. Our tools should be the natural materials around us, rocks mostly, but sometimes logs. Where the damage is gaping, we will use heavy equipment to haul and place rock fill, but for the most part, the work can be done by hand.

We can prevent future problems by purposely falling standing dead trees away from the stream. If the trees fall on their own directly into the streambed, they might redirect water to less-protected soils. In addition, falling the trees reduces the likelihood that tree roots (nick points), which stabilize the streambed, will be jerked out of the ground.

Once the physical adjustments are made, we can enhance the biological glue by adding native riparian—or water-loving—plants.

The real keys to these solutions are working their way upstream toward us. Three tribal members, led by Mae Burnette, are carefully measuring and documenting the latest conditions of the stream course. Over the past year, Mae has personally visited and studied critical springs, streams, and drainages. She has witnessed springs that only the elders remembered reappearing in places where the fire removed dense vegetation. She has also witnessed the damage caused by the record runoff from the barren slopes.

Mae raised the initial alarm regarding this particular drainage, and through her constant surveillance, alerts our staff to other sites that need some intervention to prevent major erosion problems. Through the dedication of Mae, her co-workers, and other tribal members who pay attention to the land, we interact with the landscape, admire the powerful natural restorative processes, and step in with a helping hand when we think we can make a difference.

 SOWING THE SEEDS OF
A FUTURE FOREST
May 2004

No bigger than a black-eyed pea, the ponderosa pine seed gives no hint of the massive tree it can become if given plenty of sunshine, adequate water, and whole lot of patience. In our attempt to replace the forest, we try to give these seeds a head start. Having just refurbished the five greenhouses on the Fort Apache Reservation in McNary, the tribe is now proud surrogate parents of approximately 360,000 pine seedlings, sowed in as many twenty-one-cubic-inch containers just weeks ago.

Come fall, we will carefully place the six- to ten-inch-tall seedlings in the ground at those extremely damaged places where fire killed all of the trees. Although we plan to plant around two hundred trees per acre, on average this is only the equivalent of two trees per acre for the most severely burned land.

The task of reestablishing the forest is daunting. Although many of the homes this fire burned have already been rebuilt, even with the 650,000 tree seedlings we planted last fall, we have barely begun to replace what was once a beautiful, productive forest.

The greenhouses at McNary were first built by the Bureau of Indian Affairs in 1974. For fifteen years, the agency grew tree seedlings to plant on burn areas (Carrizo, Penrod, McNary, and Pinetop fires) and spruce clearcuts. Through the years, foresters honed this craft of establishing new trees. They found that fall planting yields the most reliable survival rates for our latitude and elevation. In the greenhouse, they learned to inoculate rooting medium with mycorrhizal fungi found naturally in forest soils. Staff developed the ability to grow seedlings with well-balanced stems and roots. Although the greenhouses have not seen much activity over the last decade, we are in a good position, pending adequate funding, to make a long-term commitment to reforestation.

Building upon this wealth of knowledge, and factoring in our current drought conditions, we continue to learn lessons the land offers on how to jumpstart the long effort toward replacing trees.

First we start with the seed. The seeds are germinated in a rooting medium of peat moss and vermiculite packed into crates that hold eleven four-parted planting envelopes. One to two seeds are sown in each cell, and then the crates are placed on elevated benches in the greenhouses. During the first few weeks following germination, crews thin and replant each cell so each basket grows forty-four trees.

On chilly mornings the greenhouses offer a tropical retreat. Warm and humid, the greenhouse environment is closely regulated. The trees are watered with a traveling boom that evenly distributes water, mycorrhizae, fertilizers, and herbicides. Lighting, carbon dioxide levels, temperature, and humidity are carefully controlled to maximize seedling development.

The goal for the next three months is to focus on height growth. Once the trees reach the desired six-inch height, diameter and root growth are emphasized through induced water-stress events. Each step requires precise understanding of the seedlings' growth patterns.

The trees are then moved out of the greenhouses to shade houses where they are toughened up for field conditions and held until planted in the fall. The transition from pea-sized seeds to quality seedlings is just the first step in a long journey toward reestablishing the future forest.

FENCING FEATS
July 2004

The ground is rocky up by the Rabbit Ear, the extreme northwest portion of the reservation. It takes approximately twenty thrusts with a post pounder to plant a steel t-post deep enough to support four strands of barbed wire. Developing a rhythm of grasping the welded handles on each side of the thirty-pound steel cylinder and lifting and slamming it down on top of the metal fence post, I contemplate the effort that has gone into this almost completed fence project.

The fire destroyed 65 miles of boundary fence, which excluded off-reservation cattle from grazing on tribal lands. Since protection of recovering vegetation is critical to burn-area rehabilitation, an additional 51 miles of fence was needed around the fire perimeter to exclude tribal cattle from the burn area as well. This short section of fence my employees and I are working on is the final piece of what has turned out to be 120 miles of fence construction.

Our section may be short, but the effort is extraordinary. We drove five hours one way to get near this remote section, left the vehicles on an opposite ridge, and packed in three hundred-pound rolls of barbed wire, twenty-five steel t-posts, and assorted fencing supplies. Our crew of seven is smaller than we planned, the majority of our staff being redirected this morning to fire suppression.

Although BAER employees initiated and are finishing the fence, the true credit for this accomplishment goes to tribal contractors who built most of the fence in eight months. During this effort, nine tribal entrepreneurs established businesses and contracted fence construction in one-mile sections, hiring four to ten employees each. The BAER program provided materials, oversight, and administrative support including small business management workshops. In addition to building fence, we hopefully have built some businesses that can continue to contract various forest management activities.

My partner and I have pounded in at least a dozen t-posts in the past few hours and I have a few new blisters to prove it. Yet our efforts seem insignificant to the nearly forty thousand steel t-posts that have gone into this project. I think back to the semi-loads of fence supplies, and try to take stock of what else we have used: almost two thousand rolls of barbed wire, over two hundred bags of t-post clips, hundreds of pounds of stay wire, at least five pallets each of metal and wooden stays, and approximately one thousand pounds of staples. In addition to purchased supplies, there are thousands of assorted posts, cross-braces, and stays that have been cut on site.

As the day shifts into evening, I realize our small crew will not complete the task. It will take yet another day to "finish the fence." I advise the crew that we will pull out once the sawyer and swamper finish the chainsaw tasks. They will return in a few days to finish the posts and string the wire.

There really isn't an end to "finishing the fence." We have fourteen cattle guards to install or clean and some water gates to construct. Since the area is dominated by dead trees prone to wind throw, fence maintenance will be an ongoing task for many years to come.

Shadows get long as we hop rocks across the creek and trudge up the long hillside to the trucks. It will be close to eleven p.m. before we get home. Although an impressive effort, the initial construction of the fence is another small step in the rehabilitation efforts of what has been Arizona's largest fire.

LAND LESSONS
August 2004

Years ago my Pueblo friends would advise me that there was a season—a specific time of year—to share stories with others, and the rest of the year, when thunder might be listening, we would keep these stories safely snug in our hearts.

Now it has been raining for several weeks, and it seems clear the monsoon season is well entrenched. Leaders at Fire Management are no longer staffing large weekend patrols to prevent the next "Big One," so I feel I can safely tell another kind of story. This one is about fire.

The Rodeo-Chediski complex is the largest burn that has occurred in the Southwest Region. Within the fire perimeter on the tribal lands, roughly 120,000 acres of tribal lands experienced low fire severity, and may have even benefited from the fire. When I first came to this project I was told that anywhere I saw green trees, there had been some kind of forest management activity in the area's history. Being a skeptic, I have been carrying my management activity map to test this theory.

Limestone Fire Tower is a good place for the story to start unfolding. Jutting up on a ridge several miles from the reservation/national forest boundary, the fire tower hosts a spotter who cries alarm when wildfires start. Over the years, Limestone Camp has hosted crews of firefighters who, when not fighting fires, worked diligently at thinning the forest. The year before the big burn, there was a large prescribed fire. In the 1980s much of the area was thinned. Now, two years postfire, in the areas where these prefire activities occurred, the

The mottled pattern of burn severity matches the boundaries of forest management units. Unmanaged stands experienced complete tree mortality. Photo by author.

forest has tall, green pines, and a rich carpet of grasses, wildflowers, and shrubs.

From the lookout tower, more lessons can be learned. To the northwest along the reservation boundary, there are large islands of green. These patterns on the landscape match the thinning and prescribed burning project maps. Directly to the west and southwest there is another anomaly to the treeless, eroded slopes that dominate the burn. Here trees occur in clumps, sometimes isolated, sometimes not. This area deserves closer inspection.

Last week I took a group of Navajo middle school students there to observe these lessons. In a region known as White Springs we found some beautiful stands of large, yellow bark pine that had missed being destroyed, as well as several other canyons, ridges, and slopes that seem to have escaped the wrath of flames. Pulling out the management map, we learned that flames were the major part of the story. The Carrizo Fire of 1971 had burned much of the area and timber salvage harvests followed in the years after that fire. A portion of that area had burned again during the White Springs Fire of 1996. The resulting mottled mosaic of forest now represents an area that has experienced three major wildfires in the past quarter century.

There are other sections of reservation lands within the Rodeo-Chediski burn that I do not know well. On the map, the layers of timber sales, thinning projects, and prescribed fire in the Chuckbox and Bull Flat areas are tangled and complex, but happily we will not be adding rehabilitation projects to that management history. Though the fire did burn through these areas in 2002, the "damage" is minor and these areas do not require additional erosion control or reforestation assistance from my program. The story of this land will be told by others as graduate students from a neighboring university tease apart the evidence to see how forest management impacts fire severity.

The stories this land tells are complex and fascinating, with the major lesson being the need for extreme care with ignition sources during certain times of the year. On the reservation this year, we heave a deep sigh of relief because, knock on wood, we have escaped this fire season without having another major wildfire.

As the rains pour down, and access restrictions are lifted throughout the region, it is time once again to tell the other "fire" stories; stor-ies that, if heeded, might guide us back to living within a healthy forest landscape.

CHASING THE CHAINSAWS
September 2004

"When I made that first cut," Tia Tessay confided to me, "I knew I'd found exactly what I wanted to do with my life." Her crew mates laugh. "You know she has her own chainsaw—none of us have the nerve to touch it!"

She tells me the chainsaw's name—one I can't put in print.

"But he really is one, he's so hard to start!" This is coming from the same twenty-three-year-old woman who drives a monstrously ancient and grotesquely green crew crummy called "The Hulk."

In these forests of the new century, chainsaws are the conservation tools of choice. For burned area emergency rehabilitation, we use chainsaws to place burned logs along the contour, to fell hazardous trees along roads, to salvage nick points in streambeds, to cut posts for fence replacements, and to clear roads that are littered with fallen stems. On other parts of the reservation, the constant whining of chainsaw engines transform what were dense forest stands into open, park-like glades that are more resistant to catastrophic fire.

Once the sole realm of wildland firefighters, power-saw training is now a mandatory requirement for my BAER crew. Training, experience, and field demonstration of skills sort the saw wielders into three categories: "A" Fallers, "B" Fallers, and "C" Fallers, with the last category handling the toughest assignments.

One of the most dangerous jobs in the woods, chainsaw operation demands a constant vigilance for safety. As crew leader Lorinda "LT" Thompson explains, "Operating a chainsaw keeps you alert. You think about safety all the time. You know it is dangerous, but you cannot dwell on that."

In addition to herself, LT's twenty-person crew includes five other "ladies" who each navigate their own way in the male-dominated realm of saw operation.

"We tend to use our legs more," they agree, "because we do not have the same physical strength in our arms that the men have."

"The guys used to laugh at me, because they said the saw was half my weight," Tia chuckled, "but they now know I can carry it all day and keep cutting."

Most of the orange and white saws in the program have large engines and sport twenty and twenty-eight-inch bars, but there is a "baby" saw, with a fourteen-inch bar, that the crew uses for cutting stakes and delimbing logs. Regardless of size, the saws get constant attention—regular cleaning, sharpening, and adjusting. For the crew, the saws represent jobs; if the saws are not running, the crew is not working.

When cutting down a tree, our safety protocol requires that a sawyer is accompanied by a second person known as a *swamper*. The sawyer focuses on the cuts and the immediate task, while the swamper keeps an eye on the tree and the bigger picture. Since chainsaws make lots of noise, the swamper communicates with the sawyer by touch, often with a long stick. The swamper can stand a stick's length away to get better visibility, but still have immediate contact with the sawyer.

The sawyer first examines the tree for defects, leans, dead limbs, and adjacent potential places where the tree might "hang up." Once this "size-up" is completed, the sawyer identifies two escape routes to the swamper, so both know how to get away in a hurry. Anyone else within the distance of one and a half times the tree's height is asked to move.

A yell from the sawyer precedes the first two cuts, which remove a pie-slice wedge and is the first step for directional falling. The back cut, using guidelines on the saw, confirms the fall direction. When the swamper detects movement at the top of the tree, he signals the sawyer, who removes the saw and turns it off to avoid carrying a running saw. Both quickly move out of the way. For "log erosion barriers," where arranging heavy logs along the contour is the ultimate goal, the ability to place a log exactly where you want it is highly valued.

Each day, there are twenty to twenty-five saws running in the BAER program. The terrain is rugged, and the job never-ending. Only with a constant surveillance for safe operations—and the same luck that sent the five thousand firefighters on this burn home without serious injury—can we maintain an accident-free record and improve the land.

TRIBAL TREE PLANTING CAMP
October 2004

"You'll find it won't take the firefighters long to get the hang of the hoedad," veteran tree-planting instructor Anastasia Rabin explained to her peers. "There isn't that much difference between swinging a hoedad and swinging a pulaski," she added, referring to the modified axe used by wildland firefighters. Rabin is one of twelve professional tree planters invited as instructors in what might become an annual event for the White Mountain Apache Tribe.

The Tribal Tree-Planting Camp was held this fall as a kick-off to encourage tribal members to contract tree-seedling planting. With exponential unemployment rates, the lure of tree-planting jobs on the east-central Arizona reservation is strong. Tree planting may seem simple on the surface, but a planter needs special skills and tools to effectively put hundreds of seedlings in the ground each day.

Of the almost 277,000 reservation acres burned during the Rodeo-Chediski Fire, 73,000 acres are previous forested land on moderate slopes, which are now devoid of trees. In 2003 the Kinishba Fire burned an additional 25,000 acres with 2,400 acres needing reforestation. Clearly the tribe and the Bureau of Indian Affairs will need to make a long-term commitment to tree planting.

Decades of tree-planting experience in the area have shown the best survival is obtained when ponderosa pine seedlings are planted in the fall. Because of the short time frame between late summer rains and winter snows, there is only a seven- to ten-week window for optimum tree planting. Last fall the program planted over 680,000 ponderosa pine seedlings on over 5,000 acres. Contract tree planters hired off the reservation planted 88 percent of the area despite programs utilizing twelve tribal contractors, school and community field trips, and a job-training program.

This year, to jump-start the tribal member contracting program, Tribal Forestry's BAER program hosted the week-long training camp. The instructors were professional tree planters from Oregon, Colorado, New Mexico, Arizona, Texas, Arkansas, and Hawaii.

Seventy potential tribal contractors and forty tribal employees participated in the field-based training. Each day, teams were formed consisting of instructors, inspectors, and students. The program utilized the same Incident Command System used to manage large teams of firefighters, including setting up a field camp with a caterer, porta-johns, trash service, and other logistical support needed for a small community.

Evening activities augmented the program and included traditional Apache crown dancers, a horseshoe tournament, and concerts—one night, gospel, another night, country and western.

The base camp was held in a meadow known as "Little Springs." With a rich history of logging camps, the area had more recently supported burn response activities.

The field was a helicopter staging area for scattering straw mulch. Earlier in the summer, we had dedicated the tree planting in the canyon as the Rick Lupe Memorial Forest. Lupe, a firefighter who lost his life on a prescribed fire last year, played a lead role in saving the town of Show

Low during the Rodeo-Chediski Fire the year before. Apache school students have been planting seedlings in his honor.

Now with the planting season in full swing, the camp appears to have provided the desired jump-start to the tribal tree-planting program. Approximately sixty people are working for twelve tribal contractors, and each day the stockpile of trees grown at the reservation greenhouses gets a little smaller. In the past week, an off-reservation contractor has also started planting. If the snow holds off for another three to four weeks, the 350,000 seedlings grown for this year should be in the ground.

REFLECTIONS ON
A BURNED LANDSCAPE
November 2004

In early morning hours on the burn, as the day's first rays of light caress the hills, and leave each subtle swale in shadow, I am enamored with this landscape. Mother Nature is exposed, stripped of her usual cloak of forest cloth, to reveal each limestone outcrop, each dip, each rise, every curve, every scar . . . like an erotic lover posing for the artist. I steal embarrassed glances and marvel at my opportunity to love this land.

I am surrounded by magic, bugling elk, a setting moon, and fields of mullein that—when one scrunches down like a leprechaun—form forests of fuzzy-leafed stalks. The blackened skeletons of the ghost forest dance in the early morning light, casting long shadows when the golden orb peeks over the eastern ridge. Each pebble and rock beneath my feet momentarily casts a quick shadow in the initial rays.

I first traversed this spur ridge last fall when a colleague brought me here to consider erosion control actions that might save the soil. We were too late. In the spring, there had been soil, at least six inches deep, he had explained. After the late summer rains, we had to gingerly pick our way across a rock field, careful not to twist an ankle in the pavement of cobble that was now the exposed subflooring of burnt forest. On this particular slope, in a fragile geologic moment of exposure, an isolated burst from a thunderstorm had washed away soil that had been hundreds of thousands of years in the making. On nearby ridges the soil was

Early morning on the Rodeo-Chediski burn, elk calling, cool
crisp air . . . a beauty of its own. Photo by author.

spared, at least temporarily. If our meager efforts take hold, we might
make a difference in stabilizing these slopes.

My job is to coordinate multiple projects addressing stabilization and
rehabilitation in recently burned areas of the White Mountain Apache
Tribal Lands. I work in ecosystems that seem devastated, but I am continually surprised and awed by their resiliency. In the aftermath of the
2002 Rodeo-Chediski and 2003 Kinishba fires, we plant trees, monitor
vegetation recovery, clean culverts, stabilize banks to protect farm fields,
archeological sites, and roads, protect springs, build fences, catch wild
horses, and a multitude of other tasks that mitigate the impacts of high-
intensity burning on this landscape.

The initial reaction most people have when entering this realm is
one of sadness and regret. The tribal members I work with have gen-
erations of memory of this landscape when the hills were carpeted in

green forests. It was not a forest that offered views. Yet present vistas from these burned-out ridges are stunning; as are the slopes of graceful grasses rippling in the breeze; or the bubbling joy of springs that, prior to the burn, gurgled only in the memories of tribal elders.

Since the Rodeo-Chediski Fire, access to this region has been limited to those working in the area. It has been a danger zone of falling trees and flash floods. As the transition from emergency stabilization shifts to ecosystem restoration, the challenge the tribe faces is to reclaim not only the land, but the spirit of the land. In an effort one colleague dubbed "The Return of the Native," our goals include reconnecting people to the land, ensuring a natural role for fire in the newly developing landscape, and aggressively removing exotic vegetation accidentally introduced during suppression, salvage, and stabilization actions.

However, if this postfire phase is anything like the last two years, it is the land herself that will define this process. In the early morning light, as I sit gazing out on ridges and valleys with cameras, pen, and paper in hand, full moon setting, elk bugling, and the distant chainsaws of my rehabilitation crews humming, I am full of hope and awe. I am humbled by the opportunity to witness this incredible recovery as it unfolds.

CIBECUE NATIVE MANAGES RODEO-CHEDISKI RECOVERY ACTIVITIES
December 2004

He has been here since "this all started."

Raised in the community of Cibecue, Daniel Kessay grew up exploring the canyons and ridges on the west end of the Fort Apache Indian Reservation in east-central Arizona. A forest technician with the Bureau of Indian Affairs, Daniel found himself leading a crew of twenty tribal firefighters in the summer of 2002 when a fire started adjacent to his hometown.

His crew had just completed a fourteen-day assignment on the Peñasco Fire in northern New Mexico where they had been assigned to "fire rehabilitation" work. Arriving back at Fort Apache, the crew was sent home for their mandatory rest days amid the chaos of the first day of the Rodeo Fire. About the time the Chediski Fire started several ridges west of the roaring Rodeo Fire, Daniel received his next fire leadership assignment. His crew spent their next fourteen days battling the Southwest's largest fire in history in their own backyard near Cibecue.

As the smoke was clearing, Daniel returned to his regular job as a pre-sales technician, which was now anything but *regular.* In a heroic push to salvage burned timber on the extensive burn, BIA employees worked long hours to identify and prepare thousands of acres for timber operations. In addition to providing a modest income to the tribe, removing the dead trees reduced the amount of fuel that would be available in the area during future fires.

When the salvage cutting started in the fall of that same year, Daniel helped administer these timber sales. The harvesting included helicopter and conventional logging operations. Then one morning, the forester at the agency in charge of tree-planting projects announced he needed extra folks to work weekends. With his intimate knowledge of the burn area both before and after the fire, Daniel took the lead in organizing the field reconnaissance for selecting sites for tree planting. The salvage cutting concluded in the spring of 2003, and Daniel's full-time focus switched to reforestation.

The summer of 2003, Daniel and his crew visited most of the 73,000 acres of moderately sloped lands that had lost tree cover, ultimately selecting over 7,000 acres to prepare for the first season of planting.

The White Mountain Apache Tribal Forestry program worked cooperatively with the Bureau of Indian Affairs on the 2003 Planting Program. The tribe would be assuming complete control of the project under an Indian Self-Determination Contract. As the tribal implementation leader of all of the Burned Area Emergency Rehabilitation projects, I found myself relying on Daniel's keen understanding of this landscape.

Following the first planting season that fall, when Daniel was furloughed from his seasonal federal government job, I asked him to work for the tribe as our field operations manager. In addition to the reforestation activities, this job also put him in charge of our large "log erosion barrier installation" project. Ironically, this was the same activity he supervised on the Peñasco Fire, just before the Rodeo-Chediski Fire began its endless domination of his waking hours.

Daniel continues to manage the field operations on this multimillion-dollar, multiyear effort to restore the forests of his youth. Leading a team of over fifty employees and administering over a dozen contractors, the field management keeps him regularly working fourteen-day shifts with busy rest days in between.

I recently asked him what he would do with himself if we ever got out of the *emergency* mode on this project and started working normal schedules. A family man with many children, Daniel smiled and said, "Oh, I've got plans." Then he proceeded to describe how this month he will add to his busy schedule a college class that will eventually lead to a college degree in forest management.

I pity the forestry professors who will have the task of trying to impart new forestry knowledge to this seasoned field veteran.

BAER FAIRS SHOWCASE
BURN RESTORATION
January 2005

When I finally stumble into Memorial Hall that hectic January morning, the gymnasium is a bustle of activity. Heavy black tarps protect the wooden floor from traffic. Children, teachers, community members, and tribal leaders weave lines around thirty display tables. After weeks of planning, the first White Mountain Apache Tribal BAER Fair is a whopping success.

I place what now seems a paltry assortment of snacks on the food table, and wander around the hall. My colleagues and staff are articulately presenting the mind-boggling array of activities that have preoccupied our waking hours for the past two years.

Following the record-shattering Rodeo-Chediski Fire in June and July of 2002, the White Mountain Apache Tribe, in the spirit of Indian Self-Determination, chose to assume the task of stabilizing and rehabilitating 277,000 acres of charred reservation lands. Funded by the Burn Area Emergency Response program through the Bureau of Indian Affairs, tribal leadership assumed responsibility for implementing activities described in a 352-page plan.

I am one of a handful of "white people" involved in the project. All of my staff, which numbered seventy-five in the past year, are Native Americans. Looking around the fair, I proudly admire the interactions between fair visitors and BAER employees.

Most conversations are in Apache, and although I can pick up a word or two here and there, I cannot follow the flow of ideas. It seems that our program—which focuses on healing the land—is best described in the native tongue.

Ingenuity dominates the displays. The Log Erosion Barrier crew has a tabletop hillside of soil demonstrating how logs are placed along the contour to slow runoff. The detail includes a flagged-off archeological site and cardboard crew carrier that had many more amenities than its bare-bones, real-life counterpart.

At the "Bale Bombing" display, a model helicopter carries a photo of large hay bales in a cargo net. Many other photos tell the story of how straw was strewn over fifteen thousand acres of steep, erosion-prone slopes by helicopters.

Clear plastic cups sliced lengthwise make a convincing model of the greenhouses for the display that celebrates the miracle transformation of seeds to seedlings. Adjacent tables and display boards describe how over a million seedlings have been planted since the fire, as well as how difficult tree survival is amid the same drought that produced severe fire conditions.

A wood post and wire structure introduces the idea of "jetty jacks," while a tabletop display demonstrates how these structures are used to protect roads and farm fields by guiding the stream channels away from eroding edges.

Other booths tell more stories. A table of pottery pieces and artifacts impresses the importance the tribe places on protecting cultural resources. Satellite imagery with project boundaries shows how fire burned the unmanaged forest most severely, while stands that had been thinned, burned, or logged before the fire experienced low fire severity and still have green trees. Tribal employees shared photos of sacred springs and the exciting development of long-ago springs returning to the landscape. Visitors also learned about challenges with roads, range issues, and wildlife. Additional booths stress health issues because Apaches understand that the health of the people and the health of the land are inseparable.

The BAER Fair runs two days, one day in Whiteriver and the next day in Cibecue, a community about fifty miles to the east and central to the burn area. Although the fairs themselves are great successes, my staff and I learn for our interactions with the visitors that our work informing tribal members about restoration efforts on the burn are only just beginning. Our excellent work on the ground pales if tribal members are not fully informed on the successes and challenges that lie ahead for this area.

ON THE NATIONAL FIRE PLAN AWARDS
February 2005

Five years ago I spent my birthday working on forest fires—not unusual for a forester in the Southwest where May wildfires are common. Yet that day stands out in my mind as the birth of the National Fire Plan, and I was there to witness it. Over four hundred homes had just burned down in the nuclear weapon research town of Los Alamos, New Mexico. Leaders from across the nation were gathering to witness the aftermath. As a fire information officer attached to the Southwest Coordination Center, I was assigned to accompany a vanload of VIPs to Los Alamos. On the van ride from Albuquerque I marveled at how the chief of the Forest Service and various other movers and shakers worked out a strategy for addressing wildfires that would later become known as the National Fire Plan.

The National Fire Plan crosses agency boundaries and provides unified direction for goals, funding, and achievements in addressing recent catastrophic wildfires resulting from a century of fuel accumulations. The five original arms of the National Fire Plan include Fire Suppression, Community Assistance, Hazardous Fuel Reduction, Rehabilitation and Restoration, and Accountability. Collaboration, Research, and Biomass Utilization have also emerged as major areas.

I was back in Albuquerque in February with a group of co-workers and representatives from the White Mountain Apache Tribe on the eve of the Fifth Annual National Fire Plan conference. We were onstage accepting the National Fire Plan Award for Excellence in Rehabilitation and Restoration.

Hundreds of tribal members have spent countless hours in hard, backbreaking tasks to help restore their lands. When contemplating the mind-boggling losses the tribe has experienced as a result of the Rodeo-Chediski burn, the award seemed a kind gesture in tilting the scale back toward balance. Watching the proud smiles on my staff's faces as they passed around the cut-glass sculpture award, I realized the value of recognizing jobs well done.

Days before, our two-and-a-half-year-old burn area experienced major flooding. In one day we witnessed flows that were ten times the amount of the previous February's total monthly flow. The reports were filtering in, but it would be another week before I learned how extensive the damage to our roads and land actually was. The irony that we were still experiencing disasters even as we were being recognized for having effectively handled our burn did not escape me.

The evening award ceremony was uplifting. Fifteen groups or individuals were recognized for giving that extra commitment that leads to excellence. We learned about incredible folks from Colorado, Utah, Mississippi, and Idaho who, through creative collaboration, had changed the character of their home forests from dense firetraps to open, fire resistant communities. We were dazzled by a group of rappellers from the Pacific Northwest ready to fly into wildfires. The room was brimming with overachievers. From the list of nominees, it was clear this was only a small picture of the activity nationwide.

After the congratulatory events, I found myself racing off to my motel room to prepare the presentation I would make the next day at the conference. I marveled at how the pace has not slackened for me, or for others at this event or in this field, since the National Fire Plan started. I thought back to my birthday five years earlier when, after spending the day on Cerro Grande, I found myself en route to the Scott Able Fire near Cloudcroft where sixty-eight more homes had been destroyed by wildfire.

Though the enormity of our challenges at times seems overwhelming, it helps to take a moment to recognize the progress we are making.

REMEMBERING JUDITH
June 2005

JUDITH ANN MORRIS
August 2, 1984–May 27, 2005

Last month I lost an employee and a friend, and the world lost a truly exceptional human being. It is hard to imagine the sorrow that her family, friends, and co-workers feel. The void Judith leaves is immense. She lit up so many lives. If she had been wearing a seatbelt that May morning, she would still be cracking jokes and telling entertaining stories.

For a young woman headed for a career in cosmetology, Judith did not mind getting real dirty. She was a hard worker and enjoyed tough tasks including sowing seeds and growing seedlings at the greenhouse, fighting wildfires, and embedding logs in the earth to prevent erosion.

Judith was a joyful person and had a beautiful temperament. She was like a mountain spring—bubbling with enthusiasm and delighting and enriching everyone around her.

Judith loved being outdoors and took her role as a Burn Area Emergency Rehabilitation (BAER) crew member seriously, dedicating her efforts to caring for the land. She was so enthusiastic about the job! She was willing to learn anything. She even bubbled about sitting in a hard chair all day long learning computer skills, though she balked at the idea of taking on any office-related tasks.

Judith was "bezhaan."

We would tease her about her beauty, but she never really acted like she knew how stunning her smile was. Instead she'd make us laugh, telling jokes and stories and focusing on our smiles rather than her own.

On the BAER team we work hard and I ask crew members to come to work prepared to give 110 percent of their effort—but Judith always gave more. She stayed busy, worked hard, and pulled her weight on the crew.

She loved to talk about what we were doing for the land. In January she was so outgoing at the BAER Fair that even the vice-chairman remembers her enthusiasm. In April she volunteered to spend the day at the Water Fair talking about our work. She was so good talking with children and sharing her love for the land.

Judith held a special place in my heart. When she started working for me last summer and I signed her papers, I noticed that her birth date was only a few months before my oldest daughter's. My daughter Cairn Shaw had passed away while still a baby, but watching Judith and her friends I could imagine what Cairn might have been like had she lived.

I cannot pretend to know the sorrow that Judith's family is now facing, but I know that my daughter's death was one of the most difficult events in my life. Twenty years later, one lesson that remains is an undeniable understanding that life is precious and each moment should be cherished.

Already so many people have told me that Judith's passing has inspired them to live a better life. People who never thought much about seatbelts are now realizing that each moment spent buckling up is an act of love for their friends and family. Although we are sad, we find ourselves grinning at our memories of Judith and how she made us laugh. It is a legacy worth leaving behind. We want to live the way she did, follow her example, showering warmth and energy on everyone around us.

FRIGHTENING LIGHTNING
July 2005

Lightning, thunder, open ground, ridgetop, moments—short moments between flash and crash.

A piece of oshá is tucked safely in my pocket. Over a decade ago an Apache friend recommended carrying this root to avoid lightning strikes. Now that I need this protection I am wondering if I have handled it properly. It occurs to me that, according to my own tradition, this would be an appropriate time for praying.

It is also an appropriate time for running. I sprint past the lone trees and snags left on the ridgetop of this burned landscape.

My companion, Chad McKenna, admits to a history of close calls with lightning. I have my own history as well. We agree to stay apart and he drops back while I run ahead. This is a standard procedure for folks caught in lightning storms—split up so if struck, one's companions can offer first aid and get help. We meet a few times in the next half hour to decide if staying on the ridgetop making progress toward our truck is preferable to dropping off the exposed ridge and seeking refuge on the hill slopes.

We are miles away from the truck assessing vegetation recovery in the two-year old Kinishba burn. I point out that the hill slopes are blanketed in spectral, teetering fields of blackened skeletal trees. In the wild winds that accompany the thunderstorm, it is the last place I want to go. Chad suggests that our hardhats might provide protection from falling trees. We both laugh at this ridiculous rationale. I dart ahead racing up yet another incline.

It is a childhood habit, but I am counting now. FLASH. One-one thousand, two-one thousand, three—CRASH. Pause. FLASH. One-one thousand, two-one thousand, three-one thousand, four—CRASH. FLASH, one-one thousand, FLASH, two thousand, FLASH, three thousand, CRASH. CRASH. CRASH. What flash belongs to what crash?

Finally the road begins to switchback down toward the canyon below. I quickly slip off the ridge in long lopes. FLASH, one thousand, CRASH. There is no confusion now as I marvel at the momentary contact of an intense bolt of lightning on the ridge above, the same ground where I had passed by only minutes earlier.

There is little moisture in this thunder cell, alarming to the firefighter in me, but for the moment I am grateful. I failed to grab my raingear this morning when jumping into the contractor's truck. Though I am mentally prepared to get drenched, there are barely enough raindrops to quell the dust beneath my feet. We left the truck earlier in the drainage bottom where the road had washed out. Only now I am keenly aware of the mistake. I've been around large burns long enough to know the vast power of flash floods in these denuded landscapes.

I key the mike on the radio on my chest. As I run I have been listening to my co-workers report on weather and fire conditions across the reservation. Our helitack crew has aborted their mission to a smoking snag on the Black River due to lightning. The observation plane landing now in Show Low is reporting thunderstorms "all the way to Phoenix" and "it looks like very little moisture is reaching the ground." Some of my employees have found a fire near Cedar Creek about five miles away from my location. They have felled the burning snag, put a line around it, and are now involved in their own race back to vehicles dodging lightning.

I report my position and the fact that we are getting ground strikes without moisture.

"Do you see any smoke?" the helpful dispatcher responds.

"No, it's getting dark and I am currently in a dead run trying to get out of this storm," I explain. "I recommend an aerial recon in the morning."

"Copy that," the dispatcher replies, and I hope my colleagues monitoring the radio manage to slip in a few prayers for my safety between their bouts of laughter.

When I reach the canyon bottom I turn on the head lamp. Like many drainages in recent burns, the bottom is a scoured rock field. It would seem ironic to survive the ridge exposure without harm and then twist an ankle in the final sprint to the truck. I consider slowing down, but remember stories of ball-lightning moving down similar drainages. The safety of the rubber-tired truck lures me on.

Finally we are both in the truck and bumping our way through the canyon bottom, still aware of the threat of flash floods if more moisture has reached other parts of this watershed. Our stories flow, our respect for lightning renewed. We have each been thrown by lightning. Chad's incident included a fatality—he was at an outdoor concert when lightning hit a tree nearby. I've been luckier, both times in wilderness and no one was seriously hurt. We talk about the ozone smell, the noise, the strange way our hair levitated in our near-strike experiences.

We both know firsthand how lucky we have been.

FLASH FLOODS
August 2005

"Apparently Mother Nature did not get that memo," I replied to the distant government agent reminding me that the official deadline for emergency postfire activities had passed a month earlier. I supported my case by relaying images of the past week's flash-flooding incidents.

In Cibecue the crew had helped a neighbor mop six-inch-deep mud from her roadside house. August monsoon runoff from the burned lands above the town swept over the bank and past the decaying straw bales into her home. Green metal fence posts used to stake the bales marked the long line of composted hay. Clearly the flow was anticipated by the hydrologists who addressed emergency concerns immediately after the burn. However the straw wall did not last as long as the threat from flooding.

The day before, another August monsoon storm washed logs down from the 1999 Rainbow Fire and rolled them across the highway north of Whiteriver. Traffic was stopped both directions until loaders could move the debris aside. Several yards were flooded and cornfields damaged. Walls of water poured off the cliffs in the Alchesay Fish Hatchery area.

A few days later—and a different storm—flash-floodwaters raced through the communities of Cedar Creek and Canyon Day, this time coming from the burned lands of the 2003 Kinishba Fire. Fortunately no damage was reported to the houses downstream, but roads in the burn area were severely washed out.

Flash floods occur with storms of intense rainfall and extended duration. Although any land can experience flash floods, the frequency is elevated in areas that have experienced severe wildfires. On the tribal lands of the White Mountain Apache, large burns in the past decade have significantly changed the landscape, and flash flooding is a serious threat. While scientists are reevaluating their assessments and extending their predictions into decades for this elevated response on burned lands, Congress is shortening the timeframe for emergency spending following burns.

In 2002, when the Rodeo-Chediski Fire occurred, the deadline for Burn Area Emergency Response programs was three years. In 2003 when the Kinishba Fire occurred, that deadline had been readjusted to two years, with emergency stabilization projects given a one-year deadline. Unfortunately, there are no earmarked funds to address the long-term burn-related issues.

In addition to damage to roads, bridges, culverts, wells, walls, buildings, and other costly improvements, flash floods pose a serious threat to human life. Since 1990, over ten thousand people nationwide have lost their lives in flash floods. At least six people died in flash floods in Arizona this year.

Flash flooding can be tricky to anticipate. Often isolated thunderstorms high in the watershed cause flooding miles downstream and hours later. In the burn areas, debris can accumulate in drainages, forming temporary dams that may break hours later, sending an unexpected rush of water to downstream communities.

When moving water picks up energy, debris is often carried along. These debris flows are capable of moving large boulders and even vehicles and houses. Even six inches of moving water can take an adult off his feet. Children are especially vulnerable to flash floods because of their small size and their tendency to play near creeks and in drainages.

The best strategy for avoiding flash flooding is to be aware of the weather, especially upstream, and keep to the high ground when there is a threat of flash flooding. Avoid canyons or stream channels during, and for at least two hours after, intense storms. Floodwaters generally subside quickly, so stay high until the danger has passed.

If asked to evacuate, residents should rapidly comply with the request and take important documents with them. Keeping legal papers, such as titles and insurance policies, photographs, medication, and other irreplaceable items together in an easily assessable location, can save time during a true emergency. Evacuees should take the safest route to high ground and avoid crossing drainages.

Flash floods can happen anywhere, but are more frequent and intense in and downstream of burn areas. Mother Nature is not heeding any legislated guidelines on how long burn effects present hazards. All people living near burn areas need to be aware of the hazards of flash flooding.

BEAR SCARE
September 2005

Perhaps I should have found another solution last weekend when my crew leaders radioed me about an elk carcass in the planting area. We were getting ready for the second annual White Mountain Apache Tribal Member Tree Planting Camp. The next day the woods would fill with a hundred tree planters—novices, advanced beginners, veterans, instructors, inspectors—focused on the finer points of "getting the green side up."

Our first tree planting camp in the fall of 2004 had been a wonderful jumpstart to the planting season, pairing seasoned tree-planting veterans with tribal members looking to learn new skills and work for a few months. We hoped to repeat the program and this year focus on tribal members who had already spent a season or two "hoedad-throwing."

The hoedad, a narrow shovel mounted at a right angle to the handle, allows planters to cheaply place tree seedlings in the ground. Like any tool, experience brings expertise, and good instruction can bypass years of trial-and-error learning.

I keyed the mike radioing back a flippant remark about using the elk as a microsite. Burying the carcass had been suggested, but it seemed like a lot of work and I reasoned that predators would just dig it up anyway. The tree-planting specifications require planters to place seedlings with shade on the south and west sides. This placement is known as planting microsites. The tree planter adjusts the grid distance to find stumps, rocks, brush, and snags that will give a small seedling that surviving edge of shade. Not only would an elk carcass provide shade, but I rationalized that the decaying carcass might be a long-term source of nutrients.

We needed to avoid disturbing the site since our Wildlife and Outdoor Recreation Department law enforcement officers would investigate. The bull had been shot and his antler's sawed off, clearly the work of an illegal poacher.

When we found an eagle feather next to the elk the next day, I should have known that other predators were soon to follow. Predators in the planting unit were not my only concern. The first day of camp we shut down early due to multiple dehydration cases as our water supply waned. We had also found a large rattlesnake and encountered multiple ground bee nests. Tree planting was proving to be a dangerous sport.

Tuesday saw continued dehydration cases and bee stings.

"We've sent one person a day to the emergency room," I complained Wednesday morning. "Let's be safe out there and break this record."

The morning started with a tree-climbing demonstration by seasoned cone collectors. As a veteran climber scaled to the top of a seventy-foot-high tree, more adventurous tribal members were trying on the harnesses and using the set ropes to pull themselves into the canopy of a smaller tree. I was relieved when the crews headed to the field, certain that the day could not get more exciting.

By lunchtime the radio was cackling with talk of bears. A bear had been spotted. A huge bear, according to the radio chatter. There was also a bear carcass near the elk now. No one could approach to investigate because a live bear was standing guard. The crew leaders started pulling people back, and the safety officer snapped some pictures of the long-eared, young adult boar. Eventually the game warden arrived and closed down the program. He needed to clear the area to bring in dogs and either run off the bruin or tranquilize and transport him to a different site.

Knocked out of the planting area, we had a horseshoe tournament back in our camp. Once it grew dark, traditional crown dancers entertained the campers, and the singer spoke of the strength of bears. I ended the day around the campfire, listening to many bear stories. It is the lore of human-bear encounters that lend bears great respect, and the need for distance. By Thursday our bear was gone, and we were back to learning to put trees in the ground.

Friday we shut down again when wind gusts started blowing down the three-year-dead standing snags. The blackened trunks of burned forest are now reaching a point of decay where even on a calm day an errant wind gust can land a tree quickly on the ground.

A half-million ponderosa pine seedlings wait at the greenhouse to be planted this fall. Hopefully the season facing us is much calmer than our first five-day training program.

CONE COUNTING
October 2005

This is a story about pinecones and numbers. Although there are many reasons math nerds get excited about pinecones, cone counting can get even more exhilarating when one climbs eighty-foot-tall trees to collect them. Tree climbing is not for the faint of heart. Generally there is a breeze up there, and the tree not only sways in response to the wind, but also from the climber's movements cutting the cones from the tips of branches. Still, the idea of making a living climbing trees appeals strongly to the twelve-year-old kid inside of me.

Cone counting is not for the faint of heart either. Working with numbers that have more than a half-dozen digits can also be pretty exhilarating. At least that's how I consoled that kid in me who stayed on the ground while over 1,500 bushels of pinecones were collected on the reservation this past month.

To date we have planted over a million seedlings since the 2002 Rodeo-Chediski burn and the 2003 Kinishba burn. What seems like a major undertaking pales considering the lost forest we are trying to replace. Roughly 150,000 to 180,000 acres have had at least 75 percent tree mortality from the burn. If these forests supported an average of 200 trees per acre before the burn (actually many of these acres had much more than that, which is a story of its own for another day), then we are facing replacement of 30 million to 36 million trees at maturity.

With survival rates roughly around 25 percent (tree planting during a drought in burned country is quite challenging), it will take between 120 and 144 million new trees to replace the burnt forest. Mother Nature is doing her part where live trees are nearby, but much of the area had no seed source. Our million-seedling effort seems hopeful, but in the face of the problem, rather small.

Prior to the burn, the seed stored in refrigerators of forest offices seemed adequate. No one expected the huge reforestation efforts needed on many recent landscape-scale fires. Now what had seemed like a twenty- or thirty-year supply of seed is rapidly disappearing. Therefore, even though we did not experience a bumper crop of pinecones this year, we needed to replenish the seed.

Cone collecting is tricky business. The cones must be collected when the seed is mature, but before the cones open and disperse the seed. Usually there are only about ten to fifteen days when the cones can be collected. The timing of this biological event varies from year to year. I felt like an expectant mother waiting for birth, collecting cones and cutting them open all through September looking for signs of mature seeds.

Historically, when cones were collected on the reservation, the trees producing the cones were cut down, the cones were gathered and the logs went to the reservation sawmill. This year we wanted to gather cones as close to the burn and within the burn so that the seed matches the location where we will plant the seedlings. Since these trees grow either in stands that had survived the burn or were already thinned, we chose not to cut trees down. Rather, we contracted professional tree climbers to gather the cones.

While my heart would rather have been climbing the trees, my job was to figure out how many cones we needed to collect. First, there are around 40 to 70 healthy seeds in a cone, providing the various insects and diseases that jeopardize seed production are at normal levels. If current germination rates hold for our newly collected seed, we will need to sow about 66 seeds for the 44 trees we grow in each basket in the greenhouse.

Therefore we need to collect one pinecone for each basket of trees we want to grow. Each greenhouse table holds 56 baskets, and each greenhouse has 28 tables. We can grow two crops each year in the five greenhouses, so we need about 15,000 cones to gather enough seed for one year of maximum production. There are approximately 60 cones per bushel, so we need to collect 250 bushels for each year. Allowing for approximately 10 percent mortality through the seedling production phase, our maximum in-house capacity permits us to grow and plant around 620,000 seedlings each year.

The reality is that we won't collect cones every year, and so we tried to collect all the cones we could get in the short time frame we had to get them. If our assumptions are correct, we collected about six years' worth of seed this year. Our challenge this winter is to separate the seeds from the cones and winged tissue that surrounds each seed. Again, the task seems challenging, and I'm looking forward to a whole new set of fascinating numbers, inspired by pinecones.

CHEDISKI ORIGIN MYTH
November 2005

I am as guilty as the next guy for telling this tale. It seems plausible, until you are sitting at the base of the rock outcrop that took you fifteen minutes to scramble up to, through thorny New Mexico locust and loose rockslides on the sixty-degree slope. The myth in question starts like this: A lost hiker started a fire that attracted a media helicopter covering the Rodeo Fire and was thus rescued. Now as far as I know, this much of the story is undisputed truth. The next part of the story, which I fell for as well, was that the helicopter rotor wash then fanned the flames of the fire and sent it out of control.

My scrambling companion in this quest to visit the origin of the 2002 Chediski Fire is my co-worker Reginald Armstrong. Reggie and two of his fellow helitack crew members were the first firefighters to arrive on the fire scene. He has fought fire all of his adult life, spending the past thirteen years working primarily with helicopters.

Helitack crew members generally spend much of their career fighting small fires because they are the first firefighters to arrive on-scene. The helicopter deposits a few expert firefighters as close to remotely located fires as possible. Reenforcements arriving by driving and hiking can be several hours behind this elite crew. By flying the firefighters in, the fires can often be "caught" before they become large. The morning of June 20, 2002, Reggie was in the first group dropped off at the fire started earlier that morning by the lost hiker.

When I catch up with Reggie, he has reached the Chediski Fire's origin. I look back down at the steep slope we have ascended to the flat canyon bottom below. There are only two clearings that have juniper trees similar to those in television tape where the media helicopter landed and both are some distance below our vantage point. This is when I realize the story of helicopter rotor wash fanning the fire while picking up the hiker can't be true. If rotor wash was to blame, the helicopter would have had to hover next to a steep canyon slope to have such an effect.

"Reggie," I ask the helicopter manager, "do you think when that helicopter landed, its rotor wash could have fanned this fire?"

"No way," he answers.

We are seated at the base of an outcrop of rock that looks similar to ones pictured in the television coverage of that day. I am reminded of the account in Norman MacLean's book *Young Men and Fire* about the 1949 Mann Gulch Fire in western Montana that claimed thirteen firefighters. MacLean and Mann Gulch survivor Robert Sallee go looking for Sallee's escape route twenty-nine years later. I relate the story to Reggie, telling him that even though the landmarks did not seem quite right, Sallee convinced himself he was in the right spot. Further research sent MacLean back up the mountain to look again, and this time he found a different chute that matched Sallee's memories.

Reggie grins at me and reminds me that it was only three years ago and he is pretty sure of his memory. He flags the spot he remembers as the origin. He finds his old fire line. Then I recall that author John MacLean, Norman MacLean's son, revisited the Mann Gulch Fire with Sallee years later and in his book *Fire and Ashes* allows that Sallee's memory may have been more accurate that his father's logical deductions.

I think about how many times I have heard various accounts of the story of this fire's origin. Along with the Rodeo fire that started ten miles east, the Rodeo-Chediski Complex burned over 467,000 acres and destroyed 468 homes. Both fires were started by individuals, and those people whose lives are impacted by this disaster can't help but spend time thinking and talking about the mistakes made in igniting these blazes.

We speculate on what might have happened that morning that would have prevented this disaster, if only for the lessons that can be learned. Clearly this is a stupid place to start a fire. Surely, it should have been put out once the helicopter was signaled, rather than assuming others would be able to suppress it hours later.

The role of the media helicopter's rotor wash is not the only misconception about this place.

Many of the same folks who muse about the causes of these fires also argue on the proper pronunciation and spelling of the name Chediski or Chedeski. I find it humorous to hear area "locals" from Phoenix argue about whether the first, second, or third syllable gets the emphasis.

My Apache crew members tell me the word is the made-up attempt by a mapmaker years ago to capture the true name of this place, Tséé łigai, which translates as "White Rock." The presence of white rocks along the canyon walls verifies this interpretation. Being here with Reggie, and seeing the situation for myself, I feel pretty confident I can put the rotor wash myth aside as well.

 ## MOIST MICROSITES
October 2006

There is a way of being in the woods that is about awareness and observation. It is the skill of noticing small items that help you piece together the big picture. I call this practice "Reading the Land." Learning to read the land is similar to learning to read a language. Start first with an alphabet; learn how to put letters and sounds together to make words. Words become sentences, sentences paragraphs, paragraphs pages, and a whole new world has opened up to the reader.

In the woods you notice little things, a track here, a partially built but abandoned nest there, a place where water runs downhill, a place where runoff ponds and grass seeds take root. When you put these things together you can, without actually being there, picture what happens on a burnt hillside when a thunderstorm is hurling torrential rain across the landscape.

There is a way of working in the woods that is also about awareness, observation, and then action. Formally, we call this concept "Adaptive Management." Simply, it is being aware of what is working and what is not working, and changing our operations so they work better.

Midway into our fall tree-planting season, we are adapting our planting practice to do a better job of putting seedlings in places where they may survive. These places are called *microsites*, and recognizing microsites means thinking small. Consider the landscape from an ant's perspective. A small dirt mound a person absentmindedly steps over becomes a large mountain the ant must ascend to cover the same terrain. If a tree is planted on the top of this mound, the soil there will dry out faster. If the tree is planted at the base of the uphill side of the mound, the mound will provide a natural dam for surface flow, and the spot will stay moist longer.

Our contract requires tree planters to select microsites that provide shade at two o'clock p.m. This means locating the tree with shade-producing objects to the southwest of the seedling. Out on the burnt landscape, shade for an eight-inch-tall seedling may be a snag (standing dead tree), a downed log, a stump, a rock, or a bush. If there is no such refuge available within our spacing guidelines, the planter can make shade by putting a few limbs or rocks to the south and west of the tree. Not only does the shade cool the seedling in the heat of the day, but soil in shady areas stays moist longer. In burned areas, microtopography may be as important to soil moisture as shade.

Tree planters can improve the microtopography by moving a log or large rock, after planting the seedling, to create a mini-erosion barrier. The object needs to be at least a foot long, in full contact with the ground, and oriented along the contour downslope within a foot of the seedling.

Our contractors must average fifteen feet between seedlings, but actual distances vary from seven to twenty feet. This latitude allows the tree planter to find the best microsite for the trees, and avoids having a forest planted in uniform rows. When planters put trees too close together or too far apart, the contractors are docked financially.

Focus back on being in the woods, looking small and thinking big. Our reforestation challenge is monumental. On tribal lands, the Rodeo-Chediski Fire killed the majority of trees across 60 percent of the burn, or about 170,000 acres. About half of those acres are near surviving trees and will reforest naturally. Half of these remaining acres once supported forests while the other half supported woodlands. Without some human intervention here, it may take thousands of years before trees migrate back to these canyons on their own.

Currently we are only funded to plant trees in the areas that were considered "commercial forests." That means we have around thirty thousand acres to plant. We have planted the nine thousand acres we were funded for, and expect to complete another two thousand acres.

We could pat ourselves on the back for a job well done, if we were in a different decade and a different situation. However, we are trying to plant trees during the same long-term drought that made this fire so extreme in the first place. We are planting in the most damaged part of the burn where soil loss has been catastrophic and soil movement is ongoing. Our survival rates have been varied, but mostly poor.

Our need for trees in these watersheds is immediate. Instead of giving up, we need to hone our craft to provide the greatest chance of success. Therefore, midseason, we come to our tree-planting contractors and ask for one more shift in their operations. Think about where the moisture will stay in the soil longest, and plant in that spot. Read the landscape. Adapt your actions. With this special care, and perhaps some luck, we may stand in the future shaded by the seedlings planted today.

 COOKING REPORTS—
A CULINARY APPROACH
January 2007

For the past four years I have worked with many exceptional folks from the White Mountain Apache Tribe stabilizing and rehabilitating forests, woodlands, canyons, and ridgetops burned in the 2002 Rodeo-Chediski Fire. We have accomplished a lot, through bouts of laughter, tears, sweat, screams, songs, dreams, prayers, and just plain hard work. Looking back, the miles of fences built, acres of logs contour-felled, baskets of seedlings planted, miles of culverts cleaned, pounds of seeds scattered, and a seemingly endless collection of dozens of projects, add up to amazing accomplishments and some darn-good stories to tell.

We should write a book, I told my staff. The impact of the fire will live with Apache people for hundreds of years. These stories need to be written down so their great-grandchildren will understand how Apaches responded after this fire. The first time I suggested this task, I was met with disbelief. One staff member reminded me that Apaches live by an oral tradition. Few Apaches write Apache. Writing is not a favorite task when it comes to communicating in English. Not true, I rebutted, reminding them of the detailed and sometimes hilarious accounts in the daily logs kept during the planting season. Still, though we liked the idea, we weren't sure how to begin.

So, instead of planning a book, we started planning our annual Thanksgiving dinner. Some folks would bring turkeys or hams. Others would bring mashed potatoes or yams. There would be cranberry sauce, dressing, salad, and pies. Those who were better off staying completely out of the kitchen would pick up cases of soda, or plates, cups, and silverware.

The event was a fine feast, but the meal also served as inspiration. Look what we've done, I exclaimed. This is just like writing a book! We should look at each of our projects like it was a meal. It needs meat and potatoes, but some sides will spice it up.

The meat for each write-up will describe the task—what we set out to do. For example, for low water crossings we will describe how culverts are removed and replaced with rock-armored dips less likely to wash out when flash floods come raging through the canyon bottoms. When we write about fence building, we will explain how the boundary fence was destroyed by the fire and how we wanted to keep cattle off of the burn for three years to give the vegetation a chance to recover.

The potatoes will be the part that explains what we ended up doing. For tree planting, we will describe how we rebuilt the greenhouses, collected seed by climbing trees, grew seedlings, and finally where we planted the trees. We can include lots of pictures of helicopters dropping straw, crew members sawing logs, excavators moving rocks, and schoolchildren planting seedlings.

The side dishes will be the other stories that go along with each project.

Some stories will be healthy; for example, in the section on Log Erosion Barriers, one sidebar story may describe how to fall a tree along the contour with a chainsaw. Other stories might be more like dessert, such as relating what happened when a group of workers ran into a bear and the guys took off running, leaving the girls to face the charging bruin.

Winter is a traditional time for storytelling. With snow piling up in the woods, we are sharpening our pencils and flexing our fingers on the keyboards. Each day a new idea comes in. We should write about how we used our operation plan when we needed to get a rescue helicopter to an employee who was stung by bees. We should let readers know that flash floods are still damaging people's homes, even four years after the fire. We need to include a section on Planting Camp where tribal members were transformed into tribal entrepreneurs who contracted tree planting.

For the government, we need to write a final report. If we get into the heart of the story, perhaps there will be more readers than just the government bureaucrats interested in the tale. It will be hard to write a book. Yet everything else we have done has been hard, too. Challenging.

Each time we gather, Phil Stago, our tribal natural resource director, likes to remind us that sharing food is an important Apache tradition. So if we have some stories to share, thinking of them as meals may be the tastiest way to avoid writer's block.

TRANSITIONING TO TRIBAL FORESTRY
May 2006

I accepted the Rodeo-Chediski Implementation Leader for the Burn Area Emergency Response (BAER) program because of my keen desire to have a positive influence on damaged landscapes. My position was to oversee a large, but short-term, stabilization and emergency rehabilitation effort. I would be done in less than three years. I accepted the job as a short-timer with a focused agenda.

In conversations with tribal leaders and my rapidly expanding crew of forestry laborers and technicians, I learned Apaches have a different relationship with the land than most Americans. They were affected by the tragedy of the burn in ways that mainstream society did not comprehend.

Then-Chairman Dallas Massey explained to me that the Apache words for mind and land are pretty much the same word—what we call might call a homonym—words sounding the same but with different meanings. However, for the Apache, mind and land are so closely related that really they are more like synonyms—words that have the same meaning.

The lesson is that people and land are so closely related it is difficult to separate them. When the land is sick, the people are sick. When the people are sick, the land is sick. Likewise, healthy forests mean healthy people, and healthy people mean a healthy forest. The destruction of almost one-third of the tribe's forest over a three-week period was unimaginably tragic.

The next Apache land lesson I learned was given me by Vice Chairman Johnny Endfield. On my first day he told me I should plan to stay around a very long time. He laughed at how silly the government was to think we would solve all of the emergency issues caused by the fire in only three years. Although nationally the government-funded program has a short-term mentality, my employer—the tribe—expects me to take a long-term perspective and approach to our work.

Perhaps the most important lesson I have learned is that by taking care of people, we are most successful in our quest to take care of the land. Like the land, a short-term mentality is not appropriate. Like the land, we need to consider that our responsibility to the people extends for decades.

The Rodeo Fire was started by a tribal member, a casual-hire firefighter who could only work when a fire was burning. As uncomfortable as it is to consider that one of our own firefighters ignited this blaze, it is not wholly unbelievable. At the time of ignition, the unemployment rate in the community of Cibecue—where the fire starter lived and the fire originated—was close to 60 percent. Since then the community's sawmill closed its doors because fire destroyed the timber resource. Unemployment has escalated to 80 percent. The twenty-five jobs in my supposedly temporary program currently held by Cibecue residents are incredibly important to the community. The concept that when we finish expending the remaining BAER funding, I am supposed to collapse my crew and organization is incomprehensible. We have no alternative except to find additional work to keep people employed.

In addition to healing the land, we are using the BAER opportunity to foster job skills and futures for Apache people. We have invested in training, established facilities to base operations, and acquired tools and vehicles to accomplish tasks.

Now comes our greatest challenge. We are transitioning from a separately funded and singularly focused emergency response organization to merge with our parent Tribal Forestry Department. We must find work to do and money to pay for that work. We need to adapt, change, and operate outside the box. We want to take on new projects including timber marking, thinning, and increased fire management responsibilities. Our future holds a combination of adventures. The ability to contract work off reservation is at the top of the list.

Fort Apache Indian Reservation is not alone when it comes to under-utilized forestry workers. Throughout Indian country, many talented, motivated people cannot find meaningful, rewarding forestry work. On national forest lands, over 60 percent of firefighters (including AD casual hires) are Native American. However, for other woods-related work, that figure drops into the teens.

Our next challenge is to build a self-supporting Tribal Forestry organization. As forestry workers, my staff can share their Apache perspectives and land-based ingenuity to help other natural resource managers throughout the West. If we are successful, Apache crews will be instrumental in structuring a country whose healthy forests support healthy people.

 A VISIT TO YALE
March 2007

Towers and turrets. Courtyards with archways. Stairways to massive doors. Buildings rumored to have secret passages. Years of tradition amid the ivy-covered walls. I am reminded of the Hogwarts School of Wizardry and I keep looking for Harry Potter. My host describes the "Residential College" system followed by Yale University undergraduates, and I wonder if the colleges are named Slytherin and Griffindor, and where is the Quidditch field? We laugh, but recognize that the same English institutions that inspired the famous children's series have also influenced the American "Ivy League" universities. Underlying our banter, underlying the purpose of our visit, underlying the mission of the Yale School of Forestry and Environmental Studies (F&ES) is a strong sense of global connections.

My boss, Paul DeClay Jr., and I are guest speakers at the Yale Forest Forum Leadership Seminar hosted by the Global Institute of Sustainable Forestry. Paul is the tribal forest manager for the White Mountain Apache Tribe and one of ten tribal members who have earned a bachelor's degree in forestry. The tribal lands span 1.6 million acres and stretch from two thousand feet elevation at the Salt River to almost eleven thousand feet at the summit of Mount Baldy. It is a forester's paradise.

The Yale School of Forestry and Environmental Studies is the oldest forestry school in America. Now one of eleven professional schools at Yale, the program only offers graduate degrees. Yale F&ES serves as a preeminent conservation think tank, with a strong global focus. We are guests because the school also has the vision of embracing domestic diversity. Last spring we hosted a group of graduate students from Munich, Germany, and Yale on a tour of our forests in Arizona. Now it is our turn to visit them on the New Haven, Connecticut, hill that rises on the east end of the Yale campus.

Representing the White Mountain Apache Tribe, we have many stories to share. Our aggressive forest management programs include supplying the tribal sawmill with timber, protecting reservation and adjacent communities through intensive fuel treatments, and providing aesthetic forests through intensive uneven-aged management that then host thousands of visitors each summer. In addition, we have been actively responding to an extremely large and catastrophic fire that impacted a third of the reservation's forest and woodlands in 2002. As a part of our rehabilitation efforts on the Rodeo-Chediski burn, we operate five greenhouses and have planted over a million and a half ponderosa pine seedlings.

Yale faculty and students pepper us with questions. In addition to the luncheon presentation, we are guest speakers in a few classes. We attend a seminar by another native visitor, Holly Youngbear-Tibbets, dean of Outreach and Sustainable Development Institute, College of Menominee Nation, Keshena, Wisconsin. The three of us participate in a well-attended roundtable discussion focusing on forest management in "Indian Country." We fill the rest of our two-day visit with one-on-one discussions with members of the Yale staff, faculty, and students.

One take-home message is that our daily struggles with self-determination issues and the challenge of developing tribally directed forestry programs are common to indigenous people throughout the world. As Yale ramps up their participation in native forestry, we look forward to the professional support and mutual learning that Yale F&ES has promoted worldwide.

The Yale visit challenges us to raise the bar for White Mountain Apache Tribal members. Not only do we need more tribal members pursuing bachelor's degrees, but, to be prepared for the complex environmental issues facing the reservation, we need some students to pursue postgraduate degrees as well.

Wandering among the Yale buildings on our last night in town, I am still thinking of Harry Potter and wizards and the sense of tradition that emanates from long-established institutions. I pass by the famed "Skull and Bones" tomb that is rumored to house Geronimo's skull, allegedly stolen from his grave as an early twentieth-century prank. I smile at the thought of Apache foresters, possibly even Geronimo's relatives, earning Yale degrees and building a tradition of global respect for native communities.

CONFIDENCE AND COMPETENCE
May 2007

Early one morning several White Mountain Apache sawyers are heading from the remote reservation village of Cibecue to the neighboring Apache-Sitgreaves National Forest to work on a contract for the U.S.D.A. Forest Service. They notice a single-engine plane on a hillside near the dirt landing strip outside of town. Wings intact, good chance of survival of passengers, they immediately take action, starting with making the right communication contacts to bring emergency services quickly to the scene.

I'm in another state at a coffee shop with a friend. He is intently watching me field the cell phone call, catching snippets . . . down plane . . . crew is walking up the hill to investigate . . . yes, they have already taken care of notification, and, yes, they have first aid supplies . . . sure they will keep me posted as they can.

"So what do think?" he asks as I hang up.

"If there are survivors, they are very lucky. I really can't think of a better group of people to be first on the scene of such an incident."

I beam with pride thinking of the crew I work with. They aren't just sawyers, they are wildland firefighters, tree planters, helitack managers, incident commanders. They have written and maintained our department's ninety-page operation plan that includes detailed directions for handling emergencies, in addition to job hazard analyses, department policies, and every phone number and radio frequency they might need to insure rapid communication. In the past four years, we've had our own share of crises, and with each challenge we learn and grow stronger. I have no doubt this crew is up to the challenge of responding to the early morning aircraft disaster.

Meanwhile other crew members are loading our greenhouses with seed and soil to grow seedlings that will be ready for fall planting. A third "fuels" crew is marking and thinning trees to reduce hazardous fuels and establish forests that can withstand wildfire without catastrophic results.

A group of forest technicians are heading out to collect global positioning system (GPS) information on the reservation's stock tanks for our tribal hydrologist. Other forest techs will be gathering woodland data for a long-term woodland inventory. Amid all this activity, there are trainings, physical fitness tests, and fire shelter practices to insure that everyone is ready for what may be a challenging fire season.

As a midlevel manager, my nose is buried in the budget, as the tribe's fiscal year starts May 1. In a few months, we will have completed a five-year, multimillion-dollar project implementing the Burn Area Emergency Response (BAER) that followed the 2002 Rodeo-Chediski and 2003 Kinishba fires. My challenge is to find the projects and funding to keep this clearly competent and confident crew working. There is no lack of project work; the challenge is finding the funding to accomplish it.

A few years back we developed a strategic plan to help us make this transition. We identified four directions we wanted to pursue to build our program.

First, we want to take more responsibility in managing the tribe's forest resources. The Bureau of Indian Affairs is the federal agency that has the trust responsibility to oversee forest management on the reservation. Via Indian Self-Determination contracts, the tribe can assume the responsibility for various functions in this mission. Our fuels crew is an example of our self-determination program.

Our second direction is developing our firefighters to be versatile and cross-trained in several aspects of wildland firefighting. Our priority is to support our tribally managed Southwest Fire Fighters program that provides temporary firefighting employment for hundreds of tribal members. In addition, we field an "Initial Attack" firefighting hand crew, as well as crew members who participate in helitack, hotshots, and engine operations.

Our third path is to secure grants and funding to continue restoration of the severely burned lands on the reservation. This spring we sow the greenhouses with the last of our BAER funding; with faith we will find funds by fall to plant these trees.

Our fourth direction is to find projects off reservation, utilizing our talented crew and skills to assist other landowners with forest management activities.

The pilot was the sole occupant of the downed airplane, and he has walked away from the wreck. The sawyers are in the field working by midmorning, keeping our first Forest Service contract operating efficiently. I can only hope our survival as a program is as fortunate and successful.

SAWING INTO THE
TRIBAL FOREST PROTECTION ACT
April 2007

"It's pretty clear from the majority of stumps out there, that the sawyers on your crew know what they are doing," the Forest Service contract inspector tells me. There is a story in every stump, told from the holding wood, the face cut, and the back cut. The stump tells of experience, knowledge, care, and skill. In the area we are discussing, the challenges of cutting the dead standing trees are complex.

Tribal crews fall trees along the fence line, in a tribal/Forest
Service project implemented using the Tribal Forest Protection Act.
Courtesy of Daniel Kessay.

These tribal sawyers are working on our first Forest Service project
contracted under the 2004 Tribal Forest Protection Act (TFPA). The
act was passed in response to several tragic southern California fires
in 2003. The legislation clears the way for tribal crews and resources
to assist with management activities on neighboring national forests.
Tribes can recommend projects that will protect their interests on public
lands. If the funding is available, they can noncompetitively contract
with the agency to complete the work.

For this first project, our Tribal Chairman sent a letter to the
Apache-Sitgreaves Forest Supervisor recommending that we partner
together to protect the newly constructed boundary fence in the 2002
Rodeo-Chediski burn. The towering dead pine trunks were rotting and
falling on the new fence at alarming rates. Clearly the trees needed to be

put on the ground. The Forest Service agreed and found some funds to start the first twenty-one miles of the project. The tribe provided funds for the reservation side of the fence.

The contract was signed last fall, but winter snows kept the crews out of the woods. As soon as the roads dried out, tribal saw crews spent a week completing the nine miles not restricted by Mexican spotted owl activity. Any dead tree within a tree height of the fence was cut down, as long as it could be safely accomplished. On the Forest Service side, which did not have a postfire salvage sale, many trees were large and had been dead for four to five years. Rotten wood reduced the grip of the saw chain's teeth and comprised the holding wood's ability to guide the timing and direction of the tree's fall.

The sawyers have a mix of experience, including working as loggers and advanced firefighters. Rated by firefighting standards based on field tests, "A" sawyers are novices who have size limitations and need additional supervision, while "C" sawyers are "elite" saw wielders. For this project, our crew included one "C" sawyer, a few "A" sawyers, and a logger who hadn't yet been classified, but the majority fell in the "B" sawyer category. The Forest Service also uses the same standards and safety guidelines for their saw work.

The tribal crew leader carefully monitored the costs and kept accurate records, allowing the tribe to charge the Forest Service only for project-related expenses. The crew follows guidelines in the WMAT Tribal Forestry Operations Plan, which includes OSHA job hazard mitigations, emergency procedures, and policies that protect cultural resources, guide work ethics, and provide for a drug- and alcohol-free work environment. The crew worked quickly and efficiently, determined to convince the neighboring agency to rely on their expertise.

In addition to this first TFPA contract, the tribe has recently signed a "Participatory Agreement" with the national forest, which will allow the federal agency to utilize tribal forestry employees on as "as-needed" basis. When the Forest Service identifies projects and funding, they can develop a simple plan, signed off by the line officer and the tribal forest manager, and put tribal employees on a project with a minimum of paperwork. The employees remain on the tribal payroll, but the costs are reimbursed to the tribe by the federal government.

This win-win situation allows the tribe to focus on employee development and provide uninterrupted benefits to employees, while allowing the Forest Service access to a work force that can shrink and swell as project funds are available. Meanwhile, tribal employees, who are also trained firefighters, are available to the forest as initial-attack wildfire resources. One of the Forest Service's objectives is to expand tribal employees' knowledge of Forest Service operations, thus increasing the opportunity for cooperation between the organizations.

Continuing our discussion on stump stories, the Forest Service inspector has noticed a few less-experienced sawyers on the contract. We quickly fess up, explaining that we are using the contract work to provide some on-the-job training to less-experienced sawyers. The crew leader explains that he tries to keep our "A" sawyers on the reservation side of the fence where the trees are smaller and not as closely spaced together. We all agree that sawyer safety is our top concern, and that the contract is proceeding well, efficiently, and in a safe manner.

I can only hope it is the beginning of a long and active chapter of Forest Service and tribal cooperation.

FIVE YEARS AFTER RODEO-CHEDISKI
June 2007

An August afternoon last year, standing in Amy's living room surveying the damage. Unfortunately it is not my first, nor do I suspect my last, postflood visit to this house. This time the couch is propped on plastic milk cartons to avoid too much mud splatter. Mud coats the floor of each room, bedrooms, bathroom, washroom, kitchen. My staff has been here helping mop up the mess. Community members are filling sandbags to protect this and the other forty-two Cibecue, Arizona, homes that have had persistent flooding issues each time it rains upstream on lands burned during the 2002 Rodeo-Chediski Fire.

According to government policies, postfire issues are no longer eligible for emergency funding after a year. It is difficult to explain this policy to the woman whose home has now flooded five times.

Last year we built a three-foot-tall cinderblock wall to hopefully hold back the floodwaters. This was to replace the hay bales that had originally been placed here right after the fire. Unfortunately, when it rained, water surged through the community, overflowing the small streambed next to her house, overtopping the wall, and oozing mud through floorboards and thresholds. The neighbor's car floated across his yard. The owner, one of my employees, was out of town fighting fires in another state.

Not all of our efforts have been so frustrating. For example, we have planted over one and a half million pine seedlings since the burn, and we have collected enough pinecones from trees that survived in the area to grow an additional twenty million seedlings.

Each fall we have hosted community field trips for people to visit the burn and help plant trees. I have shed tears with tribal members who view the burned land for the first time. Still there are many who stay in town, for whom it is too painful to tour the blackened forest.

As a forester, I stutter when asked how long it will take for the forest to return. In many places the topsoil that supported the previous vegetative communities has washed away. Some places are miles from the nearest surviving seed tree.

"It will not be the same," I explain, not for hundreds or perhaps thousands of years. We will continue to plant trees, but a seedling planted by a ten-year-old child today will not produce seeds until that child is a grandfather, and will not reach full maturity until his grandchild is a grandfather.

There is a new beauty on the landscape, however. Looking out over a place called Grasshopper I am struck with the contrast of perception. In this gentle terrain at the base of the Mogollon Rim, there are vast stretches where no trees survived the blaze. The blackened skeletons of the ghost forest transition a break between earth and sky. For some, this is what they see—a burnt forest.

Yet in contrast to the "moonscape" of those immediate postfire weeks, the earth is no longer bare. From a distance, a dense blanket of grass appears to cloak the hillsides, though on close-up inspection there is only a plant or two per square foot. Many of the grasses are species whose seeds were dropped from airplanes over 170,000 acres of the burn. Since these species are also native, it is hard to claim definitively whether the seed came from the sky or from the land. Only four wildflowers were seeded, and yet almost two hundred different plants have been identified postfire in our studies of the land.

We have seen an amazing response of wildflowers, rainbows of color, and prolific sprouting of shrubs that often lend dense vegetation to the steep hill slopes. We have been in this area planting trees and monitoring the results. The ground is easy to dig in, and so it is a favorite place to bring the schoolchildren from Cibecue to plant more trees. Among this cornucopia of vegetation, we can point to pine seedlings ankle-high, knee-high, thigh-high, all planted in the past four years.

I find the Apaches' respect for Mother Nature profound. Our rehabilitation efforts are a partnership. If several hundred acres of recently planted trees are washed away in flash floods, well, we should be more careful about where we choose to plant trees. Mother Nature tells us what to do; it is our job to read the landscape and respond accordingly.

Our projects have been many and varied. We have laid logs on the contour, and then found a few years later that the soil arrested behind them makes nice places to plant pine seedlings. We have replaced fences destroyed by the fire, and then found that falling trees within a tree's height of the fence can continue the damage. We have worked in drainages, moving thousands of thousands of tons of rock. Although there have been a few failed projects, we have had many successes at protecting roads, bridges, and springs.

Springs: the proverbial silver lining of the dark Rodeo-Chediski cloud. Prior to the burn, there were eighteen sources of permanent water identified within the fire perimeter. Once the vegetation was removed from the land, the water returned. Tribal watershed technicians found their best source of information on where to find "new" springs lay in asking the elders where the "old" springs were "back in the day." Now forty-one water sources have been mapped, but many need long-term protection and monitoring.

Through an Indian Self-Determination Contract, the White Mountain Apache Tribe assumed the responsibility and funding for implementing the Burn Area Emergency Response program. Legally, this allowed the tribe to utilize the funding over a five-year, rather than a three-year, period. The tribe was also able to create jobs and contracting opportunities for tribal members. In the process, the tribe has developed a capacity for handling additional program responsibilities.

Prior to the fire, there was approximately 40 percent unemployment on the reservation, and 60 percent unemployment in the remote community of Cibecue. Today, with the Rodeo-Chediski-related closure of the sawmill in Cibecue, unemployment is up to 80 percent in that community and 60 percent reservation-wide. If we release the fifty individuals who have been working on the BAER project in the next month as we complete this program, the problem will be exacerbated.

Over the years we have approached our political leaders for help, but other issues such as the country at war and disasters like Hurricane Katrina take precedence. We have not received long-term funding necessary to continue our response to the ongoing impacts of what has been the most catastrophic fire in the Southwest. We are optimistic that we can create avenues to continue to provide jobs and contract opportunities for the White Mountain Apache forestry technicians and laborers who have responded to this postfire assignment. Like the landscape, our future is a matter of perception and how one chooses to view it.

It is hard to be optimistic standing in the mud-drenched living room of the tribal member who had believed, with you, that a cinderblock wall would afford protection. In the fall at a conference, I ask a scientist, who is the expert in watershed response to fire, how many years Amy will be flooded.

"If she lived in the Northwest, it would only take about three to five years for the hydrologic response to level out to preburn levels"—his look is grim—"but down in the Southwest, it is different. You might be looking at a few decades. We really don't know for sure."

GREENING THE SUPER BOWL
December 2007

Two hundred thousand pine seedlings are staged ready to plant on the vast denuded regions of the 2002 Rodeo-Chediski burn. Most of the trees are in the shade house at the McNary greenhouses, but many baskets are staged in the woods next to planting units. The melting snow is saturating the soil, leaving perfect planting conditions. Seven tribal entrepreneurs have signed contracts and are ready to plant when the roads dry out enough to get into the remote areas.

Unfortunately, we are low on funds. I am signing paperwork to lay off thirty-one employees. I am telling the contractors to have hope. I am trying to find it myself.

The tribal leadership has focused for years on trying to find money to plant more trees. The tribe asked the Bureau of Indian Affairs's Fort Apache Agency to help find the half-million dollars to plant these seedlings. At the end of the fiscal year, government officials found $147,000, enough to plant one-fourth of the trees that are waiting. The tribal leadership made several trips to Washington, D.C., to speak with our congressional delegation. So far they have come home empty-handed.

There is a bright spot in our situation. In C-1 Wash tribal entrepreneurs are still planting trees thanks to Super Bowl XLII. One of the efforts oriented toward hosting the February 3, 2008, event in Phoenix is the concept of "greening the Super Bowl." The National Football League's (NFL) Environmental Program, in addition to recycling and other conservation efforts, is hosting several tree-planting projects including forty-two acres on tribal lands of the White Mountain Apache.

With special postfire rehabilitation funding available immediately after the fire, the tribe has planted 1.5 million trees on approximately ten thousand acres. However, over 80 million trees were killed by the fire. In areas where some trees survived, the forest is naturally regenerating, but many of the tribe's canyons along the Mogollon Rim burned so hot that no seed trees remain.

When faced last spring with the funds to grow more seedlings, but no secure funds to plant them in the fall, I took the "Field of Dreams" approach. Grow them and the money will come.

Our hopes now lie in telling our story and hoping our tale will connect us to resources for tree planting both immediately and in the long run. We hope visibility of our program with Super Bowl XLII will help us find additional grants and donations.

The NFL's Environmental Program partners with the Arizona Super Bowl XLII Host Committee, the Arizona Department of Environmental Quality, the U.S.D.A. Forest Service, Arizona's Office of the State Forester, the Arizona Cardinals, and the Salt River Project. They are also sponsoring tree planting with schools in the Phoenix area and an additional forty-two acres on the north end of the Rodeo-Chediski burn on the Apache-Sitgreaves National Forest. These projects reduce the environmental impact of hosting the Super Bowl. Restoring forests creates a wide variety of economic, aesthetic, and environmental benefits and leaves a permanent legacy of Super Bowl XLII in Arizona.

As part of the postfire economic recovery, tribal members have received training in small business and technical skills so that they are able to run their own businesses. Three local contractors directly benefit from the Super Bowl planting.

Approximately thirty thousand acres in the burn still need to be reforested. The tribe would like to plant a half-million to a million trees annually for the next twenty years. A long-term tree-planting program will provide economic opportunities to tribal members who live in the communities that have been devastated by the fire. Not only is the tribe focused on healing the land by planting trees, but by fostering tribal members as contractors, tree planting becomes a pathway for healing people, too.

10   BAER GROWLS
March 2008

The program is no longer called BAER, it is BAR. BAER stood for Burn Area Emergency Response (or Rehabilitation, depending on the agency and the year). The acronym, pronounced like the animal, lent itself to obvious connections with the other fire bruin, as if to say "see what happens if you play with matches."

The new acronym, BAR, for Burn Area Rehabilitation, conjures up the room downstairs at the hotel that will draw conference participants like magnets when the meeting ends.

"Not sure what we will do about our large, growling mascot," a bureaucratic program manager apologizes at a national meeting.

"We can still find *growlers* at our new image," I whisper to a comrade next to me.

The change in terminology does not reflect the lack of emergency in the postfire environment, especially in the large mega-fire landscapes of recent years. It may, however, reflect the omission of the government's recognition of the tragic condition of these lands.

My son writes from a House Appropriations subcommittee hearing on wildland fire management. He is a college intern working for

Representative Tom Udall. Today he is taking notes for the environmentally astute congressman. A devoted son, he jots a note to his mother thanking her for his breadth and depth of the material at hand. A bureaucrat from the Department of Interior is arguing that no additional money needs to be spent on burn areas besides those funds already designated under the BAER program. My son hears my voice over his shoulder protesting, but stays with his role of college intern, note-taker. Not his battle today.

When a fire burns outside of the range of normal variability, when the fuel conditions are misconstrued by a century of fire exclusion, the damage on the landscape redefines the concept of disturbance ecology. This branch of science studies the response of ecosystems to infrequent, large-scale activities such as floods, fires, and hurricanes repeated through millennia and influencing evolutionary development of species and communities. The scale and scope of mega-fires exceed evolutionary boundaries.

A reporter covering the 2002 Rodeo-Chediski Fire described the event as having *wreaked havoc* on the landscape. How does the land recover from such havoc?

For the people, animals, and plants, recovery is a holistic process, a complex twisting of rainstorms, soil movement, successes, failures, flash floods, overnight creation of rills, gullies, canyons, disappearance of roads, culverts, trees planted in hopes of future forests, reappearance of flowers, medicine, new views, a new landscape to learn to love.

For the government it can be broken into three stages: stabilization, rehabilitation, and restoration. The former is funded immediately postfire with the same emergency dollars that fight fire; the latter is not funded, though agencies are instructed to use their normal operating budgets to continue to manage these ravished lands.

Rehabilitation dollars are limited, distributed through twisted policy so skewed most fires come up empty. Postfire challenges rise for years and decades beyond the flames in an ecological timeframe that extends well past the short duration of stabilization and rehabilitation dollars.

These government funds are focused on the protection of lives and property. The emphasis is on soil stabilization projects. Holistic ecosystem recovery is not considered.

We stand at a log embedded along the contour of the hillside. The area behind the log is filled with soil from the bare ground above it. These few cubic yards of dirt did not wash off the mountain. The spot provides an obvious refuge for a luxuriant patch of grasses and wildflowers and an ideal microsite for improved survival of a planted pine seedling.

By BAR standards the log erosion barrier is a failure. It is no longer damming up the runoff and improving infiltration.

We seem oblivious to lessons from decades of failed government programs that focused on single-resource management issues. We are using only one bar to judge success. We are treating only one aspect of the disaster. The voice of the government bureaucrat assures our congressional representatives that all is fine on the postfire landscape.

It makes me want to growl.

CHANGING WOMAN
April 2008

At the Fort Apache camp, the spring winds are calm. The blue sky is crystal clear. Nearby, the East Fork of the White River runs cold and swollen from the abundant winter snowmelt. Buds burst forth on the cottonwood branches. Out on the dance grounds, several Apache families are celebrating one of the first sunrise ceremonies of the year.

Spring is in the air.

We are reminded by this coming-of-age ceremony that change is a part of life. In Apache tradition, through this four-day celebration the girl becomes a woman. She becomes Changing Woman. She is instructed on how to conduct herself through life's stages. This weekend, the dance honors Ashley Kessay, the daughter of our field operations manager. In the ensuing weeks, there will be many changes for our staff. In a sense, Ashley is paving the way.

I have accepted a new job with the New Mexico State Forestry Division. I am leaving Whiteriver, Arizona, and moving back to Placitas, New Mexico. I once worked for State Forestry for six years, primarily as the timber management officer for the Bernalillo District. Now, sixteen years later, I am returning as the state timber management officer. Many of the programs I worked with then, such as private landowner

Ashley Kessay is painted by crown dancers during her Sunrise Dance.
Courtesy of Daniel Kessay.

assistance, are still active. However, there will be plenty of new challenges and learning ahead: plenty of change.

My time with White Mountain Apache Tribal Forestry, not quite
five years, has been amazing. Although the majority of my energy has
been focused on the Rodeo-Chediski burn rehabilitation, I have dabbled
in almost every other forestry activity on the reservation including firefighting, prescribed burning, timber sales, thinning projects, fuels treatments, sawmill issues, and greenhouse operations. More importantly, I
have learned thousands of lessons from hundreds of people.

The drumming on the dance ground paces my heartbeats, my steps, the movement of my body. I am joined by a friend from a neighboring community. She points out that we are the only white people at the ceremony. Being among so many friends and colleagues, I have forgotten to notice. Yet, as I break the news that I am leaving to my staff and coworkers, I am greeted with congratulations and enthusiasm. There are no expectations that I would remain in this community that feels like a second home.

I sense a slight intrepidness from our leadership team. For years, we have worked toward this time when they will take the torch and strike out on their own. There is strength in their commitment; strength in their resolve to create better opportunities. Our department is changing whether I leave now or not. Considering what we have accomplished in the last half decade of postfire disasters, I have no doubt the staff will stand tall to any new crises they face.

I work the bread dough between my hands to make fry bread, tortillas, and bàń ditanè. Producing only one flattened piece for every four or five the Apache women put on the open fire, I still smile that I have finally learned to "make bread." It is an incredible honor to stand in the early morning light, making bread and getting lessons in Apache language and culture.

I am also a changing woman. Although I am sad to be leaving my life on the Fort Apache Reservation, I am grateful for the friends, memories, and lessons I will hold next to my heart for the rest of my life.

CHAPTER FOUR

Environmental Education

Summer 1993

"Mom," my six-year-old son is calling after me, "the chokecherries are ripe!"

I stop midstride and turn to the little man who is motioning us back to him. My companion is Jim Youtz, the woodlands forester with the Fort Apache Agency. Jim is showing me treatment areas to improve woodland health. Since I'm a home-schooling parent and consulting forester, my kids are part of a package deal. A teenage babysitter travels with us, but at this stop, Roland did not want to remain at the truck playing Barbies with his twin sister, so he is tagging behind Jim and me.

"Honey," I start, in a delicate attempt to honor my son's developing role as a naturalist, "it is the right time of year for ripe chokecherries, but we are up in the dry pinyon woodlands, dear, and chokecherries grow down by the creek."

Standing over a pile of bear scat, full of cherry pits, Roland retorts, "Yeah, but the bears poop the pits up here in the woods."

That night I write in my home-schooling journal that Roland is using advanced cognitive skills to reason that pits in poop mean ripe fruit down by the river. Although my kids may not be reading words yet, their naturalist intelligence is beyond their peers. Perhaps when our society was based on hunting and gathering, every six-year-old child would see messages in poop. These days though, many kids never notice a pile of feces in the forest, and when they do, after an exclamation of how gross it is, they still have no clue how it got there.

Sunlight pours through the fall foliage of a Rio Grande cottonwood. Courtesy of Mark Higgins.

As a freshman at Oklahoma State University in Introduction to Forestry, a college professor commented that if we were looking for a career that would keep us isolated in the woods and not dealing with people, we should transfer out of forestry. Later, as a senior at the same university, another professor echoed the message: "Foresters need to be out in their communities constantly sharing what they are doing and thinking," the wizened Dr. Robinson explained. "No other profession has such a profound need to bring the public abreast of their actions and aspirations. If your public is not behind you, you cannot practice your profession and help the land."

I took this lesson to heart.

Environmental education started taking a prominent place in natural resource management with the first Earth Day in 1970. Many agencies support efforts that teach young people how to care for our earth and her inhabitants. Project Learning Tree (1976) was a landmark program that paired resource managers and teachers to create curriculum materials rich in content and delivery techniques. Later Project WILD (1983) came forth from similar origins. Within the next decade projects abounded: Project WET (Water Education for Teachers), Project Soil, Project Archeology, and many local ecosystem-based programs.

This marriage of resource managers and teachers mirrored my own. My husband, the teacher, and I shared our enthusiasm for environmental education in this creative atmosphere. Together we operated a small business committed to improving environmental education both locally and nationally.

In New Mexico, on separate occasions, I served as interim state Project WILD and Project Learning Tree directors. Midwifing various educational materials into the world, my favorite child was the Bosque Education Guide. My work included running outreach programs, teaching for the Rio Grande Zoo's BioVan, developing citizen monitoring projects, and participating in environmental education professional organizations.

For many children, environmental education experiences provide their essential link to the natural world. A standard philosophy underlying many programs is to create a sense of *awareness* of the environment first. Once children have developed an *appreciation* of nature, they are more receptive to gaining *knowledge* that leads to *understanding* of ecological concepts. Only after students master these steps are they ready to take *action* to make changes that support a healthier environment.

I was nurturing a love for the land in others long before my work with the White Mountain Apache exposed me to the deep connection between land and people. This bond is not unique to native populations, but rather the core element of being human. Environmental education offers a holistic approach to shaping a society that honors both land and children.

When natural resource agencies commit time and money, dismal education budgets are enhanced. Because children are more likely to adapt lifelong behaviors that show respect for the earth, agency impact is greatest when targeted toward youth. Over the last three decades, natural resource managers have become major partners in education and in shaping a mainstream society that fosters respect for the environment.

Our citizens must understand the environment to address issues like global warming and limited energy reserves. Authors including Al Gore (*An Inconvenient Truth*) and Richard Louv (*Last Child in the Woods*) are reaching mainstream audiences. The rallying cry of educators is becoming "No Child Left Inside."

The following essays capture some of the excitement of this critical branch of natural resource management.

2 INSTILLING THAT LOVE FOR THE LAND
October 1997

In a favorite childhood memory, I am lying on my back in the warm autumn sunshine, gazing up through the golden coins of aspen leaves at the clear turquoise sky. My mother usually accompanies me, and espousing profound motherly wisdom, says things like "Mary, this is what life is all about." As a youngster, these words wash right over me. I am engaged in the movements of a spider or in determining how deep I can bury my fingers in the black, cool earth.

As I reached junior high, I would chalk this philosophical chatter up to the corniness of adulthood. I enjoyed these seasonal journeys to magical mountain groves of white-barked trees. As a young adult, when moments spent with Mom seemed fewer and more precious, I began to understand that my mother and I share a deep love of nature, particularly the beauty of New Mexico.

I went on to college, studied forestry, hiked many miles, made many friends who shared my love of backpacking and forests, and remained enchanted with the splendor of our state. I married a man with similar interests, started my career as a forester, and then became a parent. One of my strongest desires has been to find a way to pass that love of nature and New Mexico on to my own children.

The task seems daunting. I did not want my kids to end up like

Mary with her son Roland Shaw help with a community project near the Rio Grande near Alameda, in the north valley of Albuquerque, New Mexico. Courtesy of Jim Dickey.

my baby brother who, as a kid, never liked the outdoors much. Born into a family of adventurers, my brother was scooted up many trails at an early age. By the time he turned ten, he announced that he was done with backpacking and preferred to stay at Grandmother's house while the rest of the family went hiking. I wondered if the kid didn't like getting outdoors because it was his nature, or because we pushed him too hard.

"You know," he recently confided, "this may surprise you, but I really do like to go camping."

My own children have had the opportunity to spend significant time outdoors. Working as a consulting forester for the past six years, my kids often accompany me on excursions throughout New Mexico and Arizona. When they were younger, I traveled with a teen-age babysitter who would watch them while I worked in the nearby woods. They built forts, gathered wildflowers, spent hundreds of hours playing make-believe games out in the forest.

Yet I wonder if these kids, who are forced to go on outings by the nature of my work, will develop that lifelong love affair with the land. When my ten-year-old son whines about having to go to the bosque again, I feel as if the school-based field trip we are leading is more of a prison sentence than a special opportunity.

Maybe I needn't worry too much. I only have to watch my kids to see they are proud of their naturalist heritage.

"I've been going to the bathroom in the woods since I can remember!" my daughter explains to her friend on a recent hike. She is more than comfortable moving along the trail. She is at home.

I think back to a frightful morning when our daughter was two years old. We awoke to find her missing. She wasn't in bed, or anywhere else in the house. Finally when her father stepped outside to continue the search, he found her curled up in the yard with our big black dog.

"I am just watching the sunrise with my dog," she explained, as if the event was the most natural way to greet the day.

Love of nature is a part of the human experience. If we provide the opportunity to get outdoors, our kids will naturally share our fondness for towering mountains, moist forests, babbling brooks, and spacious deserts. We can nurture this call of the wild by allowing our children the freedom to experience its pull.

If appreciation of our natural world is instinctive, why has humankind allowed the environmental degradation for which we are responsible today? Why do we have politicians who fish, bike, run, and hike in the outdoors, but back within the walls of their offices continue to endorse policies and regulations that provide for more pollution, more habitat destruction, and more stress on the environment?

As parents and community members we shouldn't be satisfied if our children love and recognize the beauty of our natural environment. Our challenge extends beyond instilling this love for the land. We must also make sure that our kids can make the connection between their actions and the effect of those actions on the environment.

NEW MEXICO FORESTRY CAMP
June 1991

The elk calf rises on wobbly legs, apparently the first time on its feet, having just been born on the roadbed deep in the Baca backcountry. Fifty New Mexico Forestry Camp participants watch from the school bus in total awe. Scheduled midway through the weeklong program, the field trip to the private Jemez Mountain ranch exposes campers to private forest management. As evidenced by the elk calving ground doubling as a roadway, visitors to this valley are rare.

The day's agenda includes tours of a current timber sale, a recent fire, a geothermal site, some older timber sales, and an old-growth stand. Each stop offers seldom-seen landscapes: wide, grassy calderas bordered by high-elevation forests; large, widely spaced pines towering over thick grass carpets; meandering creeks, easy to step across but several feet deep, cutting lazily through vast meadows. For some campers, this is their first experience visiting a totally litter-free environment. Not a dirty diaper within the private boundary fence. By evening the campers, though exhausted, are excited. This week full of unique opportunities will inspire their memories for years to come.

New Mexico Forestry Camp is a five-day workshop for youth to learn how New Mexicans use, care for, and appreciate their forests. The idea for the camp arose from members of the Cuba (New Mexico) Soil and Water Conservation District. In the fall of 1989, Betty Jane Curry, one of the district's supervisors, suggested the Cuba SWCD sponsor a youth camp to teach about forestry. The board was expressing concern that too few New Mexicans understood forestry issues. In the summer of 1990, forty-three youth between the ages of twelve and eighteen gathered for a week in June with about as many foresters, wildlife biologists, teachers, range managers, and others interested in youth and forestry.

The camp is held at Rancho del Chaparral Girl Scout Camp in the Nacimiento Mountains outside of Cuba. Students are taught *how* to think rather than *what* to think about forest issues. Campers arrive on Sunday and settle into the canvas tents on wooden platforms that will be home for a week. Tent assignments insure that urban and rural students get opportunities to mix and make friends.

On Monday the teenagers head out in small groups on hikes to learn about the plants and wildlife of the area. They also get to know each other, the staff, and the natural resource managers leading the hikes. In the evening, campers experiment with survival skills like modern fly-tying or prehistoric atl-latl throwing.

The next day campers rotate among six different stations. Each stop focuses on an aspect of natural resource management such as wildlife, range, forestry, archaeology, search and rescue, and aquatic biology. The program goes on the road on Wednesday for a field trip, which varies from year to year, alternating between national forest and other land ownerships. Come Thursday, the group splits into day-long work projects. One group might collect wood to study tree rings while another group is shocking fish in the stream to assess aquatic conditions. Meanwhile, other campers build check dams to address erosion problems associated with trails. Each year there are about six different projects.

The learning culminates on Friday morning with a role-playing exercise. During the week, roles are assigned, research is conducted, and on the last morning a mock congressional hearing is held to discuss various issues on a fictional national forest. Campers debate, often supporting viewpoints they may not agree with personally. The exercise provides an assessment of the knowledge and ideas the campers have processed through the week.

The camp is hosted through the grassroots support of individuals, communities, agencies, organizations, and businesses. Sponsors point toward a bright future for the camp and the long-term management of New Mexico's forests. Through a process of developing awareness and knowledge about various functions of the ecosystem, students develop the skills to take responsible action to protect and manage the forest.

Postscript: The New Mexico Forestry Camp is still sponsored by the Cuba Soil and Water Conservation District and held at Rancho del Chaparral. Over the years, the program has introduced hundreds of youth to forestry and natural resource management in New Mexico.

RIVERS OF COLORADO
WATER WATCH NETWORK
October 1991

Parked at a fork in the road in a high mountain watershed, the Indigo Girls are singing about a similar spot on the radio. I am on my way to the Keystone Science School. What waits for me is the magic of the Colorado Division of Wildlife's Rivers of Colorado Water Watch Network. As an aquatic education consultant for the New Mexico Department of Game and Fish, my job is to develop a similar program in our state. If the Indigo Girls can sing about watersheds, certainly the time has come to make sure that "watershed" is in our students' working vocabulary as well.

In these days of waning budgets, educators are looking for tools (such as laboratory equipment and computers) to provide a modern education. Meanwhile, resource managers want to develop thorough, reliable databases to track water quality. In Colorado, the answer to these dilemmas is the same: set up high school classrooms as Environmental Protection Agency (EPA) certified laboratories to collect regular, consistent data on Colorado's water quality.

Water-quality monitoring provides a meaningful project for both schools and clubs. When taught in the context of water-quality issues, chemistry, physics, biology, and mathematics are no longer dreaded topics. Laboratory exercises become real-life science projects that affect our environmental health for years. When schools establish an official monitoring station, students take many water samples during the calendar year. They learn to identify normal fluctuations in water quality, as well as spot problems in their own environments.

In traditional high school science classes, laboratory exercises often look for known values. Water monitoring determines unknown values in real situations. A student may ask how much dissolved oxygen is in the water. The results may guide her to question the impact of low levels of dissolved oxygen on animals that live in the water and all other life in her community.

Through the Rivers of Colorado Water Watch Network, more than one hundred schools have established laboratories—run by students—to monitor rivers in their neighborhoods regularly. Not only is the collected data reliable, it has even been used in court to help determine the outcome of water cases.

The Colorado Division of Wildlife's commitment to this program is impressive. Each school receives more than seven thousand dollars' worth of resources, including a computer, pH meter, and laboratory equipment. At the start of each school year, teachers and a handful of students from each school attend the division's four-day workshop to learn how to conduct the tests, what the tests mean, and even how to take appropriate action should they encounter dangerous water quality.

Down at the Keystone Science Center, the energy level is high. Each participating school has sent students who will be the peer instructors for their classrooms back home. The students are intent on every concept presented. Most participated in previous years, and pose complex questions to the water-quality professionals. They discuss mining wastes, agricultural runoff, and effluent from sewage plants. These Colorado students are concerned about keeping the image of "Rocky Mountain spring water" a reality rather than a myth in this mountainous state.

The program is funded primarily from a federal excise tax on fishing equipment. Outdoor recreation is huge in Colorado, and available dollars for aquatic education in New Mexico from this fund are a fraction of available monies in Colorado.

Despite the disparity in funding, I leave the workshop excited about the future of water-quality monitoring in New Mexico. We will do things differently in our state. For one, our New Mexico Department of Game and Fish partners with other agencies, including the New Mexico Museum of Natural History and the New Mexico Environment Department's Surface Water Quality Bureau, in the dream of establishing a similar water-quality program. Working together, we will find a way to create programs and opportunities that will bring ideas like "watersheds" to the forefront of classroom discussions.

When the Indigo Girls come to town and sing about forks in the road, hopefully we will have chosen a path that has informed a large number of young New Mexicans on the importance of water quality in our watersheds.

PROJECT DEL RIO
June 1992

Secchi disks, D.O. kits, TDS meters, phosphates, nitrates, fecal coliform, parts per million, percent saturation, q-value, quality control, non-point source pollution.

Some high school students were easily wielding these vocabulary terms as they participated this spring in a pilot water-quality education program called Project del Rio. The Water Education Working Group of the Environmental Education Association of New Mexico sponsored the project for six northern New Mexico high schools.

The working group includes representatives from the New Mexico Department of Game and Fish, the New Mexico Museum of Natural History, the New Mexico Environment Department's Surface Water Quality Bureau, Amigos Bravos, the Randall Davey Audubon Center, and Project del Rio. The short-range goal of the group is to support existing programs and then build extensive student-focused water-quality monitoring networks throughout the state.

Last year several southern New Mexico schools participated in a new international project focusing on the Rio Grande. This spring Project del Rio, an affiliate of the Global Rivers Environmental Education Network (GREEN), geared up for its second season in a five-year project to link schools located along the Rio Grande throughout New Mexico, Texas, and Mexico. Lisa LaRocque, Project del Rio director, welcomed the working group's efforts to expand the project throughout the river's stretch in the state. The working group's six northern New Mexico schools joined twelve additional schools located from Truth or Consequences, New Mexico, south into Texas and Mexico.

Project del Rio explores water-quality issues affecting the Rio Grande along its length. The bilingual program, which encourages contact between students from both countries, requires participating schools to gather data on the same day. Using computer networking, students share and compare their sampling data and discuss their results.

Students collect data on ten different water-quality parameters. From these tests students calculate a water-quality index that can compare changes in a river, or compare the Rio Grande with other rivers throughout the world.

Water-Quality Terms: What Do They Mean?

Here are some of the parameters studied during Project del Rio.

Dissolved Oxygen: DO is a form of oxygen in the water needed by many aquatic plants and animals. The absence of DO indicates severe pollution. Higher DO levels represent healthier waters.

Fecal Coliform: Although fecal coliform bacteria are not dangerous themselves, they are often found with pathogenic organisms such as disease-inducing bacteria, viruses, and parasites. These pathogens are scarce in water and difficult to monitor, but high levels of the more measurable fecal coliform (from excrement) are a good indication of their presence.

pH: The scale to measure acid or base levels of water is the pH scale. The pH of pure deionized water is 7.0. Most natural waters have a pH between 6.5 and 8.5. Below 7.0 the water is acidic, and above 7.0 the water is basic. Most aquatic animals can tolerate a certain range of water pH. If the pH drops or climbs beyond that range, those animals are no longer present in the water.

Biochemical Oxygen Demand (BOD 5-day): The BOD test measures the aerobic bacteria that use oxygen while decaying organic material. If the demand by these bacteria for oxygen is high, the variety and quantity of other aquatic organisms that need oxygen will be low.

Temperature: Temperature affects many river functions, including levels of dissolved oxygen, rates of plant photosynthesis, and the presence of aquatic wildlife.

In a three-week curriculum, students learn how to conduct water tests, what the tests mean, and how they are related. The monitoring day is midway through the program. Although students are encouraged not to base their overall judgment of the river's condition on just one day of sampling, they do focus on learning about land-use patterns that may contribute to the conditions they discover.

At the conclusion of the three-week study period, five students and a teacher from each school attend a student congress at Chamizal

Total Phosphates: Both organic and inorganic phosphates contain phosphorus, necessary for plant and animal life. Too much phosphorus can cause algal blooms. Excess phosphates can come from human, animal, or industrial wastes, or runoff from disturbed lands.

Nitrates: Excess nitrates also cause algal blooms, a sign of eutrophication, which is an increase in plant growth accompanied by a decrease in animal diversity and water quality. Improper use of septic tanks is one source of excess nitrates.

Turbidity: This is a measure of suspended particles in the water, or water clarity. Murky water heats up faster than clear water, as particles absorb heat from sunlight. Warm water holds less dissolved oxygen. Suspended solids include clay, silt, plankton, sewage, and other waste.

Total Dissolved Solids: Dissolved solids include calcium bicarbonate, nitrogen, phosphate, iron, sulfur, and other ions. These materials are important building blocks for plant and animal life. A too-high level is counterproductive, as in the case with many other water-quality parameters.

Total Solids: Total solids are a combination of suspended solids and dissolved solids. Some outside sources that affect the level of total solids include urban runoff, wastewater treatment plant discharge, and sediments from soil erosion.

International Park in El Paso. Near the banks of the concrete-lined Rio Grande, students meet in a bilingual atmosphere to discuss the condition of the river. In the morning, they explore issues ranging from agricultural runoff to sewage disposal. In the afternoon they attend action-oriented workshops guided by professionals from several disciplines.

Through this pilot project, students learn to appreciate the large, international perspective of water-quality issues. Several schools continue to examine water quality in their own neighborhoods. The Water

Education Working Group will continue to work with these schools this fall.

A long-range goal is to create, under a loose umbrella, a collection of materials, services, programs, and computer technology to build core and supplemental curricula for schools interested in interdisciplinary water-quality education. The vision will result in a community of students and resource managers sharing information that will lead to a cleaner river.

 ## PILGRIMAGE TO BOCA CHICA
January 2002

Do desert rivers have deltas? Will the river be shallow and wide at its mouth? Will I be able to stand in the middle of its waters? These are the questions coursing through my mind as I run along the deserted ocean beach. Another question is one of distance. From the imprecise scale on the map provided at the airport rental agency, it is hard to judge how far it is from where the paved road to Boca Chica Beach ends to where the Rio Grande empties into the ocean. Is it one mile? Ten miles? How long do I need to run?

I am on a mission to see the mouth of the Rio Grande, which is known as the Rio Bravo south of the United States/Mexico border. I have a personal fascination with this river. I was born next to the Rio Grande, and have lived much of my life within its watershed. The river itself stretches almost two thousand miles . . . the actual figure varies depending on how finely one counts the changing meanders.

Despite years of river rafting, I believe one only knows a river when one knows the river's watershed. Simply defined, this is all of the land where falling rain or snow can ultimately feed the river. Watershed boundaries are natural delineations. They tie us together. We can define our citizenship by town, county, state, or country, yet the watershed community is more functional. To know our watershed is to understand the people, cultures, and ecosystems that are supported by the life-giving water that gathers to form a river. The Rio Grande/Rio Bravo watershed includes three states in the United States and five states in Mexico. It is huge, and so, for a citizen, there is a lot to learn.

Last July, I stood at the top of Stony Pass on the Continental Divide in Colorado. Considered the origin of the Rio Grande, this spot is the farthest point where falling raindrops could *theoretically* reach the Gulf of Mexico via the Rio Grande.

Heavy emphasis on the *theory.*

In this age of water allocations for agriculture, industry, and urban sprawl, Colorado raindrops do not stand a chance of reaching the ocean. By the time the river reaches Fort Quitman, south of El Paso, the river-bed is often dry. Farther downstream, the river is recharged by the Rio Conchas coming in from the Mexican side. The Conchas provides water to the Rio Grande just in time to flow through Big Bend National Park.

On that late summer day on Stony Pass, we were in the clouds, experiencing a cool monsoon typical of the season. This morning's weather is similar, as ocean fog lying on the beach limits visibility like that low-lying mountain cloud. Wet weather is unusual for most of the Rio Grande watershed. Typically a sunny, desert region feeds this river.

It is the river that has brought me to the Brownsville area today. I have just attended a training and celebration of a new curriculum guide to help educators teach about the river. The guide, called *Discover a Watershed: Rio Grande/Rio Bravo,* is published and sold by The Watercourse, a national educational organization in Montana. It is the second guide in a series. The first one was on the Florida Everglades. Guides for the Missouri and the Columbia rivers are underway. This spring, work will start on the Colorado River watershed guide.

Several years ago, the Montana writing team assembled a group of approximately one hundred people from both Mexico and the United States to help compile information and activities for teaching about the Rio Grande. Now, we have reassembled to receive the guide.

After the workshop my airplane was overbooked and I opted to wait a day to leave South Texas. This gave me time to visit the mouth of the Rio Grande. I am expecting something grandiose. Palm trees. Jaguars. A mixing of fresh and salt water. The early morning sky is overcast and the fog is just beginning to lift on the sandy beach. About three miles into my solitary run, I meet a few fishermen and inquire about the river.

"You are almost there." I follow the extended hand pointing to what looks like a pond. I am confused and it must show on my face.

"There is not enough water to make it to the ocean," I am told.

I run on to a sport utility with familiar green stripes on a white background. The officers with the Immigration and Naturalization Service caution me from continuing past a pathetic line of drift logs, litter, and survey stakes that mark the border.

I complain that I was expecting a river.

The end of the river is in sight, about a hundred feet from the ocean. The Border Patrol agents tell me that the sandbar that separates river from ocean had a channel dredged in it a few years earlier. It filled back in rather quickly. It is not so much an issue to be solved by engineering, but by water politics.

If the river is to reach the ocean, enough water has to be left in it to get there. That means we, as citizens of the watershed, need a society, on both sides of the river, that appreciates the river for the river's sake. I am reminded, standing there at the drift log border, why I, as a forester from the mountains of the American Southwest, am so committed to spending time teaching about the Rio Grande watershed. I am sure if people love their river, they will find a way to keep it alive. Perhaps someday this river will flow again, and its fresh waters will mix with the salt waters of the ocean.

Maybe there will even be a delta.

EXPLORING THE HUNDRED-ACRE WOOD
January 1999

As we enter the hundred-acre wood, a coyote hops out of the brush to greet us . . . or at least cross our path. Not being Navajo, I choose to take this as a good omen. This is Dan Shaw's first ambulatory exploration deep into the heart of this bosque landscape, and Dr. Cliff Crawford and I have been granted the privilege of sharing this event with him. Dan is a science teacher at Bosque School, whose future campus is adjacent to these woods. Dan's teaching is centered on bringing kids to the bosque to conduct scientific research.

A retired biology professor, Cliff Crawford's concept of retirement is to organize a large network of monitoring sites along a two-hundred-mile stretch of forest besides the Rio Grande. I, through the fortunate circumstance of being married to Dan, am a forester who has been pulled into this awesome adventure.

Like any bosque I've encountered, the landscape begs interpretation. Brush piles from projects of yore. Different ages of coyote willow. Lush stands of yerba mansa. Native grasses. Introduced grasses. Old cottonwood logs felled by the ghosts of beavers past. Charred stumps and logs that hint at fire histories.

We are excited with the opportunities for monitoring. There is a large, open field where the brush has been cleared. Windrows of the original trunks and limbs have been stacked in long piles stretching one or two hundred feet and reaching twenty to thirty feet wide. The landowner maintains the openness through annual mowing with a brush hog. We discuss establishing paired monitoring sites. Will the groundwater be more sensitive to the river level in the open site? How will insect diversity differ between the open areas and the thick bosque? We relish finding answers to our questions.

Standing on the riverbank, we talk numbers. What's the river running? Five hundred? . . . Eight hundred? . . . our units are cubic feet per second and you really need two thousand for a good float trip. How far down is the water level? Six feet? Seven feet? Eight feet? Too far down to have a natural flood.

Dr. Crawford utters his usual mantra, "I've never seen a bosque quite like this before."

Dan and I smile.

Dan says, "You say that every time you come to a new piece of bosque."

The bosque is diverse, and, as Cliff can attest, the more you visit and study the bosque, the more you see this diversity.

A WINTER'S DAY IN THE
PUEBLO OF SANTA ANA'S BOSQUE
December 1998

We are going out to the bosque again. It feels right. This is day two of our winter break Bosque Education Program at the Pueblo of Santa Ana. We plan to follow the format suggested in the *Bosque Education Guide*. Yesterday we took our discovery field trip. Today's plans are to stay at the Santa Ana Pueblo library and start the classroom portion of the project. Plans sometimes deserve to be ignored. Our only repeat customer from yesterday's field trip is Desirae, and the sixth grader has brought her nephew A.J., a bright kindergartener who is expecting to go to the woods. It is going to take word-of-mouth success to build a clientele for this optional program. My colleague Laura and I convince another teacher, Elaina, to join us. The five of us walk toward the river.

We cross the bridge that spans the drain, stopping to admire the refuse left by dining birds. Crayfish claws. Freshwater mussel shells. All treasures to be taped to the covers of our study guides.

As we crest over the levee and drop into the bosque, the memories flood over our small group. Elaina remembers when her grandfather brought her to the river to bathe when she was five months pregnant.

"A shower just doesn't cool you down when you are pregnant," she recalls. "Your body has so much heat. A bath in the river is what you need."

A.J. and Desirae recall a fishing trip with A.J.'s father.

"Remember, A.J.?" Desirae emphatically urges. "You were sitting right there." She points to a spot on the bank of the river.

"Yeah," A.J. recalls beaming proudly, "and my dad carried me across the river."

We spend time exploring the bosque, looking for animal tracks, interesting leaves, pretending we are trees. Always we are confronted by the trash we find. A couch here. A chair there. Cardboard boxes holding who knows what. A pile of cow bones. Some magazines.

"Look up there at the tire." I gaze up, and hanging about twenty feet in the air, suspended from the cottonwood branches, is a bicycle tire.

"How do you think it got there?" I ask, secretly wishing the answer had something to do with a grand flood, the kind of annual cleansing event under which this ecosystem evolved. I know with our systems of reservoirs and water management that this kind of event is not possible now, but I enjoy the thought for the moment.

"Oh," Desirae explained, "someone just threw it up there."

The evidence is all around us. This is a bosque that has been used. The land is littered with shotgun shells, bones and carcasses, and trash of all kinds. I watch A.J. notice and retrieve the granola bar wrapper that falls out of his pocket. There is hope for a more reverent approach to these woods.

As we leave the bosque, A.J. spots a huge bird and declares it is a bald eagle. From its dark silhouette, I wonder for a moment if the bird is just another crow. It turns into the sunlight and its white head and tail signal back to us. The six-year-old boy knows his birds. Goose bumps slide down my back as we watch the eagle float back up the river.

Postscript: This essay was written in December 1998. Since then several community clean-up events have been held in this bosque, and much of the debris noted here has been removed. The Pueblo of Santa Ana has also done extensive restoration in their bosque, removing exotic species, restoring hydrological functioning by lower banks, and establishing an outdoor classroom. Tribal member Laura Peña heads an excellent outreach program to inform tribal members on environmental issues, including bosque management.

5 THE BOSQUE EDUCATION GUIDE
January 2003

I'm sitting in a coffee shop with Tish Morris working on a teacher's guide about the bosque. As two of the four main editors, we have worked with approximately one hundred individuals who have contributed some vision or writing to the book. The six-hundred-plus-page final draft of the second edition is sitting in front of us in a three-ring notebook.

A group gets up from a booth across the room. I recognize a woman who has helped with the update, a task that has taken several years. I wave her over. She approaches the table and, gazing down at the *Bosque Education Guide*, she reverently whispers, "So this is it."

She surprises me when she leans over and kisses the cover, and yet it seems an appropriate gesture.

In the past ten years, the bosque has transformed from an ecosystem at risk to an ecosystem with hope. Although restoration of the bosque is far from complete, recent activities on the ground provide encouragement and enthusiasm. The decade has seen government at its best, working together among local, state, and federal entities to address declining riparian health. The Middle Rio Grande Bosque Initiative, an effort supported by Senator Pete Domenici and funded through the U.S. Fish and

Wildlife Service, has sponsored much of this work including the development of the *Bosque Education Guide*.

Interest in bosque restoration started in 1991 when Senator Domenici appointed a nine-citizen committee to examine problems facing the bosque. As part of their recommendations, in 1993 a team of federal and university biologists wrote a report about the past, present, and probable future of the cottonwood forest growing along the Rio Grande in central New Mexico.

The Middle Rio Grande Ecosystem: Bosque Biological Management Plan described a forest in immediate trouble. The cottonwood forest, long dependent on the cycle of annual floods and meandering river channels, was rapidly fading. Human alterations to the ecosystem had created conditions that were hostile to native plants and animals and promoted exotic species. An array of dams and ditches had changed the way water operated throughout the system. The cottonwood tree, which grows from seed on damp, bare soil, was no longer regenerating naturally in the river valley. Several exotic trees, such as salt cedar and Russian olive, were increasing throughout the existing forest.

The plan boldly outlined a strategy to recover essential elements of the ecosystem. Inspired by this technical document, and knowing increased community support would be essential for the plan's success, a group of us started brainstorming about how to teach others about the bosque. Within months, we had a grassroots team of educators and resource managers developing ideas for classroom teachers. The resulting *Bosque Education Guide* was first published in 1995. Since that time, over five hundred educators have attended training and used the guide to help students understand bosque issues more clearly.

Meanwhile, bosque managers were completing projects based on recommendations in the plan. Activities included pole plantings of cottonwood trees, removal of exotic species and excess fuels, lowering of riverbanks to allow overbank flooding, and managing the river flow to support elements of the ecosystem, including the endangered Rio Grande Silvery Minnow. Within five years, we realized the *Bosque Education Guide* needed a stronger emphasis on restoration. We had also been asked to expand the guide's age range, add more subjects and themes, and provide additional activities. In 2000, we started revamping the guide.

Now the light is blazing at the end of the tunnel. The second edition of the *Bosque Education Guide* will be ready by mid-February. We hope to distribute the first three hundred guides this spring (2003) to educators in New Mexico.

The guide is more comprehensive than we ever expected. It includes a correlation for grade levels from kindergarten through high school with state education standards for all subjects, over twenty-five completely new activities, many revamped and revised lesson plans, and expanded sections on bosque ecology, service learning, teacher essays, and appendices.

At the coffee shop, Tish and I discuss some final changes suggested by teachers who field-tested the final draft of the guide. After some congratulatory words, the reverent woman walks away, leaving us to complete our tasks. For a moment, I contemplate the important role this guide will have in shaping our future river system. I am honored to be a part of this process. I, too, want to lean over and kiss its cover.

THE BEMP INTERN PROGRAM
September 2002

On the first day of fall semester, students are gathered around a tan felt blanket lying on the classroom floor in the university biology building. One of four instructors, I have just asked them to take off their shoes and stick them under the blanket to create mountains to form a valley. Soon students are walking all over the blanket in stocking feet, laying out strips of blue cloth to represent a meandering and braided river. They place paper cottonwood trees, marshes, grassland and shrubs along the river to learn—in a hands-on way—how the changes experienced by the river today differ radically from the type of changes that the river has experienced over the last hundred thousand years.

This three-semester-hour class is unlike any other course these graduate and upper-division college students have ever taken. In the next sixteen weeks, these students will participate in a wide variety of activities. They will spend days in the field collecting long-term ecological data for an ongoing monitoring project, often assisting younger students from second grade through high school with the task.

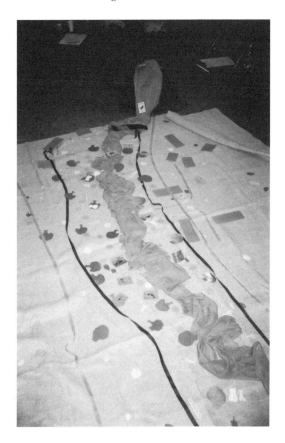

The river model is a flagship activity in the *Bosque Education Guide.* Courtesy of Tish Morris.

Through lectures, discussions, and guest speakers they will learn about the bosque—or riparian gallery forest—along the Middle Rio Grande. As interns visiting the younger students' classrooms, they will assist with data processing or other environmental education activities. As scholars, they will read and write about many scientific papers in biology and environmental education. In the field, they will take notes and be responsible for data sheets. Other program management projects might include grant writing, presentation making, equipment maintenance, or data collecting and processing.

By the end of the semester, the students will look back on the experience with a sense of awe and accomplishment. One or two might even enroll in the same class for the next semester because "there is just so much more to learn . . ."

This is the twelfth semester of the Bosque Ecosystem Monitoring Program (BEMP) Intern Course. Although dominated by biology students, the class is a favorite among education majors as well, especially from the environmental education program. Any student, or anybody, is welcome, and often the class attracts working professionals including natural resource managers, teachers, and environmental educators.

For the biology students, often the biggest challenge is learning to work with younger students. Yet, when they graduate and land their first jobs, these same biologists are better prepared for the "outreach" aspect of their new employment. On the other hand, education majors frequently state that their largest obstacle in class is their own fear of science. The hands-on approach and involved discussions of background information and data interpretation usually help these students overcome their fears. When these educators find themselves in classrooms after graduation, they are often looking for ways to involve their own students in real-science applications.

The BEMP intern class evolved out of a need to implement a quality assurance/quality control aspect to the newly established monitoring program. We needed ways to insure data was systematically and accurately collected and recorded. With a growing number of BEMP sites, we wanted more people instructed in the collection process to supervise the effort. Being a university-sponsored program, the obvious source of people-power was students. Quickly the class developed into a much richer experience for both the students and the program.

The first intern class had a more-or-less self-study format involving three students in the fall of 1998. By the spring of 1999, the class was meeting formally with nine students. One of the course assignments included a final report in which students were urged to make recommendations to improve the class or the program. From student input since then, an intense course curriculum has evolved. Field trips, lab exercises, writings on readings, and special projects have all been added to the class at the urging of past students. Over the years, course handouts have grown, and this semester students were greeted on the first day of class with an Intern Handbook that spanned over two hundred pages of instructions, readings, site maps, data results, and other program-related information.

The class textbook stands out as an oddity among the technical bulk of biology texts on the University Bookstore shelves. The trade paperback *The Geography of Childhood*, by Gary Paul Nabhan and Stephen Trimble, is a collection of the authors' essays on why children need to spend time in the outdoors. In the intern class, students discuss the value of having kids learn in outdoor settings.

The class has been held every semester, except for the summer of 2000 when severe fire conditions limited access and staff availability. The class size ranges from four to eighteen students, with an optimum size being around a dozen. Each season offers its own variations to the experience. Fall interns experience a strong emphasis on program instruction, as the younger students they work with are also new to the program.

Vegetation transects offer field opportunities for students to work alongside trained botanists. Spring students add cottonwood sexing to their experience, as interns are sent out to identify male and female trees based on catkin morphology. The course is somewhat compressed for the summer students, who get less hands-on experience working with younger children because many of the school groups are out of session.

The teaching team includes Professor Emeritus Cliff Crawford, environmental educator Mary Dwyer, data manager Kim Eichhorst, schoolteacher Dan Shaw, and myself, a forest ecologist. Course participants have both informal and formal access to a wide berth of ideas and perspectives on the bosque.

With nontraditional teaching styles and a commitment to fun learning, perhaps the course will inspire more university classes to be conducted in stocking feet.

6 ALAMEDA TAI CHI
October 1999

Of the current BEMP (Bosque Ecosystem Monitoring Program) study areas, the Alameda site is, perhaps, the most daunting to navigate. The towering cottonwood canopy shades a dense jungle of New Mexico olive. The smooth, not-quite-white-but-somewhat-green-barked multiple stems of this native shrub crowd together in an almost impenetrable thicket.

Yet penetrate it we do. Hordes of us. Mostly sixth graders from

Bosque School who monthly gather leaves and twigs that fall into the litterfall tubs, measure groundwater levels located in an array of five wells, and record and empty precipitation gauges.

Unlike the introduced shrub Russian olive, which in other places in the bosque crowd these cottonwood forests, New Mexico olive has no spines. Yet there is still a tendency for one crawling through this forest to be repeatedly snagged by olive branches.

Our western-philosophy tendency is to head to the woods with machetes and clear a trail to each of the ten rubber pig troughs that gather a sample of fallen leaves. However, we are trying to understand the *natural* forest, not one manicured with researcher paths. Since the majority of our researchers are twelve years old and have a penchant for breaking things, like limbs that are in their way, it takes a determined eastern philosophy to navigate these woods.

Remember Karate Kid? His mentor Miyagi taught him to avoid resistance. Move gracefully through the brush. Think of limbs as laser beams and if you can avoid passing through them, you will reach the prize. Practice Alameda Tai Chi. Flow through the woods. Be one with the forest. Amazingly, the snagging ceases.

As the names suggest, New Mexico olive is a native shrub while Russian olive is a foreigner, an exotic introduced for windbreaks and decoration. Along with salt cedar, another Asian-origin bush also known as tamarisk, Russian olive has escaped cultivation and formed dense shrub communities in the bosque. As a result, many people assume shrub-dominated cottonwood forests are human-induced ecological environments. The Alameda BEMP site, with its dense New Mexico olive understory, contradicts this logic.

These cottonwood stands with native shrubs are rare, and we suspect our monthly measurements of groundwater levels, when compared with grass-dominated sites, may help us understand why the variation occurs. The unique conditions in this stand have not stopped city bureaucrats from planning to annihilate this very spot. They want to build a diversion dam to siphon river water off for city golf courses. Hopefully the data we gather can support an argument to preserve this special piece of bosque.

Moving through the political brush field of water rights in a desert state may take the same Alameda Tai Chi mentality. Be one with the forest. Step cautiously around what is in your way. Go with the flow, but stand up for what matters.

We have our own Tai Chi master. Our own Miyagi-like leader. As director of the Bosque Ecosystem Monitoring Program, professor emeritus of the University of New Mexico Biology Department, author of the *Bosque Biological Management Plan*, and much acclaimed mentor of all things bosque, Dr. Clifford Crawford makes some phone calls. He inquires about the diversion dam plans. He explains the significance of our monitoring site. He tells us to be hopeful.

We return to the woods to collect data, moving gracefully.

Postscript: The diversion dam was moved upriver from its original plans to preserve this special piece of bosque.

7 PHILMONT FORESTRY
November 2002

In northern New Mexico, on the eastern flank of the south end of the Rocky Mountains, there is a paradise. It is a magical land of enchantment known as Philmont Boy Scout Ranch. Donated to the scouts by philanthropist Waite Phillips, the camp today encompasses 214 square miles and is accessed by hundreds of miles of hiking trails. I am proud to be one of the 760,000 people who, since 1938, have hiked and cherished the Philmont trails.

When I started my summer employment there in the late 1970s, I was a freshman forestry student. By my final summer in 1983, I had graduated and was a professional forester. In the years between, I had come to see this mountain paradise with exceedingly sharpened concern. Although fire suppression was a top priority, the forest was otherwise not being managed. In the absence of fire, dense stands of trees and massive amounts of downed logs were accumulating across the ranch. It was not a question of *if* Philmont would burn; it was only a question of *when* the tragedy would occur. I was frustrated that extensive forestry activities were not aligned with the existing recreation management directions that banned logging.

Fortunately, the ranch's management philosophy has changed.

Although recreation is still the primary objective, Philmont is now embracing the role of providing stewardship for healthy forests. Last month, the ranch hosted a grand opening of their Demonstration Forest. This forty-five-acre area displays several techniques of forest management. Created as an outdoor classroom, the area includes a covered gazebo and pit latrines. Trails roam through forests that have been logged by various methods and include riparian and meadow restoration projects. Along the trails, interpretive signs, which can be changed as the ecosystem responds, inform hikers about the treatments.

About sixty people gathered to explore the new "classroom." Participants included area teachers planning field trips for their students, neighboring ranchers interested in implementing forestry programs, and staff and members of many organizations that had joined forces to help the ranch construct the project. The New Mexico State Forestry Division provided the technical guidance; the wood for signs and structures were logged on site by Griego Lumber, milled at Quality Wood Products in Chama, and used in construction by staff at Philmont. The overriding sponsor of the project is the New Mexico Tree Farm Committee, an organization of private landowners who are committed to managing their forests and promoting forestry.

The site location is spectacular from both an aesthetic as well as a practical standpoint. Adjacent to the postcard-perfect landmarks of Cathedral Rock and Cimarroncito Reservoir, the central location is visited by twelve thousand scouts each year hiking to base camp along the Tooth-of-Time Ridge. Vehicles, including school buses, can easily access the site as well. Less obvious, but as important, the project occurs in the watershed that provides the majority of water for the town of Cimarron.

Since the mid-1990s, Philmont has been focusing their forestry activities in this watershed and the adjacent watershed that serves the summer population of over twenty thousand visitors. Considering the ranch's vast forests, these watersheds are top priority because erosion resulting from catastrophic wildfires can be devastating to a community water system. The hope is that by actively managing forests, lighter fuel conditions will mean less intense fires and watersheds that can recover faster when burned.

Fuel conditions are only part of the fire equation, as the ranch experienced this year. Early in the summer several lightning strikes ignited the

Ponil Complex, which burned over 92,000 acres—28,000 acres located on the Boy Scout camp. Even in areas where the ranch had thinned or logged, fires raged through in an intense firestorm. Extremely dry and windy weather conditions drove the blaze. Afterward, the ranch faced serious issues of having miles of blackened canyons and acres of charred slopes.

Following the tour of the Demonstration Forest, a small group of us headed north to examine some of the projects Philmont has undertaken to mitigate erosion and salvage some of the damaged timber. Standing on the moonscape hillsides of blackened earth amid charred tree skeletons, I wanted to cry.

As a forester, I see more than my fair share of the impact caused by catastrophic fires, results of our nationwide fire suppression legacy. Although I never master the emotional response these tragedies evoke, this time it felt worse. This fire burned in the Philmont paradise of my youth. My youthful predictions of destruction had come to pass. Yet now I was incredibly grateful the ranch was taking action to hopefully mitigate the impact of future fires.

CONTEMPLATING CLOSURES
June 2002

The publicly owned, national forest land is closed, and like most avid outdoors enthusiasts, I do not like it. I admit that the forest is "tinderbox" dry. Walking through an aspen grove last month I felt like I was stomping through a bowl of cornflakes. Aspen leaves—which typically in late spring are matted together in a moist floor pad formed under heavy snowpack—were individually curled and brittle. Streams that should have been swollen were mere trickles. No matter what altitude I walked around in, evidence of drought was everywhere. When I reached a vantage point, I spotted smoke from a wildfire across the valley. I knew it was only a matter of time before officials would be limiting access to our public lands.

Though I understand the arguments in favor of forest closures, I view the decisions as knee-jerk reactions. I am reminded of similar policies made with the same shortsighted management mentality that created the heavy fuel conditions now contributing to these closures. A hundred years ago, forestry officials declared war on fire and vowed to keep it out the woods. Today's catastrophic fires are strongly linked to that lack of insight. Now, forestry officials have vowed to keep people out of the woods. I think this is another policy that also shows a lack of insight.

If closures are absolutely necessary to prevent catastrophic fires from human causes, we might worry that the friction of our rubber-sole running shoe on the forest trail could spark a disastrous outcome. Yet, we each know the rule is not intended for us, but for the other guy—that gruesome, stupid other guy who would think nothing of lighting up a cigarette, a candle, or a campfire in these desperately dry conditions.

Just like in medieval times, the King's Forest is off limits to the common people. There is something that seems un-American about this reality. Some scientists are now predicting that the next twenty-five years are likely to be very dry. If these predictions prove true, and the government continues reacting in this manner, people are going to have limited access to the public forest for the next quarter century. I believe our founding fathers would have serious reservations with this old-world, edict-posting policy.

I agree the current wildfire-danger situation calls for desperate measures, but keeping people out of the forest seems as short-sighted as preventing the natural role of fire in the first place. Instead of trusting our citizens with the knowledge to behave appropriately in response to environmental conditions, we choose to further isolate our mostly urban-based population from understanding the land. Rather than exclude people from the forests and wildlands, this is the time to be linking people to these environments. We need to educate our populace on the dangers of dry conditions. Our children need to learn to associate walking through a corn-flake aspen stand with being very careful with ignition sources. We need a society that truly loves the forests, is deeply connected to the ecosystem, and will fight to protect our resources. We need these people to be out there now, patrolling the woods for possible offenders.

For that "other guy," the one who just won't get the message any other way, we need to increase the consequences for abusive behavior. Offer a thousand-dollar reward for anyone who turns in a smoker who has had the audacity to light up outdoors, or the camper who thinks she has to use a candle to keep mosquitoes at bay, or the kids who have the nerve to start a bonfire. Fine the offenders to cover these rewards and, if the infraction results in an actual wildfire, fine them for the suppression costs as well. Make it known that starting a fire through ignorant behavior will have severe ramifications.

Already the government is using increased resources to communicate closure notices and enforce the forest lockout. We could use this same amount of increased energy to educate the public on proper behavior in fire-prone areas.

In general, I believe in Americans. We have a tradition of being intelligent, self-proficient, and resourceful. If given the right information and respect, our people will be careful and refrain from starting fires in these dry conditions. Increased fire danger should challenge our resource agencies to increase environmental education efforts rather than limit our access to public lands.

9 LESSONS IN FALL FOLIAGE
October 2002

The rivers and streams are ablaze with golden ribbons of cottonwood; high mountains are hosting final renditions of aspen leaf fall. At mid-elevations oaks are painting the hillsides burnt orange. Clematis and Virginia creeper vines are adding a touch of red, highlighted by the bright yellow blossoms of rabbitbrush. The cool fall breeze offers a brisk chill to the pinyon smoke–filled evening. Sitting on my back deck, I am awed by lessons—both practical and philosophical—that fall foliage has offered me this week.

It started with a conversation with my kids' high school science teacher.

"I just can't seem to get students excited about basic things, like photosynthesis," she complained.

I suggested she takes them outdoors.

The next day I am with a group of elementary students in a cottonwood bosque. We stand by a large tree with branches drooping down toward the ground. Some limbs host golden leaves, others support green leaves. I challenge the students to determine if the leaves have a temperature difference. Although they hypothesize the gold leaves will be

Looking at aspen from the ground up. Courtesy of David Lewis.

cooler (less activity?), they are surprised to find the green leaves are significantly colder.

As we brainstorm explanations, we talk about photosynthesis. We discuss the well-publicized exchange of gases—carbon dioxide for oxygen—that give trees such good publicity. Then I tell them that another product is water, and as this water evaporates from the leaf, it cools the leaf surface. Since the chlorophyll in the yellow leaves is gone, there is no more photosynthesis taking place, so no evaporative cooling. These kids are now psyched about photosynthesis . . . I hope their enthusiasm will carry through to high school.

A few days later my mother and I take a pilgrimage to lay in an aspen grove. The aspen have turned late this year, allowing my once-resident-but-now-transplanted-in-Kansas visiting matriarch to pursue a pastime that defined my childhood autumns and has become my own annual personal celebration. As we gaze up through the fluttering golden coin-like leaves to the deep blue sky, my mom starts to share her philosophy of life. I have come to expect this; it is part of the ritual.

"This is my last time to lay in an aspen grove," the nearly seventy-year-old woman croons. I challenge her. I remind her of our long-lived ancestors who push ninety and one hundred on a regular basis.

She assures me this is more about arthritis than anticipating her demise. "It's just uncomfortable to lie on the ground and I don't look forward to having to get up."

She explains that each leaf works hard all through the summer, making food for the tree, never taking a day off, being wholly engrossed in its community. As it reaches old age it becomes outstandingly gorgeous, shimmering in its radiance with all of the leaves it has worked beside all summer long. Then one day it just lets go, and it is all alone, sliding through the sky, slipping through the canopy, dipping to the ground, dancing its way to a new existence.

My own thoughts are focused on cycles, not endings. The rich, musky forest floor is one smell that joins many others in my olfactory celebration of fall. Roasting green chile, dehydrating apple slices, pinyon smoke–filled evenings sitting on my back deck. My lesson in the aspen grove is to take the time to appreciate autumn, to surrender an afternoon each year to catching the golden coins floating through the sky, and to not let the pressures of life's daily struggles distract me from celebrating these cycles.

FIELD GUIDE TO THE SANDIA MOUNTAINS
March 2005

After years of meetings, drafts, field trips, more drafts, emails, phone calls, next drafts, hopes, dreams, heated discussions, final drafts, late-night visits to convince an artistic friend to draw a grass one more time, and incredible cooperation among a diverse team of passionate naturalists, we have a book.

The *Field Guide to the Sandia Mountains* is a labor of love for the mountain range that shadows Albuquerque, New Mexico. Written by twenty-two authors and supported by dozens more, this volume is a book of passions, a profession of infatuations, and an intended inspiration for mountain visitors, both uninitiated tourists and seasoned residents.

The field guide touches on most aspects of the natural world. Writers describe wildflowers, trees, grasses, lichens, birds, insects, butterflies, mammals, reptiles, weather, geology, fire ecology, cultural sites, and more. Each section is written by a person who is passionate for his or her field. Often a section, such as the one on wildflowers, is penned by a writing team.

The wildflower team offers a good example of the energy that went into this book. The unofficial team leader is eighty-three-year-old Pearl Burns, who was recently recognized for thirty years of volunteer service leading wildflower hikes in the Sandias. Pearl is joined by Tom Ferguson, a retired physicist and avid plant fan who has developed his own method of plant identification. Jeannette Buffett rounds out the writing group. Although Jeannette is a self-described amateur, she insures that each sentence and phrase the group writes appeals to the novice. Meeting weekly for nearly a year, the team hammered out descriptions of over one hundred plant species.

The affection the writers hold for their particular field makes the elements come alive. Art Arenholz's birds fly off the colorful pages. Rich Anderson's reptiles slither in and out of the spiral binding. Paul Polechla Jr.'s mammals howl and squeak with delight. Ernest Giese's and David Lightfoot's butterflies, insects, spiders, and other crawly things creep camouflaged against the pastel cover depicting watermelon mountains at sunset.

The field guide offers more than names. Robert Julyan sets the stage with an introduction to Sandia Mountain ecology, and other writers go deeper with discussions of weather, fire, and geology. The human influence is also recognized, including information on place names, hiking and skiing trails, and cultural resources.

The Friends of the Sandia Mountains sponsored the book. A docent group dedicated to supporting the work of the Cibola National Forest's Sandia Ranger District, the Friends identified the need for an area-specific field guide. Since I had coauthored a similar field guide for Philmont Scout Ranch many years earlier, they invited me to an evening meeting to pick my brain on how to get such a book written. I suggested they write it themselves, and offered to serve as editor. When I accepted a job in Arizona, Robert Julyan joined the project as a coeditor. Gerry Sussman provided project coordination throughout.

The book is sturdy and small enough to be tucked in a daypack. It also makes a beautiful presence on a coffee table. The writers, photographers, artists, reviewers, sponsors, and others who brought forth this book have a shared vision. As more people develop their knowledge, they will have increased respect for the mountains that shadow New Mexico's largest metropolitan area.

STRIVING TO FOLLOW IN THE FOOTSTEPS OF CARSON AND BRUCHAC
June 2002

Wooo-whaa-wooo. Heart song. The eerie notes draw our attention to the quiet man centered in front of the fireplace.

Wooo-whaa-wooo. Flute song. The hand-carved wooden flute greets us with its perfect tone.

Wooo-whaa-wooo. Word song. Sacred thoughts swirl in a language that transcends the spoken word.

First there is the voice of the flute. Seductive. Wise. A voice that speaks in the language of canyon wrens and canyon walls. Then he speaks, and before he has uttered the second line of his welcoming poem, my heart is crying "Old Friend!"

This recognition of friendship is one-sided. He is the storyteller. I am the listener. He is the presenter. I am the audience.

For many, many years, Joseph Bruchac has been telling stories, writing books, and traveling thousands of miles each year to share, through his Abenaki heritage, his message of caring for the earth. Tonight he is sharing his craft with a roomful of writers.

The workshop, perched on the edge of the Maine Coast, is held in honor of Rachel Carson, another gifted storyteller who dedicated her life to sharing a message of caring for the earth. Like the complex food webs Carson wrote about, the writers at the workshop are connected through the common passions of environment and words.

Bruchac has joined us to remind us that we are telling stories that are larger than ourselves. In an hour and a half he does an elegant job of showing us, by example, that one can impart powerful guidance through the telling of stories.

We are enthralled.

After the talk, I stand in a long line to meet the speaker—this friend who does not even know my name. When it is my turn to exchange a handshake and a few words, I tell him of the incredible influence he has had on me, as a mother, and on my children.

I tell him that I had forgotten over the years the origin of our inspiration to tell stories. Storytelling has become such a large part of our family life. I said that when my children were in trouble—and they knew it—they would defensively plead "tell me a story," and I would usually do just that. It was only when he began to speak this evening that I remembered who had given me the advice to discipline my children through tales.

I tell him that Gluscabi tales were winter bedtime story fodder for many years. I tell him we told other stories from our own family events, our own traditions, our own imaginations, and our own research.

I thank him for sparking such rich experiences for our family. My children, who are now almost fifteen, have the gift of oral tradition. I am grateful to have a chance to personally thank him for that gift.

There is a sparkle in his eye, as if the dim light in the room had gathered in a forming tear, or perhaps the tear is in my own eye.

I walk out into the drizzly Maine night and go down to the water's edge. As the water laps the rocky shore, I think about connections. Despite the huge globe we saw today in the Delorme Map Store south of Freeport, the world is really a small place. I had watched this three-story-high replica of the earth slowly revolve within the glass foyer of the store, and thought of how each inch of the structure represented sixteen actual miles—getting lost in the enormity of the concept. Yet tonight I grasp the insight that one person, one teller of stories, can make a significant impact in this world.

Rachel Carson had done that forty years ago when she published *Silent Spring*. Twelve years ago, Joseph Bruchac had touched my life making me a better mother, which in turn made my children better people. Joseph Bruchac did not know he had touched *my* life. Perhaps he must have known about me indirectly. Why else would a person dedicate his life to telling stories and teaching others to tell stories, if he did not have a fervent belief that he was making the world a better place?

Unless it is just because the stories want to be told.

I contemplate the passion of writing, especially writing about the outdoors, and the passion of people who write about the outdoors. There is a rich tradition of these writers, from Thoreau to Abbey, Carson to Williams, Emerson to Meloy, Muir to Bruchac. All of these writers have made a lasting impact on the way others think about and care for the earth.

Like most aspiring writers, I dream that someday, someone will come up to me and say that my words have made their lives more full and the earth a better place. I hope on that day, I will have the wisdom to know that the credit is not mine, but belongs to the story. A story that insisted on being told. A story that is larger than myself.

Thump-thump, thump-thump, thump-thump. Heart beat. Bruchac reminds us this is the first sound we heard before we had even breathed our first breath.

Thump-thump, thump-thump, thump-thump. Drum beat. We are reminded of our origins and our connections.

Thump-thump, thump-thump, thump-thump. Word beat. The stories flow and each of us is but a measure in the perpetual song of life.

CHAPTER FIVE

Recreation

Run the rivers, breathe deep of that yet sweet and lucid
air, sit quietly for a while and contemplate the precious
stillness, that lovely, mysterious and awesome space.

—Edward Abbey

MY FATHER TAUGHT ME A SIMPLE MANTRA: WORK HARD, PLAY HARD.
With my love of the outdoors, understandably my play time is spent outside,
too—hiking trails, running rivers, climbing mountains, collecting plants,
and so forth. Although most of the essays in this book were originally published as monthly columns, the essays in this chapter also originated from
other sources including speeches and magazine articles. Whether in travel
or play, I remain a forester, and that influences my writing.

As a child I spent days identifying wildflowers with my mother or hunting with my father. Through scouting (both Girl Scouts and Boy Scouts)
I camped, backpacked, and climbed rocks. When I was an adolescent,
climbing Wheeler Peak in northern New Mexico, my mother explained
that there was, at least in theory, a ridge that separated the watersheds of
the Atlantic and Pacific oceans. It was called the Continental Divide.

Seven years later I embarked on a hike with the dream of travers-
ing the length of the Continental Divide through the United States.
Starting in March of 1981 in the "bootheel" of New Mexico, I was flat
on my back near Yellowstone National Park in Wyoming by August. I
had contracted a water parasite called Giardia. In five months I walked
through New Mexico, Colorado, and most of Wyoming . . . around two

Mary with the twins at the Rio Grande Zoo. Courtesy of Dan Shaw.

thousand miles. During those months I developed a serious arthritis issue, which resulted in one foot swelling to twice the size of the other. The combination of these medical conditions forced me to quit the hike about a thousand miles short of my goal. The desire to "go back and finish" is constant. "Rocky Canyon Trail Building" and "Tomorrow's Adventurers" come from that serious hiker.

For three summers during and after college, I worked at Philmont Scout Ranch in northern New Mexico. "Opportunity, Privilege, and Respect" started as a speech delivered at the ranch twenty years after my tenure there. The inspirational message was originally presented to the first female Roving Outdoor Conservation School crew; however, this wisdom applies to all of us who are given the opportunity to love and enjoy this land.

When work consumes me, it is the gentle words of Edward Abbey that remind me to get out and nurture my soul. "Pico de Orizaba" is a tale from the mid-1980s, when my natural resource consulting firm,

Seldom Seen Expeditions Inc., really did lead expeditions. Another travel tale is "Tree Spirits in Thailand." The articles on the Mount Taylor Quadrathlon and whitewater river rescue capture a bit of adventure.

At the end of the day, at the end of the workweek, at the end of a fire assignment, at the end of a job, I try to take a deep, relaxing breath and recharge my passion for the outdoors. As a final chapter in this volume that peeks into one forester's world, here is the opportunity to play.

PICO DE ORIZABA: 1985–1986
SELDOM SEEN EXPEDITION
December 24, 1985

Tana's phone call last night was discouraging. I had asked my Las Cruces–based friend to buy train tickets for the mountain-climbing expedition my husband and I were leading to Pico de Orizaba (Citalcetpetl), Mexico's highest mountain, on the day after Christmas.

"Oh, Mary," she sighed, "are you really sure you want to ride the train? It's so dirty there, and the people trample each other like cattle loading on a cattle car."

On our last expedition two years ago to climb Popocatepetl, we had flown into Mexico City. The train was a new idea. I wasn't sure, but less than a week from departure of our next expedition, there was little choice.

Tana had not gotten tickets. She was told there is one man with the railroad who speaks English. His name is Señor Barraza, and although she was not able to find him, he may be able to help.

"We've got eight other climbers counting on this trip," my husband moaned.

"We still have two days before departure time." I then offered to try my luck.

Which is why I am standing in Juárez on the day before Christmas. Last night I had called family friends in El Paso, and the Pineda family said they would be glad to help me out.

Phillip Pineda had picked me up at the airport. He had just flown in the night before. Phillip lives in California and was home for the holidays.

Four years earlier Phillip and I had spent fifteen days together hiking on the Continental Divide. He was a high school student on spring break, and I was a college student on a long-distance journey to see if I could walk across the backbone of our country. During the weeks together we had become fast friends, and despite the lack of political correctness, I had taken to fondly calling him "My Chicano Boy."

Today I am noticeably nervous about getting the tickets.

"No problem," my Chicano Boy tells me, "I've got it under control."

"How's your Spanish?" I ask.

"Good as it's ever been."

I groan. For a kid with heavy Mexican ancestry, Phil's Spanish is sketchy. I remember four years ago being lost with Phillip in a Navajo farmer's field. The man spoke no English, and little Spanish. Phillip managed to secure some drinking *agua*, but we were even more lost by the time he finished with the directions. Maybe it's my imagination, but I think he said "no problem" then, too.

Phillip drives me to the Juárez train station. There is something about crossing the border that brings the Mexican out in Phil. Within moments of crossing the border, Phil has done three illegal U-turns and dashed through several precarious intersections. Both his parents assured me that Phil knows how to drive in Mexico, and, from the way the other drivers are behaving, I don't doubt it. Fortunately the train station is only twelve blocks from the border.

The station is bustling with people. We join the line at the first-class window. The hours are posted on the closed window, and we see we have arrived in time. "In fact they should be open now," I point out.

Phillip laughs. "That sign means nothing. This is Mexico. The window will open whenever the man who opens it feels like it. That might be today or maybe tomorrow."

Standing there I notice a handwritten sign in Spanish that says all reserve tickets are sold out until January 12. Tickets will be sold for the day of purchase only. Phillip tells me I am wasting my time.

We stand in the motionless line for two hours. When the window finally opens, the clerk refuses to help me. He does not speak English and has no patience for my broken Spanish. He points me to the dark office of Sr. Barraza. We find Sr. Barraza in the luggage area. Barraza probably speaks English but seems to enjoy watching me suffer with my Spanish. He assures me we will be able to get tickets at one p.m. on the twenty-sixth.

Phil and I head back to America.

2 *December 26, 1985*

On the road in the dark early morning, three friends manage to sleep while Dan and I navigate the heavily loaded Volkswagen van to El Paso.

At the Pinedas' house, we drag my Chicano Boy out of bed. His mother and sister drive Phillip, my friend Jim, and I to the border. We exchange lots of U.S. dollars for lots more pesos at a change house.

We take a taxi to the estación de ferrocarril. The window is open and I show Sr. Barraza stick figures I have drawn to help me talk to the ticket seller. Today Sr. Barraza's English is excellent. Within fifteen minutes of arriving we have the tickets. Today there are no crowds. The train station even seems cleaner. I wonder if Jim really believes my horror stories of just two days ago.

Back in the United States, we gather our fellow climbers. Tumbling out of the Volkswagen van at the border, I explain that our train leaves in forty-five minutes.

"Get your gear, get across the border, and get a taxi to the train station," I instruct in my best trip leader voice. Although we are a group of friends going climbing in Mexico, this trip is officially sponsored by Seldom Seen Expeditions, Inc., the business my husband and I have recently formed. If our first clients are good friends, we can work out the kinks in our operation before we branch out to leading strangers.

Heading across the bridge, we are each carrying a large backpack and holding assorted daypacks, water jugs, and grocery bags in our arms.

At the train station, there is a moment of confusion. The fourth car on the train contains livestock instead of sleeping berths. I ask a helpful porter for directions to our assigned Carro Quatro, and he points us to the wrong car. Threading our way through the tight aisles, intimidating any passengers coming the opposite way with our large packs, eventually we locate our "camarins" or sleeping berths.

Each room is a cleverly compacted apartment. The sink folds out from the wall. The commode is under a padded stool. The couch is more of a love seat, comfortable for two really good friends. The bed comes out of the wall. Storage space is limited, requiring creative ways to live with large packs.

The train rolls out about forty minutes past its scheduled departure. The worst news on board is that beer is seventy-five cents a can.

$\big)$ *December 27, 1985*

During the night the train rolls through Chihuahua. The countryside is arid, overgrazed high chaparral on flat plains bordered by low mountain ranges. We see vultures, hawks, prickly pear, Joshua trees, and lots and lots of creosote.

Although the train passes along this track daily, villagers in each town watch us pass. Young children run behind the slow-moving beast to beg for money from tourists standing on the deck. Our pockets are emptied of loose change.

In the afternoon, the ride gets monotonous. While several of our party take naps, Mike and Roland are restless. When the train stops in Zacatecas, they decide to buy cheaper beer. Dan and I are on the platform waiting for them when the porter asks us to board. There is no sign of Mike or Roland. The train starts moving.

Once in motion, we decide the boys must have been left in Zacatecas. Our only concerns are whether they have enough money to get to Mexico City and if we will be able to handle the extra gear on the way to the hotel.

Five miles from the station, the train stops again. We are still laughing about losing the pair and making plans to eat their dinner, when Mike comes running alongside the train and jumps for the rear door. Roland is seconds behind him.

Apparently when they heard the whistle, they leapt on the front of the train as it started moving. The second-class section they were in was bolted off from our first-class section so they were unable to get back to their seats without getting off and on.

The terrain changes to rolling hills and ravines. Consequently, the track takes many long curves to struggle up and down the inclines. As the train rumbles along the track, I find myself fantasizing about having a horse, pack saddle full of hard biscuits and jerky, and time to explore the inspiring countryside.

Towns become more frequent and larger. In general, the houses we have seen have been in shambles, but as Dan points out, the poorest people in the United States also live along the railroad tracks.

4 *December 28, 1985*

On the train yesterday, we met two children, Paco, four, and Miguel, two. This morning I met their mother. Laura speaks some English and with my little Spanish we have a good conversation. Her husband died last year, and then, last September, her home in Mexico City was destroyed in the terromuerte (earthquake). She and the boys have been living in Juárez the past two months.

We arrive in the Estación del Ferrocarril de Ciudad de México in the morning and take taxis to Hotel Metropol. There we catch up with the final members of our party, a total of ten climbers.

The food is different than Mexican food in New Mexico. We carefully avoid lettuce or unpeeled vegetables, and take Pepto-Bismol before and after each meal. We are not just tourists, but mountain climbers with a mission. Until we have bagged our peak, we do not want risk being victims of Montezuma's Revenge.

Walking near the hotel, a government information officer tells us about the earthquake a few months earlier. Two years ago on our last visit, the square block where we are standing had been the site of the Regents Hotel, a department store, and several other buildings. Now it is a square block of red pebbles.

5 *December 29, 1985*

In the morning, we take taxis to the eastbound bus station. Miraculously all ten of us find ourselves on the same bus to Puebla within fifteen minutes of arriving.

The time saved with the quick exit from Mexico City is more than made up for with a long delay in Puebla. Young men walk around the bus station yelling, "Yankees go home." Like American bus stations, the place is characterized by filthy bathrooms, rude people, and everyone looking defensive and harried.

A few blocks northeast of the bus station we stop at a supermarket. Along with crackers, cheese, soup, cookies, sardines, and tuna, we find juice boxes: jugo de naranja, jugo de piña, jugo de uva, and jugo de manzana. Once we have groceries, we walk twelve blocks to the next bus station looking for the bus to Tlachichuca.

It is market day in Puebla. The streets we are winding through are colorful and noisy. At the second bus station, we are directed to a third. Finally, all ten of us and our gear are on the same bus heading toward the mountain.

Roland, standing in the aisle of the crowded bus, decides to open a can of beer he has carried through town. He pops the top and foam spews all over the woman sitting near him. He tries to say "I'm sorry" using the Spanish phrase "lo siento" to conjugate the verb *sentir*. She misunderstands him and thinks he is asking for a seat (the verb *sentar*) and makes her son stand up so Roland can sit.

The bus stops often as we slowly inch toward the mountain. We are surprised at our first glimpse of Pico de Orizaba. The massive peak looms on the landscape.

In Tlachichuca, we get off in front of Antigua Flor. The store owner, Sr. Reyes, is renowned for providing climbers a place to stay and a ride to the climbing hut on the side of Orizaba where most expeditions commence. We are assigned a room off the main kitchen area where we spread out our sleeping bags.

Two brothers staying with the Reyes have grim and intimidating news. The preceding day, they had been preparing for their own ascent when word came down that two Austrian climbers had fallen on the glacier. The first one slid over a thousand feet and died on impact at the bottom of the ice field; the second one was still alive. First they had been told that there were plenty of people with the injured man. When they began to doubt this, they went up with supplies and discovered only one other Austrian with him. By midnight they had organized a rescue party to transport the injured man. With the full moon, visibility was good.

The man died on the way down.

Having just returned from the mountain a few hours before our arrival, the brothers were now heading for Yucatán.

The body of the Austrian climber is in a room next to ours.

We deposit our gear and go for a walk in the dusky evening. Sunset on Orizaba is beautiful. The mountain herself—although intimidating—is emitting a siren call to our climbing spirits.

December 30, 1985

The other body arrived last night, along with the other Austrians. We wait most of the morning for our ride to Piedra Grande.

I feel ill. Perhaps it is a combination of different food, travel blues, and fear of the mountain. I try to take a nap, but keep coughing and cannot sleep.

We are not the only climbers waiting today. The Austrian climbing team is waiting for arrangements with their embassy for transportation home. Several of them successfully climbed all three volcanoes (Orizaba, Popocatepetl, and Ixtacihuatl), but now this seems insignificant next to the death of their friends. They are worried about their families.

Karl speaks the best English of the group. He talks about the accidents. He witnessed both. He and the climber who died during the rescue have been best friends since childhood. They often climbed together in the Alps. Karl does not want to discourage anyone from climbing, but he pleads for everyone to be careful.

We head up the mountain. The Piedra Grande climbing camp at the end of the road is at 14,000 feet. There are two huts. The newer of the two is a large building with three stories of sleeping berths. It can hold approximately sixty climbers. The second hut only has the capacity for six to eight people.

Once at the hut, I admit I am sick. Dan takes my temperature—102.5. He wants me to go back with the drivers. I know if I go back now, I have no chance to climb. If I stay, perhaps this thing will pass. As the night progresses, I wish I could die.

December 31, 1985

Aspirin, Nyquil, water, and sleep seem to have worked miracles. I wake up feeling great. The thermometer confirms that my temperature is normal. Today we plan to go to the glacier and practice self-arrest techniques with our ice axes. This will also help us acclimate to the altitude. I am weak and my cough sounds bad, but I head out anyway.

At the base of the glacier, Roland and Mike are talking with two men from San Diego who attempted the peak this morning. They climbed to about 17,500 feet. At this point they felt the ice was too slick.

The Forester's Log

Our party straps on our crampons. Here, lower on the glacier, the conditions are great. It is hard to believe it is so desperately icy farther up. Mike, our most experienced climber, starts the "Mike Zinsley International School of Climbing."

We practice recovering from four basic positions one might find oneself in while sliding down a mountain: head first or feet first and either on one's back or front. Mike instructs how to maneuver from each of these positions to dig the pick of the ice ax into the slope. We set up a belay system so we can practice the techniques after building up momentum.

I leave the climbing school ahead of the others. This is the highest I will get on Orizaba this year. My temperature increases to 103 degrees by the time I reach the huts. In addition to being sick, I am depressed about missing the climb. I huddle in my sleeping bag while everyone else prepares for the pre-sunrise departure.

January 1, 1986

At three thirty an alarm goes off. Two more of our party opt out of the climb. The expedition heads out forty minutes later. Around nine thirty a.m. I wander down to the large hut. Several binoculars are focused on my friends. Even with magnification they are only dots on the glacier.

Along the trail and here around Piedra Grande are many memorial crosses. They are inscribed with a name or names of those who have died on this mountain. There are usually dates. January 7, 1962. November 20, 1959. 1974. I wonder how many lives 1986 will claim? I vaguely wonder why people climb in the first place when it is clearly dangerous, but I am more amazed at how sorry I am that I am not climbing today.

We watch the progress of our party; five climbers are moving up. Two people are coming down. The main party has veered to the right as we had planned. The "experts" at the hut are arguing over the wisdom of such a move. I glare at them. The armchair climbers voicing their opinions have already stated that they are not climbing the mountain. They are claiming altitude sickness or that it just doesn't feel right.

Climbing Mexican volcanoes has become so popular that many people who lack previous mountaineering experience are coming to climb these mountains. They have an impression that the mountains are easy climbs. Brandishing ice axes with price tags still hanging from them, they are learning basic knots at the base of the mountain.

I scramble back up to the peaceful solitude of the upper hut. As I am falling asleep, nine Mexican youths crowd into the building. They know ten words of English among them. By the end of our visit, they have learned at least twenty more.

My new friends are from the village down in the forest. They are interested in mountain climbing. They do not climb themselves, but they are proud of their mountain. They say Orizaba is the highest mountain in the world. I teach a short, graphic course in geography, drawing maps of Nepal and Mount Everest. They prefer the idea that Orizaba is the highest mountain in Mexico, rather than the third highest peak in North America.

Some climbers bring me a letter from Susie and Dan. Susie was suffering altitude sickness and hypothermia on the glacier. They made it to about 16,500 feet. Dan offered to help her back down. They are doing fine, but moving slow.

Meanwhile, the rest of our party nears the summit.

When Dan and Susie reach camp, Susie immediately goes to sleep. Dan says he feels like throwing up. If they are in such poor shape, I worry about the other team members.

Jim is the first one down. He tells of success. Mike, Charlie, and Roland reached the summit. Roland was coughing blood. Jim reached the rim, and Hal turned around within three hundred feet of the rim. Roland is the last to arrive at the jeep.

On the way into Tlachichuca, our driver, Luis Reyes, tells about their New Year's Eve celebration.

"Are there any traditional foods Mexicans eat at New Years?" Susie asks.

"We eat twelve grapes," he replies, "one for each month of the year."

Luis confides that he understands the need to climb. He has tried to climb Citalcetpetl several times. He has only made it partway up. Each time he returns from a climb, he says never again. Sure enough, he tries again the next year.

When we arrive in Tlachichuca, there are many stories.

Apparently Roland pooped on the glacier.

"Apparently hell!" says Jim.

"Roland pooped at 18,300 feet," Mike, always cognoscente of climbing feats, brags. Jim adds that he was happy to have his rope dragged through it. Roland reports it was a refreshing experience. The belay for this celebrated crap took at least fifteen minutes to set up, and the crap itself lasted a "long time."

January 2, 1986

We are heading to the beach today. It is tough work: riding in packed buses, lugging heavy packs, and being sick. We switch buses twice between Tlachichuca to Veracruz. When we started this trip, I was doing much of our group conversing to obtain tickets, taxis, etc. Now I have lost my voice and have been relieved of these duties.

We stay at the Mocamba Hotel. The resort is well beyond our budgets, but being privileged Americans, we produce little plastic cards from our wallets. We find ourselves in rooms opening right to the poolside. We learn later these are the most expensive rooms in the place.

Since I grew up in landlocked states, this is my first time swimming in an ocean. My East Coast–raised husband teaches me to bodysurf.

January 3, 1986

The next morning on the beach, I buy white cotton-gauze dresses. Shedding the climber wardrobe, I don tourist attire. The guys in our party buy exotic shorts depicting tropical scenes. The shorts have trouble staying on in the ocean. Regardless, we have chicken fights, dunking games, and other water fun. We drink milk from coconuts. We sit poolside, drink cerveza, bask in the sun, and broil.

That evening we stroll into Veracruz. On the square we are entertained by a mime. He starts walking behind Dan, and soon he has drawn a crowd. He forms a band with Susie as the lead singer, and Mike and Charlie for supports. Eventually we pay him and wander on.

Several women in beautiful rainbow dresses are on a nearby stage. We walk around the block and come across a sea of young people dancing to the rhythm of a large drum band. We stand near the drums, adrenalin flowing, our hearts keeping time to the African-influenced rhythm.

January 5, 1986

The air is thick in Veracruz. Due to heavy gravity, we accomplish little. Our group has started to disperse, each climber making different travel arrangements to head back to the states.

Our aspirations to go to the beach are spoiled by the weather. We lie around the motel room, cursing the rain. We head for the bus station after noon, and arrive in Mexico City around eleven p.m. By midnight we are roaming around Alameda Square, taking in the last of the Epiphany Eve festivities.

January 6, 1986

After breakfast, Dan and I go to the market to spend the last of our pesos. For two hundred pesos apiece, we go up to the observatory in the Latin American Tower. From the forty-fourth floor, the view of the earthquake's devastation is immense. Half of a parking structure resembles a stack of pancakes. The west end, still standing, provides a remarkable contrast.

Directly below us, tiny people are shoveling away at the rubble.

"Why do you suppose they are using hand shovels and not machinery?" I ask Dan. Our eyes meet with a shared guess.

"More than likely," Dan voices what we are both thinking, "they are practicing archaeology—from the fall of 1985."

How many tombs exist below us? Looking down on the piles and piles of rubble . . . how many people died? The official word is 7,000 to 8,000, but every resident we have asked seems to believe a more realistic number would be 30,000. At least 150, probably more like 200, major buildings have collapsed.

Between the piles of rubble there are tent cities. Temporary dwellings. Homeless people. Slogans sprayed on the wall convey a message of disappointment despite the printed government signs with messages of thankfulness and hope.

On our taxi ride to the airport, the driver races the wrong way down one-way streets, makes quick, squealing turns each time the "short cuts" are blocked by earthquake rubble. He is proud of his ability to defy every existing traffic code, and we are grateful to have survived the experience.

In Juárez, the night is cold and windy. Our van is forced to the side of the road to wait for an intense rain shower to pass. Crossing the abandoned bridge over the Rio Grande, an eeriness fills the empty night. A young Mormon missionary in white shirt and black tie has ridden with us from the airport. He seems spooked and he keeps muttering "just get me out of this country."

We are relieved when a smiling Gus Pineda picks us up in downtown El Paso.

"Only two of you?" he asks, remembering our large party.

"Yes, it's just us," I reply tiredly.

TOMORROW'S ADVENTURERS
June 1986

"What are all these flies doing up here? I mean what do they eat, here in the forest? Like, at home they eat our food, but how do they live out here?"

The speaker is Shannon Kelly. She is a member of my Senior Girl Scout Troop. We are hiking on the Sandia Crest Trail. The trail balances along the spine of the north-south mountain range that looms a mile above Albuquerque. We are on an overnight backpacking trip. We rode the tramway up from town, and we will hike back to my home in Placitas, spending one night out along the way.

My grandmother was a Girl Scout leader, my mother was a Girl Scout leader, my sister is a Girl Scout leader—I am now carrying on the tradition. The six girls hiking with me go to area high schools and, like me, have been Girl Scouts most of their lives.

"What's the longest hike you've been on?" the talkative Shannon now asks. I do a double take. I ask myself if she is asking this question seriously. I suppose I have not told these girls about my hike five years ago.

"Two thousand miles," I reply.

"You're kidding."

I realize, for these young women, it is hard for them to know when I am serious or when I am pulling their legs. I give some details about spending five months hiking along the Continental Divide through New Mexico, Colorado, and Wyoming.

"You should be in the history books!" Shannon exclaims.

I tell Shannon the world is full of many other adventurers like me. The multivolume encyclopedia documenting all the people who have embarked on personal journeys would fill a large library. What we share are dreams, and Shannon, too, can be a dreamer.

I was Shannon's age when I first dreamed about hiking the Continental Divide. Anything is possible. Dreams need to be nourished. Dreams make life worth living. I have friends who hike, friends who bike, friends who travel abroad. I have friends who dream of owning houses, of having children, of working on a ranch and growing old on horseback. What we share is a lust for life and a willingness to claim what we want. Our dreams sustain us.

Shannon gets it, or so she says. She dreams of reaching the end of our trail to get away from all the flies. I know she's kidding. We have planted a seed. She may not have a big dream this moment, but she'll be searching for a mission.

Someday I hope she drops me a line and lets this Girl Scout leader know what she has achieved. I think about my own Girl Scout and Boy Scout leaders who provided that ripe environment for my dreams to grow. Maybe I should send them a postcard.

ROCKY CANYON TRAIL BUILDING
July 2001

Prying rocks loose with a crowbar, I set them free to roll down the hill-side. With luck, each rock rolls only a few hundred feet, to the vicinity of the freshly cut trail below. Occasionally, the victim rock rebels and, once loosed from its original bed, builds momentum enough to sail across the work site and barrel on to a new angle of repose, far below, irretrievable for our purposes.

Across the steep ravine, my daughter, Katie, and her friend Ali are yelling at us. Tiring earlier of the grueling grunt work that comprises trail building, the girls had taken a break to explore the mountains around us. They seem to enjoy getting our attention. This is the second time within the last half hour they have been raising such a ruckus.

Twenty years earlier, as a twenty-one-year-old adventurer, I set

Mary's daughter, Katie Shaw, building the Continental Divide
Trail in the Gila National Forest. Photo by author.

out to hike the Continental Divide from Mexico to Canada. Although
Congress had established the concept of a Continental Divide National
Scenic Trail in 1978, in 1981 there was no such feature on the ground. I
backpacked two thousand miles in five months, walking across New
Mexico, Colorado, and Wyoming. Most of the way, my route followed
back roads, game trails, cross-country compass bearings, and, rarely but
most enjoyably, hiking trails.

Now I have returned to the Continental Divide down on the Gila
National Forest to participate as a volunteer in a trail-building project. Cosponsored by the U.S. Forest Service and the Continental Divide
Trail Alliance (CDTA), our project at Rocky Canyon is just one of thirty
projects sponsored this summer by the CDTA.

Last spring, while pondering a summer vacation, my fourteen-year-old daughter and I decided to go on a trip. Her father and I were negotiating divorce, and Katie and I needed quality time together. Katie, a social middle school student, quickly amended the plan to include her friend Ali. At first we thought about camping, maybe in Colorado or Arizona; then backpacking sounded more appealing. However, when the CDTA flyer arrived outlining opportunities to help build the Continental Divide Trail, our dilemma was solved. Why hike a trail when you can build one? We signed on for the project in southern New Mexico.

Our volunteer group, assembled for only a week, is paired with a seasoned Forest Service trail crew that will spend their summer on the project. We camp together along a remote dirt road at the trailhead, and walk each day up the newly made trail to where it ends, and our work begins. We bust rocks, cut trees, build rock foundations, scrape ground, and push the path a bit farther from camp each day.

The work is exhaustingly physical. For me, trail building offers perfect therapy. For days I pound my frustrations, anger, and disappointments, and, in the process, remove rocks from the trail bed that would otherwise trip an unwary hiker. On this slope in Rocky Canyon, where no trail had been before, there will someday soon be hikers—hikers who might never understand the sweat, anguish, and energy that prepared their path. I daydream about being one of those hikers.

Our volunteer group provides comic relief for the trail crew. We are on vacation; they are working their seasonal job. We organize dress-up nights, create exotic costumes, prepare exquisite meals, and act incredibly goofy. We find living in the woods with a neighboring little honey-colored black bear a novelty. The trail crew thinks the mostly grown bear cub is a nuisance.

The girls return from their hike out of breath. I am placing newly dislodged rocks to construct a foundation to keep the path on a contour. They are animated. They had come face to face with a much larger and darker black bear than the one we have seen near camp. They are upset we did not come to rescue them when they called.

Grateful the bear encounter resulted in memories and a good story, rather than injuries and a nightmarish tale, I am also pleased the girls have caught the essence of the Continental Divide experience.

We build the trail to lure ourselves into the wilderness and into our wildness.

OPPORTUNITY, PRIVILEGE, AND RESPECT
August 2001

I grew up hanging out in the mountains of northern New Mexico. My parents were mountain junkies. There I learned to play, relax, and challenge myself. In the mountains I learned to seek *opportunities*, honor *privileges* granted me, and *respect* all life that surrounded me.

By the time I was sixteen, I had already climbed New Mexico's tallest mountain, Wheeler Peak, several times and was hopelessly in love with the neighboring Moreno Valley. The eastern skyline of the valley was, for the most part, Philmont Scout Ranch and belonged to the Boy Scouts of America.

As a girl, Philmont Scout Ranch was forbidden territory, or so I thought. It was of course a *Boy Scout* Ranch, and when my mother caught my gaze shifting over to Baldy Mountain, she would emphasize the word *boy* letting me know that climbing that mountain was beyond my grasp.

The summer I was sixteen, I found new hope.

I was in the Pecos Wilderness with my Girl Scout troop. I was about four miles from our base camp at Truchas Lakes, wandering alone as I often did in the mountains. It was a typical summer day in the New Mexico highlands. The day had started out sunny, with a sky so blue it was the color of alpine forget-me-nots. By midmorning a few puffy white clouds had appeared, and these continued to build to midafternoon. In the pattern that would continue, the full-scale thunderstorm would throw a few bolts of lightning, crash a few peals of thunder, possibly produce an intense but brief downpour, and then blow on by. With luck the evening sky might even be clear again.

I reached tree line as the storm hit. I was sixteen and had enough mountain traveling experience to know better than to expose myself on an alpine ridge in a thunderstorm. I hunkered down among the Engelmann spruce about thirty feet off the path to wait out the storm.

A few minutes later a party of four hikers came up the trail. They seemed intent on moving on, so I hollered at them to come join me. These three guys and one woman hailed from exotic places like North Carolina, Ohio, Virginia, and Pennsylvania. Learning they were foreigners, I launched into my speech on northern New Mexico weather, and strongly advised that they sit out the storm with me in the shelter of the trees. They tolerated my lecture, and even seemed amused to have this young girl talking to them this way. When I finally paused, they explained that they gave similar talks on a daily basis. It was their job. They were Philmont Rangers.

I was shocked. I stared at Hannah.

"Girls can go to Philmont?" I stammered, and told them of my aspirations to climb Baldy Mountain.

We talked until the storm passed, and I promised to find a way to get to the ranch. The next summer Hannah Wilson was my Philmont Ranger when I attended a challenging individual program called Rayado. I finally got a chance to climb Baldy Mountain.

My first summer participating in the Rayado Program at Philmont Scout Ranch provided an intriguing introduction to a magical place that laid the groundwork for many of the lessons I have learned in my life. Oklahoma oilman Waite Phillips donated the National High Adventure Base to the Boy Scouts of America in 1938. The enormous generosity of that gift set the stage for a program that celebrates everything good about life. At Philmont, I learned to cherish the concepts of opportunity, privilege, and respect.

For me, *opportunity* is claimed by an individual, *privilege* is granted to an individual, and *respect* is a two-way street that flows from the heart.

I failed to get a job as a Philmont Ranger the following summer, so I returned to the ranch for another Rayado Trek. Finally, after my first year in college, I got my ranger contract. During my first summer as a Philmont Ranger I climbed Baldy Mountain fourteen times!

The responsibility for *opportunity* lies in self-motivation. Although opportunity is something that a person claims, others are often involved. I would not have my Philmont memories if it weren't for other people offering me the opportunity to seize the experience, starting with Waite Phillips himself. I sought the opportunity to first come to Philmont in a special program, and then as a staff member. When I didn't immediately get the opportunity to come back, I kept trying.

In 1978, my first year on staff, the opportunities for women at Philmont were limited. The only way a woman could spend significant time in the backcountry was to be a ranger. Working in the backcountry, or even the conservation department, was off limits for females. It was still that way six years later, my last year on Philmont staff. After my first summer on staff, I had some other opportunities to seek out, and so I did not return to the ranch until four years later.

In college I studied forestry, which has demanding expectations, especially in the summer. I was hired by the Forest Service as a cooperative education student, meaning I alternated semesters (including summers) between attending school and working in the field. I was also pursuing another dream.

From the time I was fourteen years old, I had wanted to hike the Continental Divide. In March of 1981, I started hiking in the bootheel of New Mexico. Five months and two thousand miles later, I was forced to quit my hike due to medical reasons up in Yellowstone National Park in northern Wyoming. Still, it was an awesome hike and someday I'll write that book.

However, here is a story from this hike that will launch us into our next special word: *privilege.*

One evening, while hiking on the Navajo Reservation near Two Grey Hills in northwestern New Mexico, I spotted a windmill and, being low on water, headed for it. Along the way I met a stooped, elderly Navajo woman herding goats. I tried asking for her permission to get water—which I later learned was a rather foreign concept . . . a desert people would not naturally consider denying water to any animal—but she spoke no English and I spoke no Navajo.

The windmill turned out to be near her hogan, and as I was filling my water bottles, a young woman approached me. She explained that her mother wanted to know who I was and what I was doing there. Since it was getting dark, I quickly explained my hike and asked if she minded if I camped nearby. She wanted me to camp in the yard where they could keep an eye on me.

As I was finishing my dinner Ester House, the daughter, returned to my camp and told me that her mother, Ruby House, wanted to talk to me. I entered the hogan and the interrogation began, Ester translating between Navajo and English.

"How long have you been doing this?" Ruby asked about my hike.

"Forty days," I said.

"What a waste of forty days," the goatherd replied.

I may have been slightly insulted at the remark, but I felt so privileged to be in the hogan conversing with this woman that I kept my disappointment to myself. I learned that Ruby had raised twelve kids by herself, herding goats to feed and clothe them and send some of them to college. Her kids were all scattered now. Ester, the youngest, had just returned from spending several years in California. We talked about plants and animals, moon and stars, the loom in her one-room hogan. We talked and we talked. I told of my trip.

Around two a.m. when the coffee could no longer compete with our drooping eyelids, I rose to go back to my tent, and Ruby's final words were: "I am glad you are doing this (hike) for us women."

I was honored by the complete change between Ruby's initial and final assessment of my expedition. Had anyone else suggested that I was doing the hike to prove that a woman could do it, I would have responded with anger. I wasn't hiking the Continental Divide because I was a woman; I was hiking because I love to hike! That night, I was privileged to be hiking the divide for *us women*. In the days to come when I was experiencing particularly severe pain in my foot, I would think of Ruby House, and be inspired to keep going.

Hiking the divide was a great opportunity, but I was also learning that it was a wonderful privilege as well. I impacted so many people's lives. What started out as a purely selfish endeavor on my part became a meaningful and inspiring event for many other people, including people who read of my hike in the newspapers.

Privilege is not something that *you claim*, as much as it is something that *is given to you*. Privileges can be abused. It is our personal responsibility to be aware of those privileges we are given, and to honor them.

I turned down my *sure-bet* Forest Service career while I was in college for ethical reasons that I still marvel at today. For a few years after graduating with my bachelor's degree in forest management, I bummed around northern New Mexico working for Philmont as a training ranger in the summers, and doing odd winter jobs like snow-making and avalanche control. After our final year on staff at Philmont in 1983, my boyfriend, who soon become my husband, and I offered to write a field guide for Philmont. Together with a group of artists and photographers who had been on the Philmont seasonal staff, we were granted this privilege later that year. We spent the next year and a half working on the *Philmont Fieldguide*.

Dan and I had another special project going on at the same time. About the time we got the final okay to start on the book, we also conceived our first child. Cairn was named for those piles of rocks that mark trails. There was a particular cairn in northern Colorado that had helped guide me while I was on the divide. I figured having a daughter would surely guide my way as well. I promised I would name my first-born daughter Cairn.

Cairn was a beautiful baby. She had a charming smile, but was a demanding little thing. She refused to be put down. I wrote much of the field guide with one hand on the keyboard, henpecking my way through while I held and nursed her.

We were scheduled to turn the final pieces of the book in on Saturday. However, when we awoke on Thursday morning, Valentine's Day of 1985, we found that our firstborn child had died during the night. She was a victim of Sudden Infant Death Syndrome.

I share this sad story to grant you the privilege of knowing about a special part of the *Philmont Fieldguide*. It was against the rules to dedicate a Boy Scout publication to any one person, even though we all felt that Cairn deserved that honor. In the ensuing weeks of wrapping up the final appendices of the book—in the midst of our grief—my husband found a way to slip in the dedication. In the flora bibliography section, there is a reference for a book that does not exist. It reads: Shaw, Cairn M. *A Blossoming Flower*. Albuquerque. Dedication Press. 1985.

Had Cairn lived, she'd have been just the right age to be a camper at Philmont, and perhaps, as other campers, carry the *Philmont Fieldguide* with them on the trail; she is there in spirit.

I have had a privileged career working as a forester. I spent six years with New Mexico State Forestry helping private landowners manage their forest lands. The last ten years as a private consultant have involved diverse activities. This career has been rich in opportunity including the privilege of working with the people and landscape of New Mexico. It is through this work that I have come to appreciate the third special word: *respect.*

Respect is a word that makes middle-schoolers cringe; to truly appreciate the word one must reach a certain level of maturity and wisdom. However, if we foster this concept of respect, we can, as a society, master many of the challenges we face from issues of human rights to environmental wrongs to violence on our city streets.

I first fell in love with the word *respect* while working as a Fire Information Officer on the Mescalero Apache Reservation. I was asked to help the Mescalero Apache Tribe develop a fire prevention program after a couple of kids started an eight-thousand-acre fire. I wanted to understand what the cultural links to fire were for these people so I asked many questions. One of the tribal council members put it this way:

"We teach our children to respect fire."

He of course said more than this one line. He talked about the use of fire in ceremonies. He talked about the tradition of firefighting among his people. He talked about how young people should know about the inversion layer mid-slope that can affect fire behavior in the middle of the night, but also provided their ancestors a warm place to sleep while out hunting. The essence of the conversation was that fire is neither good nor bad, but that it demanded your respect.

Respect comes from the heart. Respect is a love affair—of other people, of places, of concepts, of cultures, of processes. When we respect something, we honor it. We cherish it. We value it. We love it.

When a teenager shows up at Philmont Scout Ranch to hike with a group of peers, she comes to respect the trails. Not only does she hike them, but she helps build them. She sweats and, perhaps, even bleeds along them. She learns to respect her crew members, her guides, and the people she meets along the trail.

Eventually, some rainy morning, she wakes up to the music of a mountain creek, the musty aroma of decaying aspen leaves, and the brilliance of purples, blues, reds, whites, yellows, and greens in the lush vegetation at her feet. At this point in her trek, she is facing the reality that she cannot stay here forever; she will have to learn to carry Philmont in her heart. Then it hits her. She not only loves the ranch for the northern New Mexico mountain beauty, but for the people who are attracted to this paradise. Her heart aches as she contemplates leaving this community of kindred spirits. At Philmont, respect is as much for people as it is for place.

Philmont may have nurtured my sense of respect, but it is something that I carry through life. For example, here is a story about an animal and a plant I have learned to respect. The animal is the rattlesnake and the plant is sometimes called oshá.

Next to my cabin in the foothills on the north end of the Sandia Mountains, I built a twelve-foot-by-twelve-foot building as a small office.

The foundation was simply cinder blocks and treated timbers that leave a space between the earth and the particleboard floor. One morning, I glimpsed the triangular-shaped head of a rattlesnake darting out from under the door of my office. It was only for the briefest moment, and the snake retreated beneath the office floor. I gathered my papers for my next trip out, listening to the angry rattles beneath the thin floor. Over the years, I had shared the square feet of this office space with other *basement* dwellers, mostly squirrels and rabbits, and unfortunately a few skunks. I wondered if I could be an office mate and cohabit with a rattlesnake.

In my pocket is a piece of oshá root, which grows high up in the mountains. A powerful plant, oshá is the only cure for the common cold that I know of, but its medicine is even more powerful than that. One day, I was digging up this root while teaching a class on plants on the Fort Apache Reservation in Arizona. About that time, we heard a loud crash of thunder, which sounded uncomfortably close. Several Apaches started grabbing for the root. They explained that having a piece of this root on your body would provide protection from lightning. Since I've had a few close calls with lightning, I started carrying a piece of this root with me, especially during the monsoon season.

A few years later, back in Arizona, I was teaching about plants on the San Carlos Apache Reservation. On a hillside in chaparral, we were moving through the thickly vegetated slopes looking at various shrubs and grasses. An older Apache woman was with us but she refused to step off the road. Jeannette Cassa was a linguist and was helping the tribal botanist develop an ethnobotany for her people. We would bring pieces of plants back for her to examine. Later, back in the vehicle, Jeannette and I were talking about other plants and I pulled out the piece of oshá root from my pocket.

"Oh," she said, becoming animated, "now I know why you can run all over that mountain without being bit by a rattlesnake." She explained that oshá keeps the snakes from biting you.

Two months earlier, I had stepped on a coiled rattlesnake just outside my house. Returning from a day in Albuquerque, I realized I had forgotten one errand. A few weeks earlier, while on a field trip near Flagstaff, I had snagged my leg on a barbed-wire fence, requiring stitches. Now, ten days later, I was heading out for a week in the Jemez Mountains and needed to get the stitches out, but I had forgotten to stop by the doctor's office. Being a resourceful ex–Philmont Ranger and daughter of a self-sufficient cowboy, I decided to take the stitches out myself. The gaping wound opened right back up.

Life can be complicated, and it was right then. One of the chores I had remembered to do was to pick up several sheets of Wonderboard—a heavy concrete sheeting to lay down on the floor before installing tiles. A building contractor friend was going to install tiles in our cabin while I was away, and right then that Wonderboard was still barely tied to the roof of my Isuzu Trooper. I had almost lost the load coming up my steep and bumpy driveway, and did not want to make a trip back to town to Urgent Care with boards still on the roof. With my injured leg, I could not get them down alone. Slapping a few butterfly Band-Aids on the wound, I ran toward my neighbor's house to get some help unloading the truck.

That's when I stepped on the coiled snake. It did not move. It did not strike. I immediately moved away once I realized what my foot was on, but from a safer distance I gazed into that snake's eyes and felt a strong kinship with it. I certainly felt gratitude that the snake did not bite me.

As I related this story to Jeannette, I explained that a piece of oshá root was in my pocket.

"See," she said.

I became a believer.

The rest of that snake story is sad because my helpful neighbors not only unloaded my truck, but probably killed the snake. They said they had thrown a rock at it, and it had crawled away. I promised to move the snake, and called a friend and neighbor who was involved in the Mexican Gray Wolf Reintroduction Program.

"Peter," I said, "I've got a predator over here that no one wants in the neighborhood."

He immediately guessed I was dealing with a rattlesnake and said he would be right over with his snake stick and we could move it.

When he arrived, I was ready. I had changed into canvas overalls, my logging boots, leather gloves . . . I met Peter at the door. He was there in his sandals and cutoffs, holding a pole about the length of his arm. He laughed at my getup and promised that I could handle the snake.

When we found the snake, it wasn't moving. Peter suspected it was dead. Being a forester and thus familiar with trees that, at least initially, are hard to determine whether they are dead or alive, I still insisted on moving the snake to an unpopulated drainage nearby. Peter wanted the rattles, but I kept insisting the snake might be alive.

Peter finally pulled out his knife and sliced off the rattles and said, "Well if he's still alive he can grow a new set."

I went running the next day and checked under the bush where we had left him, and the snake was gone. I don't know whether the coyotes ate him or if he was indeed only stunned and later crawled away on his own volition, albeit without a tail.

I never saw or heard the snake under my office floor again, but I am haunted by the few seconds its head darted beneath my office door. My midnight travels between office and house are different. I no longer go barefoot. Often I carry a flashlight. Always I carry a piece of oshá root. Whether or not I get the *opportunity* to catch this snake, and the *privilege* to relocate it away from my house, I have a greater *respect* for the idea that I coexist in an environment shared with rattlesnakes.

MOUNT TAYLOR WINTER QUADRATHLON
February 2002

For the people of Grants, New Mexico, this winter was the nineteenth time they hosted the Mount Taylor Winter Quadrathlon. The event stimulates the imagination, as well as the Grants economy. There are four legs to the race, which starts and ends in town but, at its midpoint, reaches the top of the 11,301-foot Mount Taylor. Bicyclists start the event with a thirteen-mile ride—not a great distance by bike riding standards until you consider the 1,800 feet of elevation gain. Where the pavement ends, the race shifts to running. The run course is a challenging five miles uphill, often on snow or ice. As the course switches from road to trail, the cross-country skiing begins. The uphill ski course is so steep that only the uninitiated or the overconfident attempt the slope without specialized mountaineering skins attached to their skis to prevent sliding. For the last push to the summit, the skis are replaced with snowshoes. Upon reaching the top, the race backtracks, with an alternate route for downhill skiing.

Many people do the entire race on their own. These soloists draw respect. Most contestants are members of four-person teams with each team member completing one leg of the journey, both up and down. Some participants choose to do two or three legs of the race forming two-person pairs. That was my choice this year. I talked my brother-in-law into biking and running, while I skied and snow-shoed.

Grants is the perfect town to host this premiere winter multisport event. For one thing, not many towns can boast having a volcano in their backyard. There are two other critical elements that make the Mount Taylor Winter Quadrathlon click. The first, and most obvious, are the volunteers from the town that come out and support the event. The other is the Forest Service's commitment to multiple-use activities on national forest lands not designated for other specific purposes.

Since my part of the race began partway up the mountain, I started the day early catching rides. I hopped into a van that was providing a shuttle to the first transition point. Learning that our shuttle driver teaches second grade at the local school, I thanked her for giving up her Saturday to tote us around. From her knowing grin, I realized she had more invested in this project than just one Saturday.

Her radio started to cackle.

"Alicia, do you know where there are more safety pins?" the registration desk was asking.

She made a few radio contacts that insured the desk would be restocked shortly.

I asked about her job, but our conversation was interrupted by another radio message requesting trash bags.

Then it hit me. Our shuttle driver was Alicia Gallegos, the race director. I marveled that she was able to drive a shuttle van and still run the event.

"Well," she said, laughing, "it is really the volunteers that run this race, and we've been doing it so long, we have most of the kinks worked out."

Nineteen years, though, is a long time, and recruiting volunteers is getting tougher. So Alicia drives the van *and* runs the race. The radio cackles again, and this time the request is a bit more complex. The run/ski transition is requesting two hundred half-inch-diameter dowels about six inches in length. Alicia starts making calls to see if the hardware store has the dowels and can make the cuts.

At the bike/run transition, we transfer to the back of a pickup truck to complete our journey to the run/ski transition. On the way up, the conversation among the quadrathletes is of other races. There are bike rides up mountain roads, and ultra-runs across mountain ranges, but the group concludes there is nothing quite like the *Quad*. As we start to brainstorm the races we would like to see, we realize that many of places we are daydreaming about are designated wilderness where organized events are generally frowned upon. The multiple-use strategy of the national forests means more than timber harvesting and cattle grazing. It includes wild, fun sporting events as well.

There is a letter from Alicia in my race packet, welcoming me as an athlete to the event. On the back is a letter from the Grants community extolling the virtues of multiple use and explaining that snowmobiles have a right to be on the mountain as well. There is a thinly veiled reference to a conflict between skiers and snowmobilers. The letter gently reminds us that the mountain is managed as a multiple-use area. I wonder if the skiers who might have a problem with snowmobiles realize that this designation is what also makes the race a reality.

The race day was awesome. I chugged up the steep hills enjoying the fine weather. On top I paused to look around and could see for a hundred miles. Heading down the mountain at the end of the day, I made my annual promise.

"Next year," I said aloud to anyone who would listen, "I will be back!"

It will be the Quad's twentieth year. Perhaps I will celebrate by trying the event as soloist, or maybe I should come back a volunteer.

RESCUE TRAINING IN THE WORLD OF WHITEWATER
May 2002

"There are only two kinds of animals that will plunge headfirst into a boiling hole," our fearless instructor advised us, "Labrador retrievers and whitewater rescue technicians."

With this he lunged off the rock, twisted midair to avoid a submerged boulder, arched his back, and landed on the chest of his life preserver. His head, arms, and legs were extended up to avoid initial contact with the water. Immediately taking a few strong strokes, he worked his way across the rapid. We were expected to follow his example.

Recently I took a Whitewater Rescue Technician course. The course is designed to give boaters skills and knowledge to rescue people and equipment that end up in trouble on the river. My passion for rivers often lures me to pilot a boat, challenging fate and flowing water. In my household, boating is a family affair. As my teenagers are expanding their skills and interests beyond our gentle family trips, I want to make sure we are prepared to face the inevitable—dumping a boat in the midst of a rapid. I took this course with my fourteen-year-old son.

The three-day workshop was held on the Rio Grande south of Taos, near the tiny riverside town of Pilar, New Mexico. Our classmates included recreational boaters, professional river guides, and agency personnel who work on the river. The first day was indoors. We studied hydraulics, watched gruesome videos of water tragedies, tied and retied a multitude of knots, reviewed essential first aid, and confronted the fact that no amount of training can prevent all fatalities.

The next two days were spent in and on the river learning how to prevent accidents and rescue people and boats that get into bad spots. We wore wet suits or dry suits to battle the cool snowmelt waters, although we still found the often-exhausting exercises numbingly cold.

The basic rule of thumb in offering assistance is to put yourself in the least amount of danger and still get the job done. The prioritized list of responses—reach, throw, row, go, helo—is in order of increasing danger to the rescuer. The safest way to rescue a "swimmer" is to be able to reach out and grab him or her from a secure spot, such as the boat or the shore. Unfortunately, this isn't always possible. Therefore, standard rescue equipment for most river runners includes a throw bag. This stuff sack is crammed with approximately fifty feet of rope. The rescuer holds the end of the rope and tosses the bag out to the swimmer who grabs the cord and can then be pulled to safety. We practiced throwing the bag until we could accurately place the rope fifty feet out twice within twenty seconds.

Throw bags require that the subject of the rescue is alert and ready to help. Rescuers may have to go to a panicky or unconscious victim. Ideally this can be done with a boat—the "row" option. Our class spent several hours learning how to safely maneuver a boat in rough rapids by using lines managed from the shore, or from a series of ropes, called a Tyrolean traverse, stretched across the river. This is where all of our knot-tying and pulley-alignment practice really paid off.

Instructors Steve Harris and John Weinmeister help Mary practice leaping strainers (logs or other debris in a flowing river) during a whitewater river rescue class. Courtesy of Roland Shaw.

There are times when a rescuer just has to swim after a victim. We learned how to right a facedown person who could have a neck injury or how to approach a combative swimmer. While acting as "victim" during one exercise, my "rescuer" experienced real muscle cramps so we quickly traded roles. I swam him toward safety and another classmate tossed us a throw bag. It was a real confidence builder to see how quickly we could handle an emergency.

The most difficult water rescues involve using helicopters. We talked about procedures and proper use, but since this is so dangerous, we were happy not to be getting hands-on experience.

We learned how to swim in rapids, swamp and right boats, and even walk on—rather in—rapidly flowing water. My son is now compiling his own kit of rescue equipment and toying with the idea of going professional when he turns eighteen.

When it was my turn to plunge headfirst in the boiling hole, I almost balked. Then I thought of my old dog that was part Labrador retriever.

"This one's for Logan," I cried into the roaring froth. My technique might not have been as smooth as the instructor's, but I still made it across the rapids.

TREE SPIRITS IN THAILAND
March 2006

Last year my daughter spent her junior year of high school in Thailand as a foreign exchange student. She and I are now visiting the Land of Many Smiles during spring break of her senior year. She is showing me the place that has become her second home, and introducing me to her friends, teachers, and host family. It is an auspicious way to meet this foreign land. Despite trying to focus on my daughter's experiences, as a forester I cannot help but make a few professional observations as we travel the countryside.

Upon arriving in Bangkok we are whisked away to the countryside in the small town of Nakhon Nayok where Katie lived most of last year. We settle for the night at Katie's host family's compound, which includes a home-stay, much like a hostel. The cabin has a large tree growing in the center of the porch, heavy with unripe fruit I have never seen. The property is full of trees, gardens and ponds, frogs and insects, and joyful night noises that quickly lull me to sleep.

The following day we travel by train to the northwestern part of Thailand to Chiang Mai. After spending a claustrophobic night in an upper sleeping berth, in the morning I am delighted to be traveling through mountainous countryside. To my surprise most of the ground next to the tracks is blackened from recent fires. Since the canopies of the trees seem less affected by the burns, I wonder if the fires were set intentionally or if they started from sparks generated by metal on metal as trains roll along.

The next day my forester's curiosity is piqued at the mountaintop temple of Doi Suthep when I learn that in Thailand large trees are often inhabited by tree spirits or *thep-pa-pak*. Generally these thep-pa-pak are good spirits that bring good luck when called upon. People wrap colorful strips of cloth around the tree to honor the spirit. Later I read in *Thai Ways*, by Denis Sageller, that when people wish to cut down a large tree they leave an axe leaning against the trunk for two days. If the axe has not moved, the spirit has granted permission to cut the tree. If the axe has fallen over or is in a different place, the tree should not be cut down.

On the return trip to Chiang Mai, I spend hours through the night standing on the steps of the train car watching the moonlit countryside. At first I am surprised by the flames up on the mountainsides. After hours of seeing fires burning on the ridges of both sides of the long valley we are traveling through, I realize that the burning is probably intentional.

This is confirmed the next day when I ask an English-speaking woman at a Bangkok church. She tells me fire is often used and most of the burning occurs at night. I embrace this information, but the speaker—an American missionary who has been in the country for over a decade—seems concerned.

"You think the burning is a good thing?" she asks.

I explain how our forests in the United States are suffering from the exclusion of fire that has occurred since European influences have dominated the land. Through ignorance of the importance of fire to forest health, our policies to keep fire off the landscape have left us with dense and overgrown forests vulnerable to catastrophic fires. She seems relieved and says that the burning has troubled her since she arrived. As a complete stranger to this land, I cannot offer her an opinion on burning in Thailand, but I am pleased to see flames on the hillsides.

Our first night back in Nahkon Nayok, we are heading to a night bazaar with a carload of teenagers—my daughter's friends. We pass a field burning next to homes with six- to eight-foot flame lengths. I seem to be the only one in the vehicle to notice or comment. Burning here seems so commonplace it hardly gets noticed.

As a farang—or foreigner—I look for answers in my guidebooks. Again, Segaller informs me that in Thai folklore there are five goddesses and one of them is Mae Phra Plerng, the goddess of fire. Her companions include Mother Earth, Mother Water, and goddesses of wind and grain.

I am smitten by this land where trees have spirits and fire has its own goddess. I light my joss sticks with fervent wishes to return to this intriguing country full of friendly faces to learn more about the enchanting earth and culture.

LEOPOLD RETIRES
FROM FORESTRY CAREER
May 2008

He has been a constant companion. For the last five years he has lain under my desk at the Tribal Forestry Field Office or been in the woods on field days. Before we worked for the tribe in Arizona, he accompanied me each summer visiting forest ecosystems across the Southwest. He was always a hit at environmental education workshops for schoolchildren. He's been the best partner a forester could have.

His name is Leopold. Leopold the dog, named for Aldo Leopold, the forester and author of *Sand County Almanac*. This book and other Leopold writings help mold much of the ethical and ecological underpinnings of forestry and related professions.

At the mellow age of thirteen, my hundred-pound mutt has officially announced his retirement from a long career of forestry assistance. I am grateful he has made this decision, as my new job is located in a state building in Santa Fe where dogs are not necessarily daily companions. Otherwise I might have had to develop a disability that required dog assistance. Leopold, though, is the one developing disabilities.

A few weeks ago when we did the pack test to insure we were ready to fight fires for the season, he tagged along for the first mile but rode in the back of the test administrator's truck for the next two miles. He stood, though, barking his encouragement as we struggled with our forty-five-pound loads to demonstrate that we could move the required three miles in less than forty-five minutes.

A mile is a good distance for Leo, and even with retirement, he and I sally forth from our woodland home daily to give the old bones a workout. We used to run for miles and miles.

It was on one of those runs that Leopold found the injured coyote. The animal was alive, but could not move his rear end. I would have raced right past his hiding space by the trail if Leopold had not pointed him out. With the help of a neighboring veterinarian, we transported the coyote to the Rio Grande Zoo vet clinic. For weeks the zoo vets tried to help the poor animal, but finally determined he would not survive the paralysis.

Leopold always made me more aware in the woods. I imagine that if I could have gone to the woods with the famous ecologist, I would

Leopold on sandstone bluffs near Grants, New Mexico.
Photo by author.

have been shown many things I would miss if alone. Since Aldo Leopold died in 1948, and I was not born until eleven years later, I would have to suffice with reading his writings and exploring the woods with his namesake. Since then the dog has introduced me to hidden fawns, carcasses from mountain lion kills, bear scat, and innumerable evidence of animal death in the forest environment. As a forester, I might have otherwise been content to stay focused on trees and plants.

Aldo Leopold never let his attention remain tree-focused. Although one of the early foresters, he is dubbed the father of modern wildlife management. Leopold was also a leader in wilderness establishment, and crafted the basis of land ethics. In 1924 he was writing about the importance of keeping fire in ponderosa pine forests.

We have moved home, to the yard that Leopold grew up in. He seems content to spend his days curled under a juniper tree, rather than under my desk. Neither of us misses the daily struggle to get his massive, arthritis-ridden torso into the back of my Subaru Forester. Although I miss the familiar breathing beneath my desk, I am grateful to find a faithful mutt waiting at the end of the day to take a walk and see what lessons wait for us.

COPPER AND CONDORS
November 2007

Squinting in the predawn dark, I confirm the tip of the bullet I am sliding into the .270 rifle barrel is blue. My nephew, who owns the gun, left me three copper bullets to fill my cow elk tag from the White Mountain Apache Tribe in east-central Arizona. These bullets are more expensive than the box of lead ones I have shot to become familiar with the weapon. However, with deference to condors, I am joining thousands of hunters who will no longer hunt big game with lead bullets.

Although prime condor country lies three hundred miles to the northwest of me, the lessons learned from condors apply anywhere. Condors hang out in the greater ecoregion around and within Grand Canyon National Park. I once stood out on a rock ledge on the South Rim one fall day, when a condor flew a few feet above my head. Its wingspan was immense. I thought of pterodactyls. I told my companion—a bird fan who spends months each year counting raptors flying over the rim—that when I died I wanted to come back as a condor. He told me that would take really good karma. There just are not that many condors left.

The rareness of the large scavengers inspired the copper and lead lesson. The condors are endangered birds on the verge of extinction. Researchers studying the recently introduced population found alarmingly high lead levels in the birds' blood. To maintain the population, each condor is given a blood transfusion annually to prevent lead poisoning. The lead comes from the gut piles of large game left by hunters field-dressing their take. The Arizona Game and Fish Department believes that hunters can save the condors by switching to copper bullets.

A soft metal, lead bullets shatter when they enter an animal. Tiny but fatal pieces of lead are distributed throughout the tissues. When the condor, or any predator for that matter, consumes this lead, it is poisonous. Copper is a harder metal, and these bullets do not disintegrate. The flesh and guts of an animal killed with a copper bullet are less likely to poison other animals in the ecosystem.

I won this elk tag last June at a conference, but I never intended to be the one hunting. I bought the raffle ticket with the idea that my father, who was lying in a hospital bed suffering from a major stroke, would find the elk hunt in Arizona motivation to get through rehabilitation and be here himself.

When we won the hunt, I thought it was a sure sign he would recover. I had taken Dad out hunting on the reservation a few years earlier and, although we saw no elk then, we had many wonderful father-daughter days exploring the woods.

A month ago my father died.

I asked my nephew if he wanted the tag, and he suggested I use it. I had not hunted in twenty-five years. When I was married, my husband disliked hunting and guns so I had given up that part of my life. Now, despite three recent deaths in our family, going hunting was an intriguing way to honor my father.

When I step out of my Subaru on the last day of the hunt, in the predawn dark, I can hear elk calling all around me. I put a bullet in the rifle, and move off into the woods away from the car. Working my way around the herd, I settle myself on a rock ledge directly above the animals and wait for the dawn.

EPILOGUE

"Hey, Mary. Did you get the elk that morning, the one you were hunting in the last essay in the book?"

"Well, you know. There are a lot of ways a hunt can be successful. That morning was an incredibly rewarding experience. Another story for another place. But do you really think I would have written about copper bullets if I had spent the day field-dressing a cow elk?"

ACKNOWLEDGMENTS

WRITERS WILL UNDERSTAND MY DISCLAIMER THAT THESE WORDS come from an outside source, a creative muse that possesses my mind and sends my fingers racing to the keyboard. Despite my ego's desire to be filled with wholly original thoughts, I am a product of a rich fabric of influences around me. I take full credit for all of the mistakes and ideas that offend, but for the inspired thoughts that grace these pages I am indebted to hundreds of people who have influenced my thinking.

At the risk of gross omissions, I name a few.

Dick Bassett, Bruce Buttrey, Cliff Crawford, the late Paul DeClay Jr., Milo Larson, Don MacCarter, Will Moir, Manuel Molles, Esteban Muldavin, Jim Paxon, Tom Swetnam, Ellie Towns, and Maury Williams, at some critical point in my career, served as mentors, learned sages leading the way. John Goodwin, Tom Hennessey, and Dave Robinson, professors at Oklahoma State University, stood out in launching my career during my undergraduate years.

My co-workers and colleagues also honed my skills and my thinking. I especially thank Louie Casaus, Kim Kostelnik, Fred Rossbach, Greg Shore, Ken Schein, and Bob Cain with New Mexico State Forestry; Lisa Ellis, Rebecca Helianthus, and Tish Morris, my coeditors of the *Bosque Education Guide*; Mary Dwyer, Kim Eichhorst, Laura Pena, and Dan Shaw, from the Bosque Ecosystem Monitoring Program; the writing teams with Seeking Common Ground and the Field Guide to the Sandia Mountains; and Bryan Antonio, Reginald Armstrong, Rachel Endfield, Daniel Kessay, and dozens more with White Mountain Apache Tribal Forestry.

I am grateful to the editors and publishers who have faithfully carried my column over the years, especially Robert Borden and Kathleen Wiegner of the *Jemez Thunder*, Betty Jane Curry and Peggy Ohler of the *Cuba News*, Candy Frizzell of the *Aztec Talon*, JJ and Kim Duckett of the *Mountain Times*, Ty and Barb Belknap of the *Sandoval Signpost*, Sky Nez of the *Fort Apache Scout*, Dave Koch of *Smoke Signals*, Amie Rodgers of the *Maverick*, Penny Elliston of the *International Journal of Wildlife Rehabilitation*, and Sandra Martin of *Women in Natural Resources* magazine.

My writing groups in Arizona and New Mexico have made me a better writer, and I especially thank Wes and Karen Alderson, Jim Beck, Barclay Berg, Daisy Kates, Dallas Kent, Doris "Maverick Moe" Kroupa, Norma Liebman, Sheri McGuinn, and Joy Price. I am also indebted to the Lodestar Mountain writing retreat so graciously provided by Clark and Barbara Hockabout. Several readers (in addition to writing group members) improved this manuscript, including Jerry Babbitt, Barbara Davis, Gina Huda, Allen Johnson, Tom Kempton, Catherine Mullaugh, and Fred Rossbach.

Finally, I acknowledge a special group of talented writers, who are also my family. Thanks for the creative support provided by my children Katie and Roland Shaw; my brother, Hank Stuever; my sisters, Pat Graff and Ann South; my mother Sister Joann Stuever; and my father, the late Joseph H. Stuever Sr.

∞

Many individual articles in this book have appeared in monthly and semimonthly newspapers as a column entitled *The Forester's Log*. These papers include *The Aztec Talon*, *The Cuba News*, *The Jemez Thunder*, *Fort Apache Scout*, *The Mountain Times*, *The Pioneer*, *The Sandoval Signpost*, and *The White Mountain Independent*.

In addition, articles have been regularly featured in newsletters, magazines, and websites including EE Connections (Environmental Education Association of New Mexico), *International Journal of Wildlife Rehabilitation*, *Maverick Magazine*, *Sky Island Forester* (Southwest Section Society of American Foresters), *Smoke Signals* (Bureau of Indian Affairs Fire Management Program), *Timber West*

Journal of Logging & Sawmills, Wildland Fire Lessons Learned Center, and *Women in Natural Resources*.

In addition, the following articles appeared in these publications.

"The Red Belt of 1984," *High Country*, Philmont Staff Association, August 1996.

"Wildlife Management Inspires Backyard Tree Farmers," *American Tree Farmer*, January 1990.

"Project del Rio," *New Mexico Wildlife*, New Mexico Department of Game and Fish, July–August 1992.

"Thoughts on Fire and Mortality," *Wildfire*, International Association of Wildland Fire, September 1994.

"Musings of a Fire Information Officer at Grand Canyon National Park," *Nature Notes*, spring 2002.

"Single Engine Air Tankers," *Southwest Aviator*, September–October 2003.

"Philmont Forestry," New Mexico Tree Farmer Newsletter, spring 2003, and *High Country* (Philmont Staff Association), spring 2003.

"She Ran Calling 'Godiłtła,'" *A Mile in Her Boots*, ed. Jennifer Bové, Traveler's Tales, 2006.

"Five Years After the Rodeo-Chediski," first appeared as an op-ed piece in the *Arizona Republic*, June 2007.

CHRONOLOGICAL LIST OF ARTICLES

ARTICLE TITLE	DATE	PAGE
Pico de Orizaba: 1985–1986 Seldom Seen Expedition	December 1985	215
Tomorrow's Adventurers	June 1986	226
Red Belt of 1984	August 1986	61
Circle A Thinning	February 1987	62
Betty Jane Curry: An American Tree Farmer	November 1987	63
Fire—Chapter Introduction	Autumn 1988	1
Who Pays the Bill?	April 1989	34
Wildlife Inspires Backyard Tree Farmers	January 1990	68
Addressing the Wildland Urban Interface	March 1991	36
New Mexico Forestry Camp	June 1991	183
Rivers of Colorado Water Watch Network	October 1991	185
Project del Rio	June 1992	187
Thoughts on Fire and Mortality	April 1993	51
Environmental Education—Chapter Introduction	Summer 1993	177
Forestry—Chapter Introduction	Summer 1995	57
A Visit with Harry Kallander	August 1996	17
Bernalillo Watershed Prescribed Burn	January 1997	19
Respect Fire	April 1997	9
An Argument for Keeping the Baca Ranch Private	June 1997	70
Instilling That Love for the Land	October 1997	180
A Winter's Day in the Pueblo of Santa Ana's Bosque	December 1998	193
Exploring the Hundred-Acre Wood	January 1999	192
Remembering Sam Tobias	October 2000	49
Alameda Tai Chi	December 2000	200
Rocky Canyon Trail Building	July 2001	227
Opportunity, Privilege, and Respect	August 2001	230
Musings at Grand Canyon National Park	September 2001	22
This Year, Get a Patriotic Christmas Tree	November 2001	73
Green Side Up, Okay?	December 2001	76
Pilgrimage to Boca Chica	January 2002	190

Article Title	Date	Page
Mount Taylor Winter Quadrathlon	February 2002	238
Freezing Fires	March 2002	4
Rescue Training in the World of Whitewater	May 2002	240
Contemplating Closures	June 2002	204
Striving to Follow in the Footsteps of Carson and Bruchac	June 2002	210
When Firefighters Start Fires	July 2002	11
Dying Pinyons	August 2002	92
Fire Triangles	September 2002	6
Divining Healthy Forests	September 2002	88
The BEMP Intern Program	September 2002	197
Lessons in Fall Foliage	October 2002	206
Philmont Forestry	November 2002	202
Forester's Confession	December 2002	84
The Bosque Education Guide	January 2003	195
Cutting through the Tangle of Private Timber Sales	February 2003	86
A Common Vision for Jemez Mountain Elk	April 2003	90
SEATs Take No Back Seat in Air Tanker Business	May 2003	30
Fire in the Bosque	July 2003	39
The Perfect Fire on Powell Plateau	August 2003	24
Observations of a Dying Pinyon Tree	October 2003	94
Mixing in Mexico	October 2003	114
Rehabbing the Rodeo-Chediski Fire	January 2004	112
Laying a Log Erosion Barrier Legacy	February 2004	118
She Ran Calling "Godiłtła'"	March 2004	120
Stream Sense	April 2004	123
Sowing the Seeds of a Future Forest	May 2004	125
Gathering the BAER Clan	June 2004	116
Fencing Feats	July 2004	126
Land Lessons	August 2004	128
Burn Area Recovery—Chapter Introduction	Autumn 2004	109
Chasing the Chainsaws	September 2004	130

Article Title	Date	Page
Tribal Tree Planting Camp	October 2004	132
Reflections on a Burned Landscape	November 2004	134
Cibecue Native Manages Rodeo-Chediski Recovery Activities	December 2004	136
BAER Fairs Showcase Burn Restoration	January 2005	138
On the National Fire Plan Awards	February 2005	140
Field Guide to the Sandia Mountains	March 2005	208
Smokey's Wisdom	May 2005	13
Remembering Judith	June 2005	142
Frightening Lightning	July 2005	143
Flash Floods	August 2005	145
Bear Scare	September 2005	147
Cone Counting	October 2005	149
Chediski Origin Myth	November 2005	151
Oklahoma Fire Response	February 2006	41
Tree Spirits in Thailand	March 2006	243
Farewell to My Fire Boots	April 2006	42
Transitioning to Tribal Forestry	May 2006	157
Nothing Gray about Fire Starting	June 2006	15
Alaska Adventures	June 2006	45
Logging in on Forestry	July 2006	105
Habitat Typing	August 2006	98
Pining for Pinyon	September 2006	96
Moist Microsites	October 2006	153
Burning Piles	December 2006	26
Cooking Reports—A Culinary Approach	January 2007	155
Creating Cottonwoods	February 2007	77
Visit to Yale	March 2007	159
Sawing into the Tribal Forest Protection Act	April 2007	163
Confidence and Competence	May 2007	161
Five Years after Rodeo-Chediski	June 2007	166
Southwest Fire Fighters	July 2007	33
Survivor Tree Symmetry	August 2007	79

ARTICLE TITLE	DATE	PAGE
White Mountain Stewardship Program	September 2007	101
Burning Questions	October 2007	29
Copper and Condors	November 2007	247
Greening the Super Bowl	December 2007	169
Living in a Log Home	January 2008	82
In Defense of Informed, Intuitive Forestry	February 2008	103
BAER Growls	March 2008	171
Changing Woman	April 2008	173
Leopold Retires from Forest Career	May 2008	245

INDEX

Italicized page numbers indicate illustrations.

Abbey, Edward, 212, 213

Acree, Laurie Dee, 15

adaptive management, 90, 103, 104, 154

Aero Tech, Inc., 32

Alaska, 45–48

Albino Rhino, 1–2

Albuquerque, NM: bears in, 68; bosque along Rio Grande, 14, 79; as conference location, 17, 96, 140; firefighting in, 31, 36–37, 39; grazing history of, 20; Sandia Mountains, proximity to, 208, 226; tile building in, 84, 86

American Tree Farm System, 44, 63–67, 70, 203

Anderson, Rich, 209

Antonio, Bryan, 109–11

Apache-Sitgreaves National Forest, 101–2, 161, 163–66, 170

Applegate, Bob, 83–84

Arenholz, Art, 209

Arizona Department of Environmental Quality, 28, 170

Arizona Game and Fish Department, 247

Armstrong, Reginald, 151–53

Askew, Jim, 217, 223–24

Asociación Mexicana de Profesionales Forestales, 114

aspen, 58, 180, 204–5, 206–8, 207

Babbitt, Bruce, Secretary of Interior, 17, 19

Baca Ranch, the, 70–72, 183

Backyard Tree Farm Program, 68–70

BAER. See Burn Area Emergency Response

BAER fair, 138–40, 142

Bandelier National Monument, 72, 97

bark beetles, 61, 66, 88, 92, 97

Barrancas del Cobre (Copper Canyon), 115

Barraza, Señor, 215–17

Bays, Mark, 41, 81

bear, 57–59, 68, 147–49, 157, 177, 229

Bernalillo District, New Mexico State Forestry, 1, 3, 36, 37, 72

Bernalillo, NM, 90

Bernalillo Watershed, 19

Betancourt, Julio, 93

Boca Chica, TX, 190–92

bosque, 1, 14, 39–40, 192–202, 206

Bosque Ecosystem Monitoring Program (BEMP), 197–202

Bosque Education Guide, 179, 193, 195–97, 198

Bosque School, 192, 201

Boy Scouts of America, 213, 230–31

Boyer, Steve, 99

Bruchac, Joseph, 210–11

Buffett, Jeannette, 209

Bureau of Indian Affairs (BIA), 33, 35, 163; employees of, 17, 136; Fort Apache Agency, 26, 111, 116, 125, 133, 137, 138, 170, 177; Mescalero Agency, 10; in Oklahoma, 42

Burn Area Emergency Response
    (BAER): national program,
    116–18, 146, 171–73; and Rodeo-
    Chediski (RC) coordination, xiii,
    111, 137, 157–59, 162–63, 168; RC
    projects, 127, 133; White Mountain
    Apache Tribe crew, 119, 130–32,
    139, 142, 169
Burnette, Mae, 124
Burnette, Victoria, 33
Burns, Pearl, 209
Bush, Don and Carol, 69

Carrizo Fire (1971), 125, 130
Carson, Rachel, 210–12
Casaus, Louie, 1–2, 32, 37
Cassa, Jeannette, 236
Cedar Creek, 144, 146
Cerro Grande Fire (2000), Los
    Alamos, NM, 23, 51, 73, 140–41
chainsaws: operation of, 130–32, 165–66
Chapman, Jennifer, 14
Chediski Fire. *See* Rodeo-Chediski Fire
Chihuahua, 114–15, 218
Christmas tree, 69, 73–75
Cibecue: BAER project in, 136, 140, 168;
    economy in, 158, 161, 169; flooding
    in, 145, 186; as Rodeo-Chediski fire
    origin, 158; and Rodeo-Chediski
    fire, 119, 137
Cibola National Forest, 1, 20, 35, 38, 209
Circle A Ranch, 62
climate change, 45, 60, 97
Cloudcroft, NM, 49, 141
Colorado Division of Wildlife, 185–86
condors, 247–48
cone collecting, 149–51
Continental Divide, 190–91, 213, 215,
    226–27, 228–29, 232–33
Cooper, Bob, 68
Cooper, C. F., 54

Cooper-Ellis Ranch, 68
cottonwood: and fire, 1, 14, 39–40;
    biology of, 77–79, 173, 200–201; in
    the bosque, 193–94, 196–97, 200;
    fall foliage of, *178*, 206
Coyote Fire (1989), 36–37
Crawford, Cliff, 39, 192–93, 200, 202
Creel, Chihuahua, Mexico, 115
Cuba, NM, 62–63, 67, 85, 183
Cuba Soil and Water Conservation
    District, 66, 183–84
Curry, Betty Jane, 63–67, 183

Dane, Judy, 69
Davis, Hal, 223
DeClay, Paul Jr., 160
Denali National Park, 45
diameter breast height (DBH), xi
Dickey, Jim: photo by, *181*
Dobbs, Susie, 223–24
Domenici, Senator Pete, 195–96
Dwyer, Mary, 200

East Mountain Interagency Fire
    Protection Association, 37–38
Eichhorst, Kim, 200
El Huerfano Fire (1998), 114, *115*
elk, 57, *71*, 90–92, *91*, 98, 134–36, 147–48,
    183, 247–48
Elkins, Buddy, 57
Elliott, Valinda Jo, 15
Endfield, Johnny, 158
Engelmann spruce, 83, 230
engine boss, 1, 3–4
Environmental Education Association
    of New Mexico, 187
Environmental Protection Agency
    (EPA), 185
Ethelbah, Larry, 123

fence building, 126–28, 156, 164–66, 168

feral horses, 120–22

Ferguson, Tom, 209

Field Guide to the Sandia Mountains, 208–10

Finch, Michele, 41

Fire and Ashes (MacLean), 152

fire exclusion, 3, 54, 73, 103, 172

fire information officer, 4, 41, 47, 49–51, 140, 235

fire scars, 10, 23

fire triangle, 6–8

flash floods, 144–47, 157, 168, 172

forest pest management, 61

Fort Apache Agency. *See* Bureau of Indian Affairs

Fort Apache Indian Reservation, 17, 26, 33, 125, 175, 236

Friends of the Sandia Mountains, 209

Gallegos, Alicia, 239

Garcia, Maria, 50

Geography of Childhood (Nabhan and Trimble), 200

Geronimo, 161

Giese, Ernie, 209

Gila National Forest, 228

Girl Scouts, 67, 183, 213, 226–27, 230

Godiłtła', 120–23, *121–22*

Grand Canyon, 22, 25, 58, 247

Grants, NM, 57, 238–40, 246

Green, Chief Gene, Cloudcroft Police Department, 49

greenhouses: at McNary, 125–26, 134, 139, 151, 162, 169

Gregg, Leonard, 15–16

Griego Lumber, 203

habitat typing, 98–100

Hackett, Ali, 227–29

Harris, Steve, 242

Hayman Burn (2002), 118

Henley, Jack, 70

Henry, Adam, 109

Hernandez, Walter, 65–66

hoedad, 132, 147–48

House, Ester, 232–33

House, Ruby, 232–33

Incident Command System (ICS), 3–4, 37–38, 41, 47, 133

Incident Management Team, 5, 49

increment borer, 62

Indian Self-Determination, 137, 163, 168

information officer. *See* fire information officer

Intertribal Timber Council, 45

Jemez Mountains, NM: elk in, 90–92, 183; fire in, 51–53; management of, 63, 72, 78, 98–99

Jenkins, Peter, 237–38

jetty jacks, 139

Juárez, Mexico, 215–16, 219, 226

Julyan, Robert, 209

Junger, Sebastian, 11, 24

Kallander, Harry, 17–19

Kelly, Shannon, 226–27

Kessay, Ashley, 173–74

Kessay, Daniel, 110–11, 136–38, 173; photos by, *110, 164, 174*

Kinishba Fire (2003), 133, 135, 144, 146, 149

Kirkland Air Force Base, 36

Kitchen, Jim, 25

Kuponen, Leo, 50

Kurth, Tom, 47

LaRocque, Lisa, 187

Larson, Milo, 100

Las Vegas, NM, 30–32

Lawrence, David, 99

Leopold, Aldo, 17, 70, 245–46

Leopold the dog, 245–47

Lewis, David: photos by, *71, 91, 104, 207*

Lewis, Franklin, 110

Lightfoot, Dave, 209

lightning: igniting fires, 19, 22–25, 203; as safety concern, 143–45, 230, 236

Limestone Fire Tower, *110*, 128

Lincoln Logs, 83–84

Lincoln National Forest, 50–51

log erosion barriers, 112, 118–20, 132, 137, 139, 173

logging, 137, 202; as a tool, 55, 60, 65–66, 86–88, 105–8, 202–4; historic, 60

Los Alamos. *See* Cerro Grande Fire

Los Alamos National Labs, 72

Lupe, Rick, 133–4

MacLean, John, 152

MacLean, Norman, 152

Madison, Charlie, 223–24

Mann Gulch Fire (1949), 152

Manzano Mountains, NM, 37, 69

Martinez, Jose, 51

Massey, Dallas, 158

McKenna, Chad, 143–45

McNary, AZ: fuels adjacent to, 26, 98. *See also* greenhouses at McNary

Meals-Ready-to-Eat, 34

Medina, Alvin, 123–24

Mescalero Apache Reservation, 4, 10, 235

Mexico, 14–16, 187, 191, 215–25

microsite, 78, 85, 148, 153–55, 173

Middle Rio Grande, 77, 195–98

Middle Rio Grande Ecosystem: Bosque Biological Management Plan, 196

Mogollon Rim, xii, 25, 167, 170

Moir, Will, 100

Morris, Judith Ann, 142–43

Morris, Tish, 195–97; photo by, *198*

Mount Taylor Winter Quadrathlon, 238–40

Mount Vision Fire, 14

Muav Saddle, Grand Canyon North Rim, 25, 125–26

Nabhan, Gary Paul, 200

Nacimiento Mountains, NM, 64, 183

National Fire Plan, 73, 140; award, 141

National Fish and Wildlife Foundation, 90

National Football League (NFL) Environmental Program, 170–71

National Park Service, 14, 22, 45, 71

Natural Resources Conservation Service (NRCS), 66, 69

Nenana, AK, 45–47

New Mexico Cooperative Extension Service, 69

New Mexico Council of Outfitters and Guides, 90

New Mexico Department of Game and Fish (NMDGF), 69, 90, 185–86, 187

New Mexico Environment Department, 186–87

New Mexico Fire Marshall's Office, 35

New Mexico Forestry Camp, 183–84

New Mexico Museum of Natural History and Science, 186–87

New Mexico olive, 200–201

New Mexico Share with Wildlife Program, 108

New Mexico State Forestry Division: fire assistance, 1–3, 21, 32, 35–37, 40; forestry assistance, 64, 69, 72, 173, 203, 234

New Mexico Tree Farm Program, 44, 67, 69, 203

nick point, 123–24

Northern Arizona Wood Products Association, 102

Northern New Mexico Livestock Association, 90

North Rim, Grand Canyon, 22–25, 58

Nuvamsa, Ben, 116–17

Ohler, Jason, 65

Ohler, Peggy, 64–67

Oklahoma City Memorial, 79–82

Oklahoma Forestry Division, 41, 81

Oklahoma State University, 81, 178

Oregon State University, 17

Parks Highway Fire (2006), 45–48

Peña, Bob, 49

Peña, Laura, 194–95

Peñasco Fire (2002), 136–37

Perfect Storm, The, 11, 24

Phillips, Waite, 202, 231

Philmont Fieldguide, 209, 233–34

Philmont Scout Ranch, 61, 202–4, 209, 214, 230–35

Pico de Orizaba, 215, 220–23

Pinchot, Gifford, 54

Pineda, Gus, 226

Pineda, Phillip, 215–17

Pinetop, Arizona, 18

pinyon pine: dying trees, 92–98; fire ecology of, 20; habitat type, 98, 100

Pitts, Molly, 102

Placitas, NM, 4, 8, 19, 122, 173, 226

Placitas Volunteer Fire Brigade, 3, 4–5, 8, 21

plant associations, 90, 98–100

Point Reyes National Seashore, 14

Polechla, Paul, Jr., 209

ponderosa pine: as a Christmas tree, 75; fire ecology of, 10, 23, 25, 54, 246; habitat type, 89–90, 98–100; harvesting of, 87–88, 101–2; planting of, 85–86, 125–26, 133, 149, 160; red belt in, 61

Ponil Complex (2002), 204

Pool, Roland, 218, 220, 221, 223–24

Powell Fire, 24–26

Powell Plateau, 24–25

prescribed burning: conducting, 16–21, 26–28; effects of, 10, 12, 113, 128–30; fatality associated with, 51–54, 133; planning of, 29–30

Project del Rio, 187–89

Project Learning Tree, 179

Project WET, 179

Project WILD, 179

Pueblo of Santa Ana, 193–95

pulaski (firefighting tool), 132

Pyne, Stephen, 12, 24

Quality Wood Products, 203

Quay, Anthony, 109–10

Rabin, Anastasia, 132

Rainbow Fire (1999), 146

Rancho del Chaparral Girl Scout Ranch, 67, 183–84

rattlesnake, 148, 235–38

Raven Fire (1989), 35–37

red belt, 61

Regina, NM, 83

Reyes, Luis, 220, 223

Rick Lupe Memorial Forest, 133

Rinner, Dan, 32

Rio Grande: bosque fires along, 1, 14, 39–40; cottonwoods near, 77, 79; ecology of, 29, 187–89; education about, 192–93, 193–95, 195–97; monitoring, 187–89, 190–92; river, 226, 241

Rio Grande Zoo, 179, 214, 245

riparian area, 124, 195, 198, 203

Rivers of Colorado Water Watch Network, 185–86

Robertson, Helen: photo by, *80*

Robinson, Dave, 178

Rocky Mountain Elk Foundation, 90

Rocky Mountain Research Station, 20, 123

Rodeo Fire (2002). *See* Rodeo-Chediski Fire

Rodeo-Chediski Fire (2002): BAER implementation of, xiii, 111–13, 134–35, 155, 162, 166–69; BAER projects in, 133–34, 135–40, 146, 160, 169–70; fire behavior of, 24–26, 102, 106, 110, 128–30; ignition of, 11–13, 15–16, 151–53, 158

Rossbach, Fred, 62; photo by, *2*

Ruidoso, NM, 4–5, 32

Russian olive, 40, 196, 201

Sageller, Dennis, 244

Sallee, Robert, 152

salt cedar, 1, 40, 196, 201

San Carlos Apache Reservation, 236

San Juanito, Chihuahua, 114

Sand County Almanac (Leopold), 245

Sandia Mountains, NM, 37, 68, 208–9, 226, 235

Sandia Ranger District, 20, 35, 209

Santa Fe National Forest, 52, 72

sawmills, 18, 65, 83, 87, 158

Scott Able Fire (2000), 49–51, 141

Seeking Common Ground, 90–92

Seldom Seen Expeditions, Inc., 215, 217

Shaw, Cairn, 143, 234

Shaw, Dan, 69, 192–93, 200, 217–18, 221, 223–25, 233–34; photo by, *214*

Shaw, Katie, xiii, 227–29, 243–44

Shaw, Roland, xiii, 59, 177, 181, 242; photo by, *242*

Shawnee, OK, 41–42

Show Low, AZ, 101

silviculture, 60

single-engine air tanker (SEAT), 30–32, *31*

Skidmore, Norman, 111

Sky Ridge Church Camp, Weed, NM, 50

Smith, Curtis, 68

Smokey Bear, 9–10, 13–15

snag, 95–96, 143–44, 148–49, 154

Society of American Foresters, 96, 108, 114

Society of Range Management, 96

Soil Conservation Service. *See* Natural Resource Conservation Service

soil erosion: on roads, 106; prevention of, 20–21, 65–66, 118–20, 173

Sombrio Ranch, Inc., 64

South Rim, Grand Canyon, 22, 247

Southwest Coordination Center (SWCC), 140

Southwest Fire Fighters (SWFF), 33, 163

Southwest Region, U.S.D.A. Forest Service, 16, 100, 128

Stago, Phil, 157

Stuever, Joann, 67, 180, 207–8, 213, 226, 230

Stuever, Joseph Sr., 80–82, 213, 237, 248

Super Bowl XLII, 169–71

Survivor Tree, 79–82

Sussman, Gerry, 209

Swaim, Bruce: photo by, *48*

Szymanski, Jean, 52–53

Tanana Chiefs Council, 45

Tarahumara people, 115–16

task book, 3

Tessay, Tia, 130–31

Texas Forest Service, 14

Thai Ways (Sageller), 244

Thailand, 243–44

thinning, 12, 26–27, 62–66, 101, 106, 128–30

Thompson, Lorinda "LT," 131

timber harvest, 133, 137; effects of, 12, 106–7, 133; sales of, 64–66, 86–88, 101–2, 137; techniques of, 83, 203–4

Tlachichuca, Mexico, 219–20, 223–24

Tobias, Sam, 49–51

tree planting: camp, 109–10, 132–34, 147–49, 157; general instructions for, 76–77; pole planting, 77–79; and other White Mountain Apache Tribe projects, 137, 170–71

Tribal Forest Protection Act, 163–66

tribal forestry, 45–46, 101, 137, 157–59, 165, 174

Trimble, Stephen, 200

U.S. Fish and Wildlife Service, 195–96

U.S. Geological Survey, 93

U.S.D.A. Forest Service: contracting with, 161–66; employment with, 232–33; fire policy of, 16, 18, 35, 140; and forest management, 61, 99–100, 101–2; and prescribed burning, 20–21, 51–52; projects, 71, 74, 170, 228–29, 239; and wildlife management, 90

Udall, Representative Tom, 172

University of New Mexico, 20, 39, 202

Valencia County, NM, 1

Valles Caldera National Preserve, 71, 72, *91, 104*

Vista Fire (2001), 23–24

Walker, Dwayne, 102

Walking the Edge (Acree), 15

Ware, Dan: photo by, 27

water-quality terms, 188–89

Watercourse, The, 191

watershed: as a geographic feature, 19, 78, 213; as boundaries for defining communities, 67, 185–86, 190–92; flooding response to fire, 9–10, 114–16, 118, 145–46, 168–69; as source of drinking water, 203

Weaver, Harold, 17

Weeks, Harry, 32

Weinmeister, John, 242

Wester, Pat, 69–70

White, Carl, 21

White Mountain Apache Tribe: community, 13, 132, 147, 168–70; elk hunting, 247; employees, 33, 45, 119, 145, 155, 160, 161–63; forest management, 26, 28; Rodeo-Chediski burn, 120, 137–38, 146; Rodeo-Chediski fire, 15–16; working for, xiii, 111–12, 135, 174

White Mountain Stewardship Program, 101–2

Whiteriver, AZ, 111, 140, 173

White Springs Fire (1996), 129–30

White's smokejumper boots, 44, 62

wildland fire use strategy, 23, 26

wildland/urban interface, 5, 36–37

Wildlife and Outdoor Recreation Department (WMAT WORD), 148

Wilson, Hannah, 231

Wood, Tana, 215

Woolf, Alice, 62–63

Wright, Haskell and& Marie, 69

Yale University, 159–61

Young Men and Fire (MacLean), 152

Youngbear-Tibbets, Holly, 160–61

Young's Sawmill, 65

Youtz, Jim, 177

Zieroth, Elaine, 101

Zinsley, Mike, 218, 221–24